KEN PIKE
SCHOLAR AND CHRISTIAN
BY EUNICE V. PIKE

D1316251

SUMMER INSTITUTE OF LINGUISTICS
DALLAS, TEXAS

Cover design and photographs by Barbara Alvarez

Takashi Matsumara shown with Ken Pike

Order additional copies from:
Summer Institute of Linguistics
7500 W. Camp Wisdom Road
Dallas, Texas 75236

Table of Contents

FOREWORD

It is often heard that you cannot mix religion and scholarship, or that those who are deeply religious seldom excel in a secular academic field. Ken Pike is a bold exception. In him we see that reverence for God and the Scriptures need not be a deterrent to good scholarship and excellence, but rather a motivating factor. The synthesis of scholarship and deep faith in God, along with Ken's wiry drive has been the basis for his achievements.

My acquaintance with Ken began the summer of 1949 when I first attended the Summer Institute of Linguistics. At that time I was impressed by this teacher, who though brilliant and far from ordinary, was really humble. His goal in life has been to serve God and his fellow men. In the years I have been with SIL, I have benefited from his willingness and patience to teach me not only linguistics, but also administration and much more. His "Timothys" are numerous.

Ken Pike's untiring leadership of SIL has been an inspiration to all who work with him. Because of his contribution to this organization, and his example to each of us that (with God's help) a person can excel in any academic field he chooses, SIL has chosen to digress from its normal publication of linguistic and related technical books to publish this biography.

When I asked Eunice Pike to write her brother's biography, she wasn't at all sure she wanted to tackle it. She was the younger sister, always close to Ken in heart, mind and sororal affection. Could she write his story objectively?

One of her main goals, when she began to write, was to present the real Ken. I believe she has met her goal.

Frank Robbins
Executive Vice President
Summer Institute of Linguistics

INTRODUCTION

On October 26, 1973 the University of Chicago presented an honorary degree of Doctor of Humane Letters to Kenneth L. Pike who was Professor of Linguistics at the University of Michigan, President of the Summer Institute of Linguistics, and on the board of Wycliffe Bible Translators.

Dr. Raven I. McDavid, Jr., Professor of English and Linguistics at the University of Chicago was the one who presented him as a candidate to the President of the university. Part of the citation which he read at that time was as follows, "Since 1935 he [Kenneth L. Pike] has taken literally the injunction to go into all the world and teach the good news of Christ. In dedication to his mission, so that he might understand better the tongues of those to whom he went, and might teach others how to learn those tongues, he became a linguist. Student of Sapir and Bloomfield and Sturtevant and Fries, he has analyzed more languages than all those worthies; if we count the work of his students, he has probably done more than anyone else to broaden our knowledge of the tongues of man.

"Under his leadership ... the Summer Institute of Linguistics has become the best training ground in the world for field linguistics.... At the same time he has maintained his association with the University of Michigan ... and has helped maintain its distinction as a center for linguistics.

"Though his interest in linguistics arose from practical needs—and ever finds new practical application—he has become one of the most significant American theoreticians. Again, his interests are wide—phonetics, phonemics, tone languages, general theory. His work on English intonation is still a landmark. Throughout his career he has manifested a gentle modesty rare to his profession ... redoubtable in controversy but respectful toward his adversaries, poet and teacher of composition, he approaches the ideal of the Christian gentleman in his work and in his life. I ask that we make him one of our distinguished graduates by conferring on him the degree of Doctor of Humane Letters.''

Professor McDavid had known Pike since the summer of 1937 when they both were studying at the Linguistic Society of America's Linguistic Institute at the University of Michigan. In writing the citation, Professor McDavid certainly captured the dual emphases of Pike's life.

To Pike, religion is important, but science and scholarship are important to him too. He is a scholar and he also considers Jesus Christ to be his boss. He is grateful that, because of Christ, he has been made acceptable to God. He is grateful that Christ is near him every day, and that He takes care of him and his family. He even looks to Christ to supply him with a good idea now and then.

Pike's driving purpose is to obey Christ, and he notes that Christ not only said that His followers should go and teach (Matt. 28:19), but also that they should love Him with their minds (Matt. 22:37). Ken is delighted with the combination. He is delighted that as he works spreading the news about Christ, and helping others to spread it, that he can, at the same time, be making a contribution to the academic community.

Pike sometimes wonders how he is doing. The honors he has received have been helpful in that they have given him courage. They have reassured him and allowed him to think that, yes, his goals are being accomplished. Probably they have spurred him on to do even more.

Pike received his Ph.D. from the University of Michigan in the Spring of 1942; he became an associate professor there in 1948 and a full professor in 1955. Two years before he retired, in 1977, he was chairman of the Department of Linguistics, and Director of the English Language Institute. In 1966 he was awarded a Distinguished Faculty Achievement Award. In 1974 he was awarded a named professorship, that is, he was given the Charles Fries Professorship in linguistics. In 1961 he was President of the Linguistic Society of

America, and in 1978 he was president of LACUS, the Linguistic Association of Canada and the United States.

On December 9, 1978, Pike received a further honor. At the Sorbonne in Paris, he was awarded Docteur Honoris Causa by the René Descartes University. At the presentation of the degree, the citation was read by Professor André Martinet, a scholar who for some decades has led in the development of linguistics in France. He said, "First, permit me to make a personal remark. I want to express how happy I am to see our university honor my friend Kenneth L. Pike.

"Kenneth Pike comes from a generation in which one did not receive formal training as a linguist. Rather, after having studied literature or philology, one would discover a real interest in languages and in how language functions and develops.

"In the case of Kenneth Pike, his passionate interest in languages, which was enhanced by an outstanding talent for reproducing the most varied sounds manifesting human speech, grew out of theological study and interest in evangelism. Spreading the Gospel requires translating the divine message into previously unwritten languages. That explains why Kenneth Pike was the first to present the science of phonology as 'a technique for reducing languages to writing,' rather than conceiving of it in rather abstract terms as had been done in Europe.

"From the start he saw that reducing a language to writing is not a matter of noting the physical properties of sounds. Rather, it is necessary to symbolize those features which differ from one language to another and which allow units of meaning to be distinguished one from another. This is what he presented in 1947 in his treatise entitled *Phonemics*. He thus discovered, though from a slightly different perspective, the principle of relevance which had been proposed in Europe by Karl Buhler.

"Because of his concern for the training of field linguists, he had published, four years earlier, the necessary preliminaries to any exposition of phonological method, namely, a presentation of the sounds of language. Indeed, in his book *Phonetics* he set down, for the first time in the history of science, an objective and exhaustive examination of the articulatory possibilities of the organs of human speech.

"It was this same pedagogical concern which led him to introduce the famous 'kalaba' problems; each of these presents linguistic data in a way which is inspired by a real language, but from which all sorts of nonpertinent details have been eliminated; those details, in the raw data, would have tended to obscure the true nature of the problem which students were supposed to solve. Phonology classes today are inconceivable without such artificial problems.

"Having resolved the problems relating to distinguishing units of sound, he began to study (under the label Tagmemics) meaningful units and their relationships within discourse. The masterly way in which he deals with the subject matter is that of a research scholar who is thoroughly familiar with all that constitutes a language and who never allows himself to be satisfied with a synthesis of the data before having finished an exhaustive analysis of the facts in their hierarchical arrangement.

"The contrast which the study of languages has revealed to him—that is the contrast between that which is perceived as human behavior and the value which man attaches to each trait of that behavior—has led him to a new and rich vision of life in society, expressed in his most extensive work to date [entitled *Language in Relation to a Unified Theory of the Structure of Human Behavior*], appearing from 1954-1960 with a revised edition appearing in 1967. This book illustrates perfectly what interdisciplinary study ought to be: a research project, within related disciplines, starting from a discipline which has been mastered perfectly, rather than the metaphorical extension to one's own discipline of concepts borrowed from a science which happens to be popular at the time.

"The theoretical structure which governs all of Kenneth Pike's work is based on contact with concrete data of an astounding number of languages of distinct types. Nothing could be further removed from what some have more recently presented as 'linguistic science' in the form of *a priori* constructions based on logic, or encumbered from the beginning with gratuitous hypotheses about the psychological nature of the human being.

"For the past four decades, Kenneth Pike has pursued his research on an extremely broad front in a flexible but perfectly coherent manner. He has not sought to show the originality of his own points of view by means of vain controversies; and he has known how to keep a distance, on the American scene, not only from a rigid antimentalistic approach but also from irresponsible theorizing. Thanks to him and to his followers, the true science of linguistics, that which is concerned with languages, has continued to live and flourish on the other side of the Atlantic. For all this, for what he has already brought us and will continue to bring us, he merits our deepest gratitude."

Religiously oriented colleges also have honored him. In 1960, his Alma Mater, Gordon College, of Beverly Farms, Mass., presented him with the Alumnus-of-the-Year Award, and in 1967 Huntington College, of Huntington, Indiana, gave him the degree of Doctor of Humanities. In 1977 Houghton College, of Houghton, N.Y., gave him the degree of Doctor of Letters.

The honors from the non-secular colleges also encouraged him, because they appreciated, not only his commitment to Christ, but also his intellectual accomplishments. He hoped that some of their students would also use their minds for God.

Pike was well aware that sometimes when people bestowed honors on him, those honors came to him because of the good work his SIL colleagues had been doing. One example of that was in September 1974 when Ferdinand E. Marcos, President of the Philippines, conferred on him the Presidential Merit Medal. Part of the citation said, "For his deep devotion to his work which has considerably illuminated the lives of the Cultural Minorities of the Philippines, while substantially advancing research and analysis of their languages and dialects through language workshops and seminars, and thereby enriching scientific studies which in time will help the less fortunate members of our national community understand themselves and find their true place in the life of our nation...."

Pike considers that he owes much of his academic achievement to his association with the SIL team. (By 1977 field linguists who were members of SIL were studying more than 650 of the languages of the world's minority groups.) He says that his choice to serve the team in their Bible translation work has kept him from getting involved in scholastic dead ends. A big control over what he has done has been his effort to be useful to his colleagues. He figures that probably he would never have written the *Phonemics* book, and he and his wife Evelyn would not have persisted until the

Grammatical Analysis book was finished, if their colleagues had not needed those books.

Pike also received stimulus for new theory from his SIL colleagues. This happened when they were stopped because the theory Pike was using at that time was inadequate for some aspect of their linguistic analysis. Their need forced him to develop the theory further, and sometimes their intuition even pointed in the right direction. Pike says that it is not conceivable that he would have become the kind of scholar he is, if he had been working in a normal university atmosphere, largely doing his own program and largely his own research. The desire to help the SIL team has kept Pike interested in methodology and practical application. He is delighted that his linguistic theory, tagmemics, is so useful for language analysis. Professor Norman A. McQuown, in *American Anthropologist* 76.931 (1974) in his review of the book *Kenneth L. Pike: Selected Writings,* said, "Indeed, with his [Pike's] creation and espousal, over two decades, of tagmemics, as a working theory of linguistic analysis, he has guided more practicing linguists than has any other theoretician...."

Pike is also aware of a debt to SIL administration. He says that without Cameron Townsend, Founder of Wycliffe Bible Translators and the Summer Institute of Linguistics, that he would probably not have developed into a linguist. It was Townsend who urged him to study at the University of Michigan. In the years since then, many Branch Directors have opened the door to, and encouraged the study of, linguistics for the SIL members.

At the same time, Pike is conscious of his debt to the academic community. He says that no institute, no scholar, can produce in a vacuum and that no academic work is born in a vacuum; each stands on the shoulders of a predecessor.

So that's what this book is about. It is the story of how a monolingual, evangelical young person developed into a scholar renowned in linguistics, and how, through it all, he considered that his primary responsibility was to try to carry out the orders of his boss—Jesus Christ.

1 BEGINNINGS

(...1935)

Father (Ernest R. Pike, born in Maine in 1872) was a country doctor in Woodstock, Connecticut, back before there were many paved roads in the area. In our shed, in addition to buggies, we had a sleigh that Father used when the roads were covered with snow. He covered his legs with an old buffalo robe, and in real cold weather Mother gave him a hot soapstone to put at his feet. We also had a gig for use in the spring when the mud was deep. During good weather he made rounds in a Model-T Ford. No matter what the weather was, he managed to reach the sick even in the country towns beyond Woodstock.

We attended an old Congregational church where salvation and missions were not emphasized, but Father taught those things at home. Almost every day we gathered around him while he read a few Scripture verses, talked about them, and then prayed. On Sundays he told Bible stories to the younger members of the family. (We were six boys and two girls.) Ken (Kenneth L. Pike, born in Woodstock, Connecticut June 9, 1912) was next to the youngest; I was the youngest. We loved to hear Dad tell Bible stories; he really made the Old Testament characters live. He was very busy, but he made it a point to play with us on Sunday. It was his intention to make that day the happiest day of the week. Perhaps it was, at least the games were more fun when he was playing with us.

Mother (May Granniss Pike, born in Connecticut in 1873) had her influence too. She sang hymns as she worked, or while sitting in her rocking chair with two or three of us at her feet. Ken, especially, learned to love the hymn, "The Ninety and Nine that Safely Lay in the Shelter of the Fold,'' and even years later he could picture her as she sang it.

Mother helped us in any way she could, and she wanted to get us off to a good start. Sometimes the task seemed pretty big to her and she wondered out loud whether the day would ever come when all of us would be through high school—that we would go beyond that seemed too impossible to even contemplate.

Ken graduated from high school in 1928 and then he went to work in a supermarket in Providence, R.I., thirty miles from home. While he was there, early in July, Father was operated on for appendicitis. It should have been routine, and he should have been home again in a few days, but somehow a big subdiaphragmatic abscess formed. Instead of getting better, Father became steadily worse.

Security was one of the things that Dad had meant to Ken, and to him it seemed that the world without Father would be an impossible place. (He was sixteen at that time.) He prayed and promised the Lord that if Dad did not die, he'd go into the ministry.

Father did not die, but for the next five months he was in the hospital and on the danger list most of that time. It was not until the middle of December that he was well enough to be brought home. One of his lungs, and half of the other, was permanently tied down with adhesions. For the rest of his life, he breathed only with the half of the one lung that was still inflatable.

It was apparent that it was a lack of sterile technique in the operating room that had caused the problem. The surgeon knew that, and Father knew it. But when one of our brothers started to grumble about what had happened, Father silenced him with, ''My God is bigger than some sloppy scrub nurse!'' Since God is biggest, He must have permitted the carelessness; therefore, from Father's point of view, to sit griping because of what had happened was to gripe against God. That, Father would not allow.

After Father was home, the selectmen of town had an idea. They would receive gifts to help out Dr. Pike. The notice spread by word of mouth. They didn't have to solicit; the townspeople just brought the money to them. Only a few people gave as much as twenty-five dollars, more gave five or ten, and there were many one-dollar gifts. The selectmen deposited the money to Father's account at the bank and on Christmas day they brought the receipted bank deposit slip to the house. It came as a complete surprise to the Pike family and the selectmen chuckled. They had hoped that it would be a surprise, but it was hard to believe that everybody in several towns could keep such a secret. That was a happy day.

The size of the gift had been just enough to pay the hospital bill, and the people of the vicinity sighed with satisfaction. Dr. Pike had taken care of them when they were ill and now they had taken care of him. Actually the townspeople had been helping out even while Father was still in the hospital.

Many times when I was the only one at home, the doorbell would ring. I'd answer it. Some farmer would be there and he'd ask how much his bill was. I'd go to Dad's file and try to find it. Sometimes I couldn't. Maybe he had never recorded it. Maybe I didn't know where to look. Maybe it was there and I couldn't read his handwriting. Soon the farmer would get impatient. "I know I owe this to him! Take it!" So I took it. "Now give me a receipt." So I gave him a receipt. Father's only income for a year was from people like that—people paying back bills, some that had been recorded and some that hadn't. It was enough to take care of the household expenses.

In the meantime Ken decided that the Lord had met his conditions, but it took him a while to get up his courage to tell Mother and Dad that he was planning to study for the ministry. They didn't object, but at that time Ken felt so socially insecure that it was Mother who finally wrote to Gordon College of Theology and Missions, Boston [now in Beverly Farms], and asked for application blanks.

By the fall of 1929 Father had begun to work again, although on a restricted schedule, and Ken got ready to enter college. His things were packed, and the mail carrier (who also had a license to carry passengers) had agreed to pick him up and give him a ride to the railroad station seven miles away. The very morning he was to start he woke up to find that Dad was in deep pain and had been for several hours. It was Father's judgment that he would need another operation immediately. What should Ken do? He asked Mother, "Should I stay home?"

She replied, "No, Ken, go ahead; it's awfully easy to quit."

So Ken went. (Father did have an operation, but he came home from the hospital much sooner than anybody had guessed he would. The problem had been caused by adhesions from his previous operations. Some of them had stretched tightly across a section of bowel, and when the adhesions were loosened, the problem was over.)

At Gordon, Ken waited on tables for his room and board. Actually he enjoyed working with the kitchen crew. Soon he was feeling at home and swapping prank for prank with the other fellows; in his third year he was put in charge of the kitchen crew.

Meanwhile Ken was becoming more and more concerned for the millions of people in China who had never heard about Christ. Years before, he had become aware of their need when he discovered among Father's books a biography of Hudson Taylor, the founder of the China Inland Mission. Then, when Taylor's son and daughter-in-law, the Howard Taylors, spoke in chapel at Gordon, they presented the need in China very vividly. Ken began to feel that he should respond to that need. He memorized the names of the provinces and the number of inhabitants in each. He prayed for China daily, that somehow the people there might be told of Christ. Then on December 25, 1932, he sent in his application to the China Inland Mission. He was deliberately giving himself as a Christmas present to God. He intended that everything he had should be Christ's.

He graduated from Gordon in 1933 and as one of the commencement speakers, his main point was Ezekiel 3:18. The last clause of that verse thundered as he said it, "When I say unto the wicked, Thou shalt surely die; and thou givest him not warning, nor speakest to warn the wicked from his wicked way, to save his life: the same wicked man shall die in his iniquity; but his blood will I require at thine hand."

A little later he left for the China Inland Mission home in Philadelphia. He and a number of other candidates lived there for a few weeks while they were taught the mission's policies and given lessons in Mandarin Chinese. He loved hearing about China, he admired his teachers, and he wanted to learn all he could. In his eagerness he stayed up late night after night studying. That was a mistake. Without adequate rest, he was noticeably nervous—his brothers would have called him "jittery." The CIM leaders in the home began to doubt that he would be able to take the strain of living in the Chinese culture—perhaps he would crack up.

There was another problem. Mandarin has both voiceless unaspirated and voiceless aspirated stops, differences such as *pa* versus *pha*, and *ta* versus *tha*. Ken had not been able to hear and mimic that difference. "Pike," the teacher would say, "you don't hear the aspirates!"

At that time, Ken, without a knowledge of phonetics, had not been aware that there was a difference in the way English-speaking people pronounced the two "*p*" sounds of "*paper*." If he had known, he would have done a better job at mimicking Mandarin.

The CIM leaders didn't tell Ken that he was turned down because he had had trouble pronouncing the language lessons, they only mentioned the other problem—nervousness. With regret, they told him that they could not use him in China.

Being turned down hit Ken hard. It wasn't the loss of face, but the disappointment he felt. For more than a year Ken had been talking with enthusiasm about China and the China Inland Mission to just about everybody everywhere he had been. Years later, recalling those days, he told me, "China was written on my teeth!" And now? For Ken the upsetting thing was that he had been sure, no doubt whatever, that the Lord was going to use him in China. Apparently he had been wrong; apparently the Lord didn't need him there. Ken wanted, above all else, to do what the Lord wanted, but how could he know what that was?

Dad was a nice person to go home to at a time like that. He knew that Ken was nervous and that just maybe the CIM leaders were right, but now he helped Ken to pick up the pieces. They were both convinced that the Lord would use him somewhere, doing something, but where was it and what was it? What training did he lack if he were to fill the spot that the Lord had for him?

Well, he had been turned down because of poor health and someone at the mission home had suggested that he build up strength by working outdoors for a while. So Ken took a job with the CWA (Citizens Workers' Administration) in their attempt to eradicate the gypsy moth from New England. At that time the gypsy moths were causing whole forests to die. They attached their eggs in clusters to the underside of branches. The job of the crew working for CWA was to kill the eggs by painting them with creosote. Ken was one of a crew of fifteen fellows.

The problem was that Ken had always been afraid of heights. When he was six, he couldn't make himself climb to the belfry in our village church. He could go up the open stairway, but was unable to walk across the three-foot wide platform at the top. (It had no railing.) He'd sit on the landing and tremble while other six-year-olds ran on by.

Now his job was to climb one tree after another and paint gypsy moth eggs. He was still afraid of heights, and as he described it, the moths laid their eggs on branches that were more or less a mile and a half up in the sky. He'd climb a few feet, feel sick, pray, and inch up another six inches. He'd pray some more and manage to get a little farther up. He'd remember that he couldn't do any worse than break his neck, so he'd finally come within reach of the eggs. Anybody who saw him could tell he was scared.

One of his older brothers was half ashamed of this puny kid, but to Dad the tree-climbing was an encouraging sign. Ken was scared, yes, but he climbed in spite of that fact. Dad told the older brother, "Don't be concerned about Kenneth; he's got intelligence, courage, and determination. He will succeed in anything he tackles."

Well, he hadn't done very well on that tree-climbing job, and he had been rejected by the China Inland Mission, but Dad wasn't discouraged. In accordance with Eph. 5:17 ("Wherefore be ye not unwise, but understanding what the will of the Lord is.") Dad and Ken talked about the fact that Greek had always been easy for him. They talked about the training he might still be lacking to do the job the Lord had for him. Maybe it would help him to pronounce another language if he could study some phonetics. Then, if he learned phonetics, instead of being a regular missionary, he might be able to translate the Scriptures for a people somewhere.

After working outdoors for a year, Ken went back to Gordon for a postgraduate course to get more Greek and to see what the next step should be. While there he heard someone from India mention, in a casual way, that a little knowledge of phonetics could help missionaries in a short while to do better than they had done for many years. To Ken it sounded like magic.

It was also at Gordon that he met Sam Fisk, a missionary from the Philippines. Sam had just been in Arkansas and he told Ken about a tiny school, "Camp Wycliffe," that had started there just that previous summer. He urged Ken to go; linguistics was taught there, and they prepared students for Bible translation.

The more Ken thought about Bible translation, the more interested he became, so he wrote to every board on the list of the Interdenominational Foreign Missions Association (IFMA). He asked them to tell him where he could go to get training so that he could do Bible translation and technical linguistics on the mission field. The only one who replied saying that they took people specifically for Bible translation was Legters of the Pioneer Mission Agency, and he mentioned the same little school that Sam Fisk had told Ken about—it had had only two students that previous summer. According to the prospectus, a student would be taught, among other things, the description of an Indian language, some anthropology, and a short course in phonetics.

Phonetics! Here was a chance to fill in that known gap. If he took that summer course, perhaps he would be ready for the job the Lord had for him. Hoping and praying, Ken, in June of 1935, hitchhiked from Woodstock, Connecticut, to Sulphur Springs, Arkansas.

The fees for both room and board were six dollars a month. This low rate was possible because both W. Cameron Townsend and Leonard L. Legters, who had started the training camp, were convinced that missionary candidates needed training in pioneer living as well as in linguistics. They had rented a farmhouse for five dollars a month. The students made their own board beds. For a mattress, they stuffed a muslin cover with straw—they dried the wild oats that grew on the hill behind the farmhouse. (Ken was able to use one of the beds the previous students had made, but he made his own mattress.) That type of bed had one advantage—Ken pressed his best pants by stretching them out between the boards and the mattress.

Their chairs were empty nail kegs—not the most comfortable things to sit on for hours of class. Ken says he upholstered his nail keg with a little straw and a burlap sack. Without the upholstering, he wore out very soon.

The fellows did their own cooking over the firewood they them-selves had gathered, and they appreciated very much the farmers who'd bring them a bushel of apples occasionally. Especially prized were the times when one of the women of the area would invite the whole crowd over for ice cream and cake.

Townsend and Legters had started the training camp in 1934 and called it "Camp Wycliffe" in honor of John Wycliffe who had translated the Bible into English back in the 1300's.

Mr. Legters had been a missionary to the Comanche Indians but his mission board had not allowed him to learn their language, since, in those days, people thought it would be better for the Comanches if they learned English. Mr. Legters knew that they were not understanding his Gospel message, so, in hope that they would, he learned to preach to them in sign language. Later his work changed and he spent most of his time as a speaker in Christian conferences where he lectured on how to live a "victorious life." But he was still concerned for the Indians, and he made frequent survey trips throughout Central and South America. He found many groups speaking different languages who had had no way of hearing about Christ. He was convinced that Christians should make whatever effort was necessary to learn their languages, tell the Indians of Christ, and help them in other ways.

Mr. Townsend, while working with the Central American Mission, had translated the New Testament for the Cakchiquel-speaking people of Guatemala. Then he and his wife had been invalided home, he with tuberculosis and she with a very bad heart condition. They, too, were concerned for the Indians, so after Mr. Townsend had recovered from tuberculosis, he and Mr. Legters had decided to pool their experience and train young folks to translate the Bible for minority groups.

There had been only two regular students the first summer, and in 1935 there were only five. Mr. Legters, for his part of the summer course, gave about twenty hours in ethnology and anthropology, and general missionary principles. (Several people have written about those early days, among them are: Ethel E. Wallis and Mary A Bennett, *Two Thousand Tongues to Go,* 1959; James and Marti Hefley, *Uncle Cam,* 1974: William Cameron Townsend and Richard S. Pittman, *Remember All the Way,* 1975.)

Mr. Townsend gave the bulk of the grammar lectures basing them on Cakchiquel. Ken was especially impressed by a verb chart that he used. It was a strip of cardboard with a row of windows cut into it. For each window there was a list of affixes or clitics which could occur in that spot. They had such meanings as tense, voice, mode, person. The biggest window was for the stem. By pulling the lists up or down, Mr. Townsend was able to make a hundred thousand theoretically possible verb forms.

Although phonetics was taught for ten days only, Ken became tremendously enthusiastic about the subject, and those ten days helped shape his life. Dr. Elbert McCreery, who had been a missionary in Africa, emphasized the sounds that had occurred in the languages he had studied there. As part of the course, he taught the difference between aspirated and unaspirated stops—the sounds that had blocked Ken when he had been trying to mimic Mandarin Chinese. To his amazement, by following Dr. McCreery's instructions, he learned very quickly to hear and make the sounds.

He was amazed to find that the very sounds which had given him trouble when he tried to pronounce Chinese actually occurred in his own speech. One was like the first "*p*" in the English word "*paper*," and the other was like the second "*p*" of that word.

Ken still talks of the day when he finally realized that the two p's in "*paper*" were pronounced differently. It was not the difficulty of the sounds that had caused the problem, rather it was that the sounds did not function the same way in both languages. It was the clash of language systems that had stymied him.

Once he caught on, he had great fun making the sounds that Dr. McCreery demonstrated. Within weeks he was writing home to Dad and Mother telling them how to make some of them.

Back in 1899 Dad and Mother had gone to Metlaktla, Alaska, to work among the Tsimshean Indians there. Dad had enjoyed mimicking the language, and once in a while, thirty years later, he'd say a few words for us, or tell us about some of the ones that he had not been able to mimic well. Out in Camp Wycliffe, Ken got a hold of a description, by Boas, of the pronunciation of Chinook, an Indian language that used to be spoken by people who lived in the vicinity of the Columbia River. He figured that some of it would be the same as the language of the people where Dad and Mother had been working. He wrote, "Try to gargle and say o-o-o at the same time. Is that the sound you were talking about?" Dad read the letter, followed instructions, chuckled and said, "That's it."

Remembering that time in Alaska, Dad had advised Ken, "Take care of your health. You'll do people more good if you stay with them twenty years than if you stay only two." He knew from experience. He had worked too hard in Alaska, become ill, and he and Mother had had to leave. Later his health improved, but because he couldn't go back, he practiced as a country doctor in Lakeville, Connecticut. Then in 1912 he and Mother, with six children, moved to Woodstock. He chose to be in the country instead of the city because he felt more needed there.

But, in 1935, Ken's main problem was to get to be with a people at all. Mr. Townsend asked him what he was planning to do. Ken told him that he didn't know, and Mr. Townsend's response was a quiet, "Well, why don't you come with us to Mexico?"

Those were wonderful words. He was going to be given a chance at last. Of course money would be needed, but his brother Galen (ten years older than Ken) had given him the first thirty-five dollars—that was the amount that Mr. Townsend had said each fellow should have if he wanted to take a three-week trip into Mexico.

The fellows couldn't make an appeal for funds to a church because new missionaries were no longer allowed to enter Mexico. Mr. Legters, however, never forgot that they needed money, and as he traveled around the country, he would tell people informally that he knew of a good place for them to put their tithe money. Through the people Mr. Legters contacted, Ken received about thirty dollars a month. That wasn't much, but at that time it was enough.

The fellows knew that they could not be ordinary missionaries, but they did hope to translate the Scriptures. In fact that seemed so important to them that they agreed that they would be willing to do any type of work—even "dig ditches"—if while they were doing it, they could translate the Scriptures. Mr. Townsend had a very definite idea of what that type of work should be—linguistics. Even that summer he was already planning for five hundred translators who would also be linguists, and he told the five students that in ten or fifteen years the work they were about to do would make the scientists sit up and take notice. To the students, that summer of 1935, that was a wild dream, but to Mr. Townsend it was a very practical matter—he knew that God is great and he knew that there were at least one thousand groups who still did not have the New Testament.

Ken was grateful to Mr. Townsend for overlooking the nervousness that others had objected to in him, and for letting him work. He determined to give the job all he had.

2 TO THE MIXTEC-SPEAKING PEOPLE

(Fall of 1935—early 1936)

Ken and his fellow students, Bill Sedat, Max Lathrop, Brainard Legters (son of L.L. Legters), and Richmond McKinney, crossed the border with Mr. Townsend on August 20, 1935. They traveled slowly, stopping to visit with friends of the Townsends in Monterrey and in Tamazunchale. They also traveled slowly because the rains had been heavy and sections of the Laredo-Mexico City highway had washed out. In several places they had to wait while the construction crew blasted a chunk out of the mountain and then cleared the dirt and rocks off the road.

It wasn't until the 28th of August that they arrived in Mexico City at the home of the Presbyterian missionaries, Mr. and Mrs. Norman Taylor. They fed the fellows supper and gave them a place to stay in one of their schools that was closed at the time.

The Taylors knew that Mr. Townsend's group was planning to translate the New Testament for some of the Indians of Mexico and they were glad to help them. It was through them that the fellows made contact with some Otomí-speaking people. Actually within three days of arriving in Mexico City, they were out in an Otomí village.

It had been decided that Richmond McKinney would learn that language, but Ken was listening right along with him. They had to sit on the floor while they worked, but not even that dampened their enthusiasm. They studied all afternoon, and in the evening they lit a candle and kept on. Ken reveled in the nasalized vowels, the glottal stops, and other Otomí sounds. One of the reasons he listened with such fervor was because Mr. Townsend had asked him to be ready to teach a class in Indian phonetics the coming summer.

In his sleeping bag on the floor, he woke up in the middle of the night, turned, tossed, prayed and wondered what the outline of the course should be.

He was also thinking about the difference between nouns and verbs and the way a noun sometimes became a verb, etc. The next day he tried his ideas out on one of the other fellows, and later he talked them over with Mr. Townsend.

Ken was also wondering which language he himself should study, and in what village he should live. So, a few days after being with the Otomí-speaking people, he took a second-class train to Oaxaca. There he went to the Presbyterian home where students from rural towns were given room and board while they went to school. Ken was there only four days, but with the help of Miss Ethel Doctor, who was in charge, he was able to study with students who spoke two different Zapotec dialects, two Mixtec dialects, and a Mixe dialect. He even spent a few hours in two different Indian towns. He was enthusiastic about each of the languages, but decided that he would translate the New Testament for the Mixtec people.

Meanwhile, back in Mexico City, Mr. Townsend had heard that the Seventh Inter-American Scientific Congress was meeting in Mexico City. He determined that the fellows not only be Bible translators, but that they also be scientists, so he not only attended himself, but he saw to it that the fellows attended all three days too.

Of course it was very worthwhile for the fellows to make the acquaintance of Mexican officials who were interested in the Indians, but it also emphasized Mr. Townsend's point that he expected them to become competent linguists. In fact, he was already calling them "linguists." Ken determined to be worthy of the name, and he started studying Mixtec almost immediately.

Mr. Townsend had found out about an old man in the city who spoke that language, and he took Ken to his first lesson. Mr. Eulogio Martínez was lonesome and so, for him, teaching was not only a financial help, but a pleasure as well; he wanted company. If Ken had been choosing, however, he probably would have picked someone else. Eulogio had lost most of his upper teeth, so his articulation was not the best. He was blind, and was confined to bed.

Ken knew no Spanish, so he was going to have to build on the Mixtec he learned with Mr. Townsend interpreting. He had planned that, after Mr. Townsend was gone, he would let Eulogio know what he wanted by pointing to something, or by acting out a verb. But that morning when he found out that Eulogio was both blind and bedridden it seemed to him that it would be almost impossible to learn much from him. He and Mr. Townsend worked a couple of hours, then, on the way home, Mr. Townsend said to him, "Kenneth, next time try not to let your disappointment be so obvious."

Ken kept going back, of course, and even that very day he put words and phrases on slips of paper and started memorizing. He also started making a small dictionary, and lists of words in which one sound was compared with another.

Actually he accomplished quite a bit, and a month later he showed a summary of his data to Dr. Silva y Aceves, director of the Mexican Institute of Linguistic Investigations, and former Rector of the University of Mexico. Dr. Silva y Aceves was enthusiastic enough so that a few months later he asked Ken to go to Otomí country with him and record Otomí data.

But it wasn't just linguistics that Ken was learning. Mr. Townsend made it a point to take the fellows with him whenever he had reason to go to a government office, and he made sure that they knew how to act while there. He wanted them to follow Mexican rules of politeness. With the car at the sidewalk, the motor turned off, Mr. Townsend would turn to the fellows one at a time and ask, "What's your name?" Each responded with the proper formula. For example, Ken said, "Kenneth Pike, to serve you."

If the fellows became restless while waiting to be admitted into the presence of the official, or if they started to joke among themselves, Mr. Townsend stopped them, reminding them that a person had to be dignified while waiting in an office—even an outer office.

The visits to government offices proved to be very worthwhile. The officials knew that the fellows wanted to study the languages and translate portions of Scripture. When they learned that they also wanted to help the Indians and teach them to read, they gave them letters of introduction to the mayors of the towns where the fellows were going. Ken was given letters both from the Mexican Institute of Linguistic Investigations and from the Mexican Department of Labor.

With those letters in hand, Ken knew that the time had come. At his next Mixtec lesson, he thanked Eulogio and told him goodbye. In addition to getting a start in the language, Ken had also picked up tidbits about the Mixtec culture—grasshoppers for example. It was there that Ken ate his first. As a very special treat, a bagful had been brought in from Eulogio's village by his son.

At the request of Mr. Townsend, Ken was heading out for Mixtec country without knowing Spanish. Mr. Townsend had been telling the government officials that the young fellows he was bringing to Mexico would be experts in the Indian languages, and he wanted to be sure that in a few months they would be. If Ken took the first year to study Spanish, the evidence that Mr. Townsend would be able to present to the government would be small, since he was the only one of the fellows who was going to an Indian village that fall. (The other fellows had come down for the three-week trip only. One would return after he had finished school, and the other two after getting married.)

Mr. Townsend knew that many English-speaking people had arrived in a Spanish-speaking country saying that they were planning to learn an Indian language, but they had not learned it. He knew that it was possible for that to happen to the young folks who were with him. He thought that there was a better chance that they learn the Indian language, if they learned it before they learned Spanish. He wanted to start that as a policy, so he asked Ken to go to an Indian village before knowing Spanish.

In preparation for the undertaking, Ken spent the morning of November seventh in prayer and fasting. He wanted the Lord's help in choosing the village in which he should live, and he asked the Lord to help him to learn the language to such an extent that he could be thinking in it by summer, and most of all he wanted to become more aware of the very greatness of God.

In the afternoon he went to say goodbye to one of the officials with whom he had become friends at the Scientific Congress. Ken had given Professor Javier Uranga, who was secretary to the Minister of Labor, a couple of lessons in English, and he had let Ken copy some unpublished census charts listing the towns with Mixtec-speaking people. Those charts showed Ken the general area in which he would be working.

The next day he left for Oaxaca. Because Ken spoke no Spanish, Antonio Guellano Garza, an eighteen-year-old Mexican who spoke English well, agreed to go with him. They traveled the seventeen hours to Oaxaca in a second-class railroad coach. The coach had three wooden benches running down the length of it—one down each side and one down the center. At night Ken and Tony dozed, stretched out on the center bench.

In Oaxaca they called on Miss Doctor who had helped Ken on his previous trip, and she gave him the names of an evangelical family in Parián. That's the town he was heading for because its railroad station was the nearest one to Mixtec country.

They arrived in Parián on the 14th of November and immediately they sought out the friends of Miss Doctor. They were very helpful, and through them Ken and Tony were able to hire a man and his donkeys to travel with them. Ken and Tony would ride two of the donkeys, the others would carry the luggage—Ken had two heavy suitcases, a duffle bag, a bedroll, and a typewriter.

That was an exciting time, starting off early in the morning, climbing up, up, and up. Riding along on his donkey, toes turned up to keep them from dragging, Ken could look back and down, and watch the now-tiny train until it disappeared into the cactus-lined canyons. Somewhere ahead of them was the village where he would live, and the Mixtec-speaking people for whom he would translate.

Most of the trails they traveled were steep and stony. The country was arid, and the mountainsides were gashed with deep gullies. Ken and Tony went from village to village, stopping a day or two in each. Ken would inquire about Mixtec-speakers there and study a few hours if someone was available. They slept on the floor in just anybody's house, or in the townhall, and ate whatever they were lucky enough to be served. In one town they were given potatoes in addition to the eggs and tortillas they had had in the other towns. That was a real treat.

Two weeks after leaving Parián, they arrived in Tlaxiaco. It seemed like a metropolis—some streets and some stores had electricity. There was a hotel, and most important of all there was a doctor and a drugstore. Ken had a dozen infected sores on his legs which continued to bother him even after using the salve the doctor prescribed.

Tlaxiaco was also the headquarters for the district school inspector. Tony and Ken went to see him and told him of Ken's plans to study Mixtec. The inspector invited them to speak to the teachers who had come to town for a conference, and to ask them about the towns where they were teaching. Ken asked questions and told them about the different dialects of Mixtec. A couple of days later he was delighted when the director of an Indian boarding school in Chalcatongo invited him to go there to study. It seemed ideal because so many of the students spoke Mixtec.

The director gave Ken and Tony a cordial welcome. He invited them to eat with the students, loaned them a blanket, and let them sleep on the floor of his office. Chalcatongo was over eight thousand feet above sea level and at night it was cold. In spite of the blanket, Ken and Tony almost froze until Ken's bedroll caught up with them—it had been left a couple of towns back.

The students at the boarding school lived on about thirty centavos a day (less than ten cents U.S. currency). That covered the cost of the food, clothing, and supplies. Every day the food consisted of tortillas, beans, black coffee, about a square inch of meat with a little broth or tomato soup, chile, and a chunk of whole-wheat bread. Sometimes they had a little potato. At Christmas time Ken gave the director some money so that the students could have a special treat on that day.

The classes were in music, agriculture, and other practical things, and the students were being trained to go back and teach the people in their villages—they came from many different places. There were about forty-five boys, fifteen girls, nine teachers, and the director.

One day the director asked Ken (the director spoke quite a bit of English), "What does the Bible say?"

"What about?" Ken responded. The director didn't seem to know, so Ken read to him from the tenth chapter of John, and then many verses that told about Christ's love and His readiness to forgive our sins. Then, when Ken asked him to take Christ as his Lord, the director surprised Ken by telling him that he had believed the first time he had talked to him about Christ (that had been while they were still in Tlaxiaco). Later he told Ken that for three years he had attended the Presbyterian Mission School in Coyocán. He had not decided to follow Christ then, but by 1935 he was ready to do so. Ken was grateful that the Lord had allowed him to reap where the Presbyterians had sown.

Ken enjoyed his contact with the teachers there in Chalcatongo. Every afternoon he gave them a lesson in English, and he learned some of the culture from them. As he said in one of his letters, "I have seen a cockfight and eaten part of the loser."

Then Tony received word of a death in the family, and he had to return to Mexico City. He had helped Ken establish a line of friends all the way from Mexico City to Chalcatongo—about the best thing anybody could have done. Now Ken figured he could get along alone, especially since he was spending most of his time with Mixtec-speaking students.

One of them told him a Mixtec story about a skunk. It went something like this:

> There were two skunks and they had a little son. "Let us look for a godfather for our son," they said.
>
> So they went and asked the coyote, "Will you be our godfather?"
>
> "No," he said, "I do not want to have anything to do with skunks, and I have work to do."
>
> Mr. and Mrs. Skunk were very very sad. They went and asked the Honorable Mr. Fox, and he said "no" too. Then they were very very very sad. They decided to ask Mr. Lion. He was glad to be godfather. So they went to the priest and had the little boy skunk baptized.
>
> "Eat your tortillas, Godfather," said Mrs. Skunk (for they had put on a party for him).
>
> "I do not know how to eat tortillas," said Mr. Lion, "I must have meat."

So Mr. and Mrs Skunk were very very ashamed indeed, and Mr. Skunk went to look for a bull to get meat. He met a bull, jumped on its back and began to scratch. That made the bull furious. He waved his head from side to side, caught little Mr. Skunk on his horns, and killed him.

Just then Mr. Lion arrived and saw the skunk on the horns of the bull. He ran very fast and took him off, but it was too late. He took dead Mr. Skunk back to Mrs. Skunk, and they both began to cry.

They ran to call the sexton (who was the buzzard) to come and say prayers at the head of Mr. Skunk. Mr. Sexton mumbled some prayers at the head of Mr. Skunk as they buried him. The end.

Ken studied the story carefully, not only for vocabulary, but also in order to figure out the Mixtec way of putting a sentence together. With the help of the students he had made considerable progress. Now, in his enthusiasm, he thought he might be able to write up a little something in Mixtec so that the students could read it at Christmas time. He was writing about the story of John the Baptist (Mark 1:4-8) and when he needed the word "baptized," he took a piece out of the story about Mr. and Mrs. Skunk. When the students read it, they whooped with delight. He had taken too big a piece and as he had written it that day, John had baptized a skunk.

In such ways as that, Ken's language learning was going ahead at a great rate, but he was having another problem. Many of the sores that he had had on his legs in Tlaxiaco had still not healed, and he had some new ones. The sores would start from a flea bite, or from a bruise. They would scab over, then fester under the scab, and continue getting bigger. Two were an inch and a half in diameter. Some, down near his ankle were swollen and especially angry looking.

Ken went to see the nurse at the school and she told him to go to bed and keep hot salt packs on them. So, for the next three days he spent most of the time stretched out beside his gasoline lantern. It was a combination lamp-stove, and he was able to heat water on it. After three days of hot packs, the swelling was down.

It was taking Ken about an hour and a half a day to wash off and clean up his legs, and put the bandages back on again. He counted the sores, and he had more than twenty-six on his calves and ankles. But he couldn't see that his treatment was doing any good. He began to run out of bandages, time, and patience, so he made up his mind to wrap his legs up and leave them alone. He'd spend his time on language learning and making friends with the Mixtecs.

A couple of weeks later some of the students were going out to Oaxaca to study how to become rural school teachers. Ken decided that he would travel along with them as far as the railroad station and then go on from there back to see Mr. Townsend.

While they were on horseback on their way to Tlaxiaco, Ken, talking in Mixtec, told the students about Jesus Christ. Of course they talked about other things too—the United States, for example. These young folks, on their way to the city for the first time, had never heard of the place.

When he got to Mexico City and went to see the doctor, some of the bandages had been on for three weeks. It took a while to clean the debris away, and then Ken was amazed to see that the sores were better, not worse. Somehow they had started to heal while buried under the bandages. But the doctor told him that he should not go back out to Mixtec country until the ulcers were completely healed. While they were getting better, Ken went to be with the Townsends.

3   FLEAS AND DONKEYS

(Spring of 1936)

Mr. Townsend with his wife Elvira and his niece Evelyn Griset were living in Tetelcingo, a little Aztec village about sixty miles south of Mexico City. Townsend had placed their trailer in the middle of the dusty town square, and to make larger living quarters had built a lean-to using cornstalks for the walls, covering them with cheesecloth. Soon after arriving he had hired a pair of oxen and a wooden plow and had plowed up enough of the square to make a small garden. He planted cabbage and lettuce and a few other vegetables. The plants had come up in pretty rows and made a beautiful sight.

Just one small pipeline of water came into the village and it ended in a cement tank in the square. The women came there for water and carried it home a pailful at a time. The water for the garden was the overflow from that tank.

Not only women, but men came to the square too. They gathered at the town hall, or in the village store. When they stopped to look at the garden, Townsend would hand them a head of lettuce, or some other vegetable and tell them how to eat it. In that way he was teaching the whole village about vegetables and demonstrating that they could be grown in their own area.

He was also teaching some of them how to read. He had been studying Aztec with the town mayor and together they had prepared primers in that language. By the time Ken arrived back from Mixtec country, the Mexican government had published the primers, and Townsend had organized classes. Both he and Evelyn were teaching, and then Ken helped out too.

Townsend had written the language in such a way that each letter represented a specific sound, therefore Ken was able to read and pronounce the Aztec even though he did not know what the words meant. He found it fascinating to sit or squat around a dim light in a little hut and hear men reading for the first time in their lives.

At that time there was some question as to how long Ken and the Townsends would be able to stay in Mexico. In those days Americans obtained tourist papers for a visit to Mexico with no trouble at all, but more permanent papers were difficult to come by. Because of the Aztec primers and the little garden, the Secretary of Labor became convinced that it would benefit the Indian-speaking people if the Townsends and the young folks they sponsored would live among them. Therefore the Secretary of Labor saw to it that the Townsends received the necessary papers.

Ken needed permanent papers too, and it was Dr. Silva y Aceves of the Mexican Institute of Linguistic Investigations who filled out the necessary forms for him. This Institute was very much interested in any information they could get on the Indian languages of Mexico. Specifically they were pleased with the stories that the Mixtec men told Ken. He typed them up, and, with the help of the village school teachers, translated them into Spanish, and turned a copy over to them. He enjoyed talking with the men of the Linguistic Institute at the University and he went there not only to chit-chat with them, but to read linguistic books in their library. It was there that he discovered *Language* by Sapir and he kept going back until he had gone through the book thoroughly.

It was while he was in Tetelcingo that he first began to correspond with Dr. Thomas F. Cummings, professor of phonetics and missionary linguistics, at the Biblical Seminary in New York. They wrote back and forth about languages where glottal stops were found, and voiceless laterals, and other non-English sounds. Ken found the contact very stimulating.

But in spite of the good time he was having in Tetelcingo, Ken was impatient to get back to Mixtec country. He had learned a lot from the students in the Chalcatongo school, but he had begun to feel that it was time he moved to a village where everybody spoke Mixtec. He asked questions about the neighboring towns, and was told about San Miguel—he could walk to it in about an hour and a half. The students didn't recommend that village, in fact they told him that it would be dangerous for him to go there.

About eight years previous to that time, there had been a border dispute between San Miguel and Chalcatongo, the neighboring town. The state militia had been sent in to enforce peace, but the men from San Miguel jumped them and killed most of them. Then a horde of soldiers was sent in. They ransacked many of the homes in San Miguel and carried off a number of the men whom they shot in Oaxaca city—or at least that is the way some San Miguel people tell it.

Ken's friends at the Chalcatongo school told him, "You wouldn't last more then forty-eight hours there."

Telling about it later, Ken said, "I was scared." But thinking and praying in the middle of the night, he became convinced that San Miguel was the place where the Lord wanted him to go. So he went.

By the last of March, 1936, he had rented a small log cabin and moved in. Like most huts of the area, it had a dirt floor and no windows. The only light came in through the cracks between the logs of the wall. Especially at night the wind howled through those same cracks, but even though that made the nights very cold, Ken wrote, "I love to hear the wind. The pine trees let it use their branches like a pipe organ."

The roof of the cabin was made of shingles that were about three feet long and six inches wide, and in a number of places Ken could see the sky between them.

The landlords were still using one side of the room for storing some of their larger gear—for example, four huge clay pots (the smaller ones were three feet tall), an ox yoke, various baskets, and a loom which the landlord and his sons used to weave the wool blankets worn by the men of the area.

Ken's bed was a round log beside a square one and the total width was sixteen inches. One night, soon after he arrived, he awoke to hear men shouting in the distance, "Go get him!"

Looking out between the logs of the wall, he could see their pine torches and flashlights coming up from the center of town. He stopped watching and crawled further into his sleeping bag, but he could still hear the sound of many feet on the path. The men rattled the door, but he pretended to be asleep. When he didn't answer, they pushed it open and came in. They seemed to fill the room, and then they leaned over him and shook him.

"Oh," said Ken, as though he were just waking up.

They explained that they had come to him for medical help. There had been a family quarrel and their sister's head had been slashed.

Telling about that night afterwards, Ken said that he had been just as afraid as if the prediction of the Chalcatongo teachers had been about to happen. But the Lord, by means of Luke 12:32, had told him not to be afraid, and, by means of Luke 10:3, had told him that he would be as a lamb among wolves—he would not be able to protect himself. When the Lord said, "Go," in Luke 10:3, He didn't say that there would be no danger. In Luke 12:32, He had mentioned a "kingdom", but Ken noted that he would get what the Lord wanted him to have only because God would give it to him.

Even though it was several years before Ken told the rest of us how he felt about sheep and wolves and God, it was his deep belief in that relationship that took him to San Miguel.

Now that he was in San Miguel, he concentrated on learning to talk Mixtec, and making friends. The story about Mr. and Mrs. Skunk that he had memorized while in Chalcatongo was one of his props. The town president liked that tale so much that he'd walk up to Ken's house just to hear him tell it again. In the market, in the store, wherever Ken went, the fellows would ask him to repeat it for them.

Actually, San Miguel was quite a story-telling community. The men would sit around and tell each other stories, and Ken became one of the main performers. He wrote their tales down and they would shout with laughter when he read them back to them. He found that he had to memorize them to be able to read them in a way that sounded more or less like a Mixtec talking, but it was worth the time it took. It not only helped him to make friends, but it taught him the language.

He told the stories so much that his friends memorized them too. Then whenever Ken, in ordinary conversation, would use a phrase from a story, the men would recognize its origin and roar in approval.

In this way his language learning was going along at a great rate, but there was another problem that he had not conquered yet. There was still the problem of the fleas. Remembering that many of his ulcers had started from flea bites, Ken had gone back to Mixtec country well fortified against them. That is, he carried some creosol with him.

The fleas lived in the cracks of the dirt floor of his hut, and by wetting down the floor with creosol, he hoped to kill them off. There seemed to be thousands. At night he could see them jumping as they tried to escape the beam of his flashlight. As he watched, he estimated with amazement that they could jump eight inches high. It was apparent that he could not escape the fleas on his low log bed, so he decided to put his two tables end to end and sleep there. To make the bed level and more comfortable, he put a couple of boards on top. At first all went well, but the floor sloped and in the middle of the night the boards slipped. Ken and boards went down with a clatter. The neighbors woke up startled and apprehensive. Then they laughed. Ken heard them say, "Pike just fell out of bed."

Then Ken tied the boards onto the tables, but a few nights later one of the tables tipped and as he described it, his bed "became a toboggan" and he "had a beautiful ride." Again he heard the neighbors chuckle. The Mixtecs themselves slept with only a straw mat between them and the floor, and so to them, falling out of bed was especially funny. The midnight clatter finally convinced them, however, that Ken really did need a new bed, so the next day the old man, Narciso, began working on the one that Ken had asked him to make. It was to be three feet high—high enough so that the fleas could not jump to a blanket and use it as a ladder up to warmth and a free meal.

The afternoon the bed was finished Ken spent extra time "hunting the critters." He took his sleeping bag out and shook it like a rug to get rid of any fleas that might be inside. Then to be sure that none had succeeded in taking refuge in a seam or crease, he put it out in the sun. Now for a good night's sleep!

But the fleas still found him. Apparently they were dropping down from the roof.

Then Ken got mad. God could control fleas; why did He let them torment him? He knew that Ken was doing everything he could to translate the New Testament for the Mixtec-speaking people; why did He let the fleas steal his study time—making him spend hours doctoring ulcers? Ken was doing his share; why didn't God do His? It just wasn't fair!

In some such way as that, Ken complained to God for days. Then he began to think about the implications of his complaint. Just suppose God controlled the fleas so that only non-Christians were bitten. How conceited Christians would become! Ken knew that he couldn't afford to be conceited; it was dangerous to be proud. So, well, Ken decided that God's way was right; fleas should be allowed to bite Christians and non-Christians alike.

He did try greasing himself with lard—that is what the Mixtecs did sometimes. He found that the grease really helped, and he wrote home that the first time he tried it, the "pests" had awakened him "only three or four times" that night.

Old Narciso, the neighbor who had made the bed, was also the best story-teller in town. "I have a fortune," Ken wrote, "two more legends!" The old man dropped in occasionally to tell him another one. Ken paid him three times as much for one legend (about two hour's work) as the fellow would receive for working all day as a carpenter. That was about six times as much as he would have received for working as a farm hand. Narciso thought he was really getting big money for his story-telling, and Ken heard him bragging about it to the other fellows afterwards.

The legends were not only good for studying grammar, but Ken found another use for them. He typed them out and put a copy in a book where his visitors could see it. School children and young men stopped by often and studied the page to which the book was turned. When anybody asked them if they could read in their own language, they had always insisted that they couldn't. Now, given a chance to try quietly, with no loss of face involved, they were finding that they could not only read, but that they enjoyed doing it. This was a great encouragement to Ken. He figured that if the people would read and re-read a half dozen legends, it would partially prepare them for reading the New Testament some day.

If he were going to complete that New Testament for them, he would have to keep his health—he kept remembering China and the fact that he had been rejected because he was not strong. So, even while out among the Mixtecs, he worked on building up his strength.

His log cabin was located at about eight thousand feet above sea level, and not far from the cabin was an extremely steep part of the mountain. In order to increase his stamina, he'd run down the hill a couple of hundred yards, turn around and speed back up. He did that often until at last he was able to keep ahead of some of his Mixtec friends when traveling the trail between San Miguel and Tlaxiaco. That really made him happy.

He enjoyed being out with the Mixtec fellows and trying to do things the Mixtec way. He tried his hand at cutting down wheat with a sickle and winnowing it. Then one day he went up the mountain with Nalo and Leto, sons of old Narciso, to get firewood. He chopped down a tree with a machete, and cut it up into sticks two and a half feet long. He estimated the number he could carry, piled them up and tied them together with a tumpline—one loop around each end of the load, leaving a still larger loop that was to fit across his chest. While the men supervised every detail, he laid his blanket over the pack—that was to keep the wood from chafing his back. Then he ducked down and slipped his head and shoulders up behind the tumpline. Next he was supposed to stand up, raising the load as he did so. But he couldn't—it was too heavy. Then Leto held Ken's pack just off his back while he stood up under it. Gently Leto lowered it to his back again. Then off they went down the pine needle slope together.

Ken wrote that he got a lot of fun out of trying such things, but that the men had even more fun watching him. Fun or not, he wasn't tempted to try to earn his living by bringing back firewood. If, that day, Leto had sold his load of wood in the village market, he would have received only three cents (U.S. currency), in spite of all the work it had been to get it.

Ken was determined, at whatever cost, to be with the men in situations where he could converse with them. He said that "many times the cost was loss of dignity"—when he was stunting with them, for example. Something as simple as summersaults or hop-scotch would hold the graybeards—even the school teachers—enthralled. They began to consult him as an expert in games. Sometimes he flubbed, of course, and they hooted with laughter, but at the same time they were enjoying hugely his progress in the use of Mixtec.

The time Ken set aside for stunting with the men was a deliberate part of his language study program. It was as much a part of that program as the hours he spent analyzing the grammar and memorizing vocabulary. In fact his mind was becoming so saturated with Mixtec that he wrote to Father and asked him to send down some old Newsweek magazines and Reader's Digests. He wrote, "To study nothing but Mixtec is just like strumming a banjo on one string for two hours without changing your finger. My mind needs something else badly."

Of course he changed his type of activity, but as long as he was relating to the people of San Miguel, it was still Mixtec. There was one thing, however, that he described as "just plain fun." That was telling Bible stories. Old Narciso, Nalo, and Leto were the ones who listened most frequently. Ken told them, for example, about Gideon's army with its earthenware crocks and torches. When the trumpets sounded, the crocks were broken,the men shouted, and the enemy got scared and ran (Judges 6 and 7). As Ken's friends listened, their eyes opened wide with amazement. Their reaction thrilled Ken, especially because Narciso wanted to buy a Bible. He wanted the very best he could get in exchange for the three-foot-high bed he had made. So Ken ordered one for him.

But the very evening that Narciso asked for a Bible, he said, "It's better in Mixtec." He picked up the Gospel of Luke that was on Ken's desk, turned to the first chapter, and then grumbled because it was in Spanish.

"That part hasn't been written in your language yet," Ken told him. The old man insisted that he wanted to read it in Mixtec, and again Ken told him that it hadn't been written yet.

The old man held the book closer, squinted through his twisted granny-like spectacles and slowly began in Mixtec, "It says..." Ken reached for his notebook and began scribbling furiously. When he paused, his pen poised expectantly, the old man went on to the second verse. Then the third.

In the next two hours he gave a rough draft of a number of verses. Then he sighed, "This is a long story," he said.

"Yes," said Ken, "I guess we had better finish it tomorrow."

Narciso left and Ken went to bed filled with hope. (Maybe the old man was going to study the Bible until he was completely won over by the Lord.) Ken was awakened by drunken shouts coming from the hut next door. The same man who had been eagerly reading the Bible a few hours before was now uproariously drunk. Ken wrote home, "Such things seem a strange and dismaying contradiction."

Leto, Narciso's son, wanted a New Testament, so Ken let him have one in exchange for a haircut. While he was wondering how he could encourage him to read it, Leto came to weave a blanket on the loom stored in the house Ken was renting. What a beautiful opportunity! While he worked, Ken read aloud to him in Spanish from the Gospel of John. As he read, Leto wove thumpety-thump on the loom.

After each section, Ken stopped reading and retold that part in Mixtec. With the first Mixtec sentence, Leto's motion was suspended. With his feet still on the pedals, his face alight with interest, he listened, sometimes exclaiming in amazement, for example, when people picked up rocks with which to stone Jesus (John 10:31). Then when the Mixtec explanation was finished, Leto went back to work, thumpety-thump for as long as Ken was reading.

Ken kept on, straight through the book, alternating reading in Spanish with retelling in Mixtec. Leto never lost interest while Ken "stuttered an explanation" in Mixtec, but the only time he did not weave in tune to Ken's reading in Spanish was during the nineteenth chapter which tells about Christ's crucifixion. That chapter captured his entire attention in both languages. After four hours, the book of John was finished. Ken's letter said, "I was about finished too."

Ken knew that he was soon to leave for Arkansas to teach phonetics in Camp Wycliffe, and he knew that he would not be back in San Miguel for at least four months. He didn't want to be away from Mixtec-speaking people that long, and he also wanted the students to hear a speaker of another Indian language, so he asked Leto to go to the States with him.

Even though Leto was married, the San Miguel culture required that he get his father's permission before leaving home. He also had to make arrangements with his father-in-law for the care of his wife and little daughter. Ken hired donkeys, one to ride and others to carry his baggage. Then Narciso and Nalo asked permission to carry some of the load—they could pick up a little cash that way. Ken was delighted to have the men along—besides someone was needed to return the donkeys to their owner. So it was arranged.

At last everything seemed ready, the day and hour agreed upon had arrived, but Nalo had gone to buy corn. By the time he got back, the party was no longer fit to travel—the wife had served her husband and father-in-law too much pulque, the fermented juice of the maguey plant.

The next morning it was about ten-thirty before they actually got underway, and they traveled slowly—the men were finding the packs rather heavy. They stopped that night and everybody slept in a shelter usually used by donkeys—it had a thatched roof but no walls.

The second day they were off by 4:30 a.m., but Narciso was having trouble with his foot, so Ken let him put his pack on the donkey and Ken walked.

The third morning the old man and Nalo turned back with the San Miguel donkeys. Ken and Leto hired others and went on.

The fourth day was supposed to begin very early—at midnight in fact, but they were not really underway before 2:30 a.m. "No problem," the owner of the donkeys assured Ken. They would be in Parián in plenty of time to catch the nine o'clock train for Mexico City.

But the animals were slow and the driver unconcerned. Ken tried to hurry them on himself, but somehow he did not have the knack. Their speed remained the same even when he whipped them. Finally the driver got the idea that Ken was really in a hurry. He began to smack his lips in that way familiar to donkeys, and they began to jog.

Ken says, "We were high up on the side of the mountain, and could look way down into the valley where the train would crawl out."

At last they made it down to the outskirts of town, from where, in the distance, he could see the station—and there was the train just pulling out.

Ken didn't like that a bit, but all he could do was wait the thirteen hours until the next train came along. And the weather there was hot. Too hot. Especially for people who were accustomed to the high altitude and cool weather of San Miguel.

They reached Mexico City at last, and while a friend bought clothes that Leto could use in Arkansas, Ken dashed around to get the papers that would be needed when Leto crossed the border. But he hadn't started dashing soon enough. They were held up on the Mexican side of the border while the U.S. officials checked with Washington—the problem was something about labor laws.

While they waited, Leto was getting homesick. The hotel in that border town was not a bit like his home in the mountain village. Ken tried to think of ways to cheer him up, and the best he could come up with was a midnight war with a blown-up paper bag. That worked fine, but Ken told us, "The racket proved too much for the hotel, so we had to quit."

Maybe Leto wasn't the only one who was homesick—or whatever it is that makes a person long to hear his own language. Ken could cross the river to the U.S. side whenever he wanted to, and sometimes he went over to shop or to just walk around. One day when he was in Woolworth's, two American children came in talking English. They were excited about the things they were going to buy, and they were talking about how and where they would use them. Ken heard them. That happy American chatter was delightful. He found himself following them, and others, just for the privilege of hearing them talk. He was amazed at himself; he hadn't realized how much he had missed the sound of English.

Well, he was about to hear more. While Ken and Leto had been waiting in Nuevo Laredo, Townsend was waiting in Arkansas, and after a couple of weeks he wrote Ken that he really needed him. He asked him to come immediately if possible. So Ken put Leto on the train and telegraphed friends to meet him in Mexico City and see that he was safely on his way back to Parián.

Then Ken left for Camp Wycliffe. (Permission to bring Leto in to the States did arrive from Washington, but by that time Ken was already in Arkansas.)

4 A BROKEN LEG

(Summer-Fall, 1936)

The reason the linguistic school was called "Camp Wycliffe" was that the founders, Townsend and Legters, intended that the students be trained, not just in linguistics, but also in pioneer living. Even back in 1936 Townsend was dreaming, looking forward to the day when some of the students would be working in the Amazon basin. The rustic conditions found in Camp Wycliffe were, therefore, partly due to lack of funds, but partly they were deliberate. And the conditions were rustic!

That summer of 1936, Camp Wycliffe (also called "The Summer Institute of Linguistics") was located about two and a half miles from Siloam Springs, Arkansas. Classes were held in an old country schoolhouse, and when the students sat in the seats near the front, they had to park their knees in the aisle—those seats had been built for first graders.

Across the road from the schoolhouse was an old farmhouse with several sheds and a barn. The barn loft was cleaned up for sleeping quarters and became the men's dorm. It served very well except for those times when a skunk wandered in; one did every so often.

The students ate in the farmhouse—meals which they themselves cooked on an old wood stove. The students also bought the groceries, carried water, did the bookkeeping. They did all the activities of the school except for the teaching. It was part of the plan to give them experience in working together under less than ideal conditions. And as they worked together, the old farm began to perk up. Broken windows were mended, shelves were built, the kitchen whitewashed, etc.

In addition to the nine men students who were there that summer, a married couple and five young women came too. Previously Legters had strongly objected to women taking the course, because, he said, it was a school for pioneers and pioneering was too dangerous for young women. But Townsend thought they would do well and he was able to go ahead in spite of Legter's continuing objection.

The women lived in a two-story house in the center of Siloam Springs. Since the house had been unoccupied for some time, however, there was no electricity. The women used kerosene lamps, cooked over an old kerosene stove, and ironed their clothes with flatirons heated on that kerosene stove.

The people of Siloam Springs were interested in the young folks and the women of the Presbyterian church furnished the girls' home for them. One family gave the fellows a gallon of milk every day. Once in a while there would be a party, or someone would invite both student body and staff over for ice cream and cake. As a whole the students studied hard, and they enjoyed their excursions over to Cherokee country where they tried out the techniques they had been learning in class.

Ken's classes were on Indian phonetics, and he taught the students to mimic words from Mixtec, Zapotec, and Otomí— languages he had worked with during the winter months.

The star pupil that summer was Eugene A. Nida. He had won Phi Beta Kappa honors at the University of California at Los Angeles where he had specialized in morphology and Greek. Although he was officially a student at Camp Wycliffe, it wasn't long before he was giving lectures on morphology. (Later he became translation specialist for the American Bible Society.)

Ken was especially delighted. He wrote one of his college professors, "The Lord sent him to us." Gene went through Ken's grammatical materials of Mixtec and gave him some very helpful suggestions. He also introduced him to the book *Language* by Leonard Bloomfield and to this day Ken is grateful for that. It was then that he first heard the word "phoneme."

In addition to teaching phonetics, Townsend assigned Ken to the job of teaching Bill Sedat how to pronounce the difficult sounds of Cakchiquel.

Bill Sedat, one of the students, was expecting to go to Guatemala to translate for the Kekchí-speaking people. Townsend knew that Kekchí had some of the same difficult sounds that were in Cakchiquel, the language into which he had translated the New Testament. He also knew that it would be much easier for Bill if he learned those sounds before he reached Guatemala. (Townsend himself had succeeded in making the sounds when he had learned to talk Cakchiquel, but he didn't know how to teach someone else.)

First, before Ken could teach Bill, he had to succeed himself. He started studying with Joe Chicol who was also there that year. Joe was a native speaker of Cakchiquel and one of those who had helped with the translation of the New Testament.

There were some t, and k sounds that were especially difficult. They were pronounced with a little pop, made as the Adam's apple (the larynx), used as a kind of plunger, pushed the air out. The larynx could be used as a plunger only while a person was holding his breath. It took Ken hours and hours of practice before he himself learned to pronounce those sounds. Then, once he had learned, he was able to teach Bill.

But there was still another k sound, and a p sound something like it, that Ken had not learned. The k sound was used, for example in the word "fire." Ken listened and tried to say it; Joe shook his head. Again and again Ken tried. Each time he'd go back to Joe, Joe would just shake his head. Right up until the end of the summer Ken tried—and failed.

Ken had been reading everything on phonetics that he could get his hands on, and somewhere he read about "implosives," but he didn't really understand what they were. So he wrote and asked Dr. Thomas F. Cummings who taught Phonetics and missionary linguistics at the Biblical Seminary in New York.

Dr. Cummings answered, "An implosive ... is one which is formed by drawing in air into the oral cavity by rarefaction produced by lowering the larynx...."

"That's it!" said Ken. He managed to hold his breath and lower his closed larynx while he pronounced the consonants in the word "fire." They popped like a cork coming out of a bottle. That was the sound that Joe had been making, and now none of the Cakchiquel words stumped Ken any more.

So Ken had had another lesson in what it was like to struggle and fail as he tried to learn a language—and then succeed when the procedure for solving the problem was verbalized. It affected the attitude he was to have toward his colleagues and students. When they hit a roadblock, he never doubted that they could learn if somehow he himself could show them the way. (The following summer most of his students learned to produce implosives—that hollow popping sound—after studying them for one or two hours in class.)

But at the end of that summer the weeks of struggle and failure were fresh in Ken's mind, and he was not thinking of himself as a phonetics expert. Therefore, when Townsend asked him to write a book on phonetics for missionaries, Ken laughed at the idea. He, Ken, didn't know enough. Besides he had hated to write themes in college. But Townsend had asked him, so Ken did a symbol of obedience. He wrote about five pages. His attitude said, "See? It is obvious that this is no good." In that way he had proved that he couldn't write and had put the assignment behind him.

He pushed aside the thought of writing and spent his energy helping the rest of us travel down to Mexico. I say "us" because I was one of the students that summer. Florence Hansen, later Mrs. George Cowan, was another. Florrie was a Phi Beta Kappa from the University of California at Los Angeles who had majored in French, and I was a nurse from the Massachusetts General Hospital. The plan was that we would work together. Florrie with her good language background would do the translation, and I would use my medical knowledge to help the people. Our immediate task was to get to Mexico City.

There were nine of us traveling together in two cars—Ken and eight of us who had never been to Mexico before. That made Ken the old-timer. He interpreted into Spanish for us and seemed to enjoy talking with the officials. I had to remind myself that he was only one year ahead of us. (The Townsends were traveling in a third car, but they were with us in Laredo.)

The amazing thing was that, after only four hours at the border, we were on our way again, not with the easy-to-get tourist papers, but with immigration papers which could be renewed. Both the University of Mexico and the Mexican Ministry of Labor were recommending us. The University because they wanted the Indian languages to be studied, and the Ministry of Labor because they hoped that we could help the minority groups if only in some small way.

By the time we got to Monterrey it was dark and rain was coming down in torrents. The next day it was still raining. In fact the people there told us that it had been raining off and on for a number of days, not only in Monterrey, but farther on as well. Actually it had been raining enough that two bridges went out and we were caught on the stretch of road between them. We slept in the cars two nights while the Mexican army built a temporary means for crossing the river.

Even after we were beyond the flooded rivers, we traveled slowly. We were pulling heavily loaded baggage trailers and those trailers kept having flat tires. Ken and Gene did most of the heavy work of changing the tires, and the six days it took us to go from Laredo to Mexico City were especially hard ones for them. (Years later, even a bus made the trip in less than twenty-four hours.)

After we arrived in Mexico City, much of our time was spent in going with Townsend to call on government officials—people in the Ministry of Labor, people in the Ministry of Education, and others. Then one exciting day, we were told to get ready to dine with President Cárdenas.

Townsend had known that the invitation might come any day, and he had said that when it happened, he wanted to be sure and have pictures of the occasion. So Ken dashed downtown to rent a good camera. He made it back just in time to ride to the Castle of Chapultepec in one of the cars sent over for us.

We were all feeling very honored as we sat at the table with President Cárdenas, along with the Governors of Michoacán and Quintana Roo, and the Undersecretary of Foreign Affairs. The eight of us who had just arrived in Mexico were, for the most part, tongue-tied, but Ken was enjoying his conversation with the Undersecretary of Foreign Affairs. He did stop talking long enough to take some pictures, however. He took some of the whole table, and then some that included only the President with Mrs. Townsend on one side and Mr. Townsend on the other.

As Townsend sat beside the President, he managed to bring up the point that the best possible thing we could do for a people was to translate the New Testament for them. The President listened without comment, but because he was pleased that the young folks would be living in small towns among speakers of minority languages, he ordered that each one receive a salary as a rural school teacher. That was only twenty-two dollars (U.S. currency) a month, but none of us had stable incomes and that twenty-two dollars was a big help. He also ordered railroad passes for us to use on our way to our places of service.

That dinner with the President gave us a big boost in morale, and we also found that the railroad passes, etc. served as credentials which demonstrated government backing. Those credentials began to help us as soon as we were out of Mexico City.

Florrie and I headed for the Mazatec-speaking people ten days after the dinner. Ken went with us and that made the trip easier all along the way. On the train he turned two seats so that they were facing each other, then he piled our baggage in between just high enough so that it came up to the level of the seats. That made a nice place to stretch out and Florrie and I were able to sleep until 3:00 a.m. when the train stopped at the tiny station nearest to the Mazatec region.

The next morning—that is, later that morning—we rested while Ken arranged with men to load our baggage onto their donkeys and take us the twelve hours up and over the mountains to the town where we would be studying Mazatec.

When we arrived there, Ken took us to the town hall and made arrangements with the officials for a place where we could spend the night. Then the next day he started scouting up a house for us. He did it with such a flair that I had to remind myself that meeting people and making friends had never been his forte—I knew that he must be working at it, and that the Lord was helping him.

I had never thought of him as a carpenter either, but he made us shelves for the kitchen and put up a rod on which we could hang our clothes. We had brought in a kerosene stove and two army cots, so after buying a couple of tables, we were all set up.

Of course we were there to learn Mazatec, and as soon as it was evident that we could feed ourselves and sleep, Ken made arrangements for a language teacher. He listened with us those first few days and found everything about the language to be fascinating, however pairs of words which differed only by pitch were especially intriguing to him.

Not even our fascinating and intriguing Mazatec could hold him very long, however. He was in a hurry to get back to San Miguel and his Mixtec-speaking friends. He had dreams of working nonstop until a first draft of the New Testament was done in that dialect of Mixtec. In fact, he was grimly determined to translate at least the four gospels that year.

So, after being with us about ten days, he was on the trail again. Sometimes riding, sometimes walking, he traveled with a donkey team that was carrying bags of coffee beans out to the town near the railroad station. On his way he took pictures of the steep cornfields, and of a boy who was treading almost knee-deep in mud—he was preparing a mixture to be used in making adobe bricks. Ken was especially pleased at taking a picture of the driver as he tried to adjust a load that was slipping backwards. The driver did it by pulling back on the donkey's tail with one hand while he pushed forward on the hundred pound sack of coffee with the other—the donkey didn't seem to mind.

When they got as far as the driver's home, although he had agreed to take Ken all the way, he didn't want to go any farther that day. If they didn't get down the mountain that afternoon, Ken knew he'd have to wait an additional twenty-four hours in the railroad town. So he argued and urged, and finally offered a little extra money for feed for the animals. Then the driver said cheerfully, "Well, if we go faster, we will get there sooner." So they did. They made it from there in two hours—it had taken us three and a half hours to come up that same stretch of road.

The altitude of that town was low enough so that malaria-carrying mosquitos could be expected, and the truck didn't leave for the train station until midnight. Ken doused himself with insect repellent to try to discourage the mosquitos and slept until the truck honked outside the hotel door.

The second-class coach had three benches running from one end to the other. One was on each side of the car, and the third went down the center. It was about one o'clock at night, so most everyone was sleeping. One fellow was lying on his side stretched out on the center bench. He had his knees bent and the ten-or-so-inch triangle between his heels and his thighs was absolutely the only empty spot on the coach. Disgusted and sleepy, Ken gingerly perched in those ten inches. After a while the fellow woke up, sat up and started talking to the fellow beside him—in Mixtec! Ken was neither disgusted nor sleepy after that. He joined in the conversation and found that they were from San Miguel and even knew Leto.

Ken had telegraphed Narciso and Leto to meet him in Parián with donkeys to carry the baggage. Now Ken and his new friends decided to travel to San Miguel together, but when the train pulled in to Parián, Narciso and Leto were not there, neither were the forty-eight cans of evaporated milk and four boxes of oatmeal that Ken had ordered. He needed those things to perk up his San Miguel diet, so he decided to wait for the grocery order and hope that Narciso and Leto would turn up too.

He was staying with his Presbyterian friends, and he spent most of the first day and part of the second writing letters. Then he started to write an article about Cárdenas—that was the type of public-relations job that would please Townsend. But Ken got tired of writing. Besides, there was another way he could work at being a people man. When the passenger train came through, he ran down to the station for a chit-chat with the American tourists who were traveling through in the first-class coach. There was one man he enjoyed especially; he was a fellow camera enthusiast. They talked about taking pictures until the train pulled out.

On the morning of the third day he saw some laborers carrying sacks of corn from a railroad car. That was a good way to get exercise and make friends at the same time, so he went to join them.

They saw him coming and called to him in delight, "Come on, young man, carry one." He lifted one of the bigger sacks—two hundred pounds—and quickly changed his mind. The smaller ones were only a hundred pounds. He thought he could manage that. He picked one up, put it on his shoulder and started out. The men, accustomed to carrying those loads, were off at a dogtrot. Like the owner of the donkeys, their theory seemed to be that if you went faster you got there sooner. Ken had to keep up because he didn't really know where they were going. But as he tried to hurry, he stepped on a slanted rock; his foot slipped, and down he went with the sack of corn on top of him.

One look at his leg was enough—his foot was twisted to one side. Broken. About three inches above the ankle.

He motioned to the men in the distance and they came back laughing. When they saw that he was really hurt, they became sympathetic, picked him up and carried him home to his friends. The daughter immediately went to call her uncle who was recognized in town as one who knew how to fix broken bones. There was no doctor.

The uncle got Ken's boot and sock off, and covered his leg with honey—that was to give it heat or something. The mother sewed strips of cloth together to make bandage. Then, gently, they wrapped the leg, supporting it with a few thin pieces of cardboard. They offered Ken a place to stay, saying that they would take care of him until the leg was healed, but he preferred to take the train back to Puebla to a Baptist hospital there. It was about noon when he broke his leg, and the next train north would not pass until nine-thirty the next morning.

As he waited in the tiny house, Ken felt terrible. His leg ached of course, but that was not what bothered him most. He was overwhelmed with a sense of failure. What had he done wrong? He had been on his way out to the Mixtec region to translate the New Testament—certainly God wanted that job done. Why had He stopped him? Ken knew that the accident could not have happened without the Lord's permission.

Ken was also concerned for Narciso, Leto, and Nalo. They had started responding to the Gospel, and he had hoped to help them to understand still more about the Lord's goodness. Now his return to them would be delayed months.

Ken's dreams had crashed.

Then he remembered that Paul had sung praises to the Lord when all looked black (Acts 16:16-34). Ken knew that such an attitude pleased the Lord, so that evening before the family went to sleep, Ken led them through a number of hymns. The singing itself was probably not very beautiful—Ken found his voice quivering once in a while.

During the night Ken was still struggling with the problem. Why had the Lord turned him back? He could think of only one reasonable explanation. That phonetics book that Townsend had asked him to write. The one that was supposed to help missionaries and others studying foreign languages. The Lord must consider that to have a priority even over the New Testament translation for the people of San Miguel. Once Ken had figured that out, his leg didn't hurt so much.

The next morning his hostess handed him some lunch wrapped in a cloth napkin to eat on the train—it was an eleven-hour trip to Puebla. Two men carried the chair Ken was sitting on, while a third supported his leg. Somebody else went along with a board that was to stretch between two seats in the first-class coach. The board was for his leg to rest on.

Even while they were carrying him to the train, Ken was hoping that a friendly helpful tourist would be on board. Yes! There was one! He was sitting just in front of the only double seat left, and he immediately stepped forward and offered help. He was the same fellow Ken had talked with about pictures just a couple of days before. Actually he was a surgeon from Mayo clinic who specialized in fractures. (Ken thought a grateful, ''Thank you, Lord.'')

The surgeon helped settle Ken on the board and actually succeeded in making him comfortable except for those times when the narrow-gauge car snapped around some of the especially sharp curves. (Another time when Ken was riding that train, it swayed so much that the tail light smashed against the canyon wall.)

About eight o'clock that evening they pulled into Puebla and there was Dr. Dawson from the Latin-American Hospital waiting for him—Ken's friends had telegraphed ahead. In just no time he was in bed with his leg resting in a basket.

Two days later, in a kind of half-sitting position, he had his fountain pen out and was busy describing the way sounds are made. He didn't stop even when an attack of malaria sent his fever up. Two weeks later in a wheelchair, his leg in a cast, he was holding his typewriter on his lap, still describing sounds.

He wanted to be sure that people who had not studied linguistics would be able to follow the instructions, so he tried his manuscript out on the doctor's wife and on a young fellow who was helping with the lab work. Whenever there was a paragraph that they couldn't understand, he rewrote it. By the end of three weeks he had written eighty-two pages with about two hundred words to a page. Even though that was only a first draft, he had made a good start on his assigned task.

Soon after reaching the hospital, Ken had telegraphed me, telling me that he was well cared for and that I need not come in. But there was something he did want. He wanted his manuscript tested. Would it work? He'd send me twenty or twenty-five pages at a time, urging me to try it out.

Actually it helped me to understand the difference between two *m* sounds that occur in Mazatec. That thrilled him, and spurred him on to teach me still more. Was I sure that such-and-such sounds were two phonemes? He emphasized that if one occurred only at the beginning of a word, and the other only in the middle, then they were not two different phonemes. As I remember it, I first really began to understand phonology when I studied the letters he wrote those seven weeks he was in the hospital and while I was deciphering his scrawl as I typed up the one-hundred-twenty-five-page manuscript.

While at the hospital working on the manuscript, Ken discovered that, "Studying is the thing which makes me happy ... when things begin to roll." To a friend he wrote, "Working at phonetics has made the time seem useful here, so nothing to be grieved about."

Well, his phonetics did have at least one competitor.

When a visitor turned up who knew how to play chess, Ken studied only one hour that day.

5   A GOOD DIRECTOR

(Spring of 1937)

Still walking on crutches, a little more than six weeks after he broke his leg, Ken left the hospital and joined the Townsends in Tetelcingo. His shinbone had healed, but with an easily visible notch in the front of it. (That notch is still there.) He used crutches for a couple of weeks more and then switched to a cane. But he could get around! That was what seemed important to the rest of us. We were especially anxious to have him available at that time since we were all scheduled to give papers at a "Linguistic Week."

The Linguistic Week had been organized by the Mexican Institute of Linguistic Investigations in co-operation with the Linguistic Commission of the University, the Ministry of Education, the Academy of Aztec and Otomí Languages, and the infant Summer Institute of Linguistics. Just to read the list of organizations sponsoring the linguistic week impressed and frightened us. We felt much more confident about giving our papers after Ken had read them and made a few suggestions. Ken himself was especially glad that Gene Nida was there. He was the one who read and helped shape the papers on grammar.

Actually that week, January 18 through 23, went off very well. We profited by hearing the lectures given by the other people, and some of our crowd, Ken for example, liked exchanging ideas with them during the in-between times. The week also reminded us that we really were a linguistic organization. Well, a linguistic group of people anyway. The Pioneer Mission Agency in Philadelphia was urging us to organize.

The Pioneer Mission Agency had been forwarding us the money that our friends had sent to them for us, but according to their charter, they were not supposed to forward money to individuals. Therefore, they wanted at least a committee to deal with.

Since we had already gathered for the linguistic week, Townsend suggested that we take the opportunity to organize. The first question was what we should call ourselves. At least a year before that time, he had chosen the name "The Summer Institute of Linguistics," and the Mexican government referred to us that way. Mr. Townsend liked it because, he said, it was "unpretentious." Now he persuaded the group to adopt it officially.

There was resistence to some of his suggestions, however. The fellows who had graduated from seminary thought that seminary should be a prerequisite to Bible translation. Therefore, they argued that no one should be allowed to join the Summer Institute of Linguistics who was not a seminary graduate. That would have excluded Ken and most of the other fellows. The girls, of course, would either be sent home or married off.

The seminary men also wanted it written into the constitution that nobody could do a translation unless he knew lots of Greek. Mr. Townsend argued that members could get help from lexicons and commentaries, and so didn't need years of Greek. In fact, someone with no knowledge of Greek at all could translate enough to tell the people of a minority language that God had made the heaven and earth, that He loves them, and that Jesus Christ died to save them. He gave an example. Suppose you saw a starving man when all you had was a ham sandwich. Of course you would like to offer him a T-bone steak and a piece of apple pie. Would you refuse to give him anything because you didn't want to disgrace him by offering him the ham sandwich?

With such arguments as that, Townsend persuaded the young folks to write up a constitution in which neither a seminary education nor a knowledge of Greek was a requirement—it didn't even say that no single woman need apply.

For a second time in less than two years, it was because of Townsend that Ken was allowed to work. This time it was the seminary graduates who had been considering sending him home.

In spite of the opposition that Townsend was facing, he insisted that the constitution be set up in such a way that the director be responsible to an executive committee, and that the director be elected by the membership. At the very time that some of the members were in part hostile to him, when he was having active opposition, Townsend, the leader, put the final authority into the hands of inexperienced young folks. He did it because he was afraid to have excessive power in the hands of any leader. Ken was very conscious of the power that Mr. Townsend was giving up, perhaps because he had so recently rescued him from the axe that the seminary students had hung over his head. Looking back, Ken says that, in his opinion, that decision was one of the greatest moral decisions of all missionary history.

Mr. Townsend was elected the director, of course, and for the most part he ruled by persuasion. He was always taking the members by surprise, as he did when he told Ken to prepare to go to the University of Michigan to study under Sapir (see Chapter VII). The courses of the Linguistic Society of America were to be held there during the summer of 1937.

Ken had already been reading and digesting any linguistic book he could get his hands on. Now, thinking ahead to a summer at the University of Michigan, he began to make an even greater effort to get anything that had to do with phonology. He had gone to the American Book Store in Mexico City, looked at their copy of *Books in Print,* and ordered everything he could find that was about phonetics. Then he sent a list of twenty-two more linguistic books to the Pioneer Mission Agency and asked them to get them for him.

The cost of all those books added up to a considerable sum and Ken's income averaged less than fifty dollars a month. He received twenty-five dollars every month from a Mr. and Mrs. Abrahams who had become interested through Mr. Legters. The rest was from others who sent occasional gifts—his family, friends, and certain evangelical churches. Some people who didn't give money were nevertheless a great help financially. For example, Dr. Dawson didn't charge for his medical services. (Ken's entire hospital bill was only sixty-one dollars.) The Reifsynders and Taylors, Presbyterian missionaries, gave him room and board for more than a month. Later Mrs. Hull let all of us stay in her house, rent free, whenever we happened to be in Mexico City. For years H. T. Marroquín of the Sociedad Bíblica de México, received our money as it was sent down from the States, changed it into Mexican currency, and forwarded it on to us when we were out in the small towns. Because of helpful people like these, Ken was able to spend half of his income on books that season. He considered books to be worth at least half his income and he was convinced that the Lord, too, wanted him to have them. In part he came to that conclusion by correlating the dates of the larger gifts with the dates of the larger bills. The month when the bills for his biggest order of books came was also the month that he received twice as much money as he had received for any of the preceding six. He figured that the Lord, knowing about the bills, had nudged his friends into sending him extra that time.

In his enthusiasm Ken wrote a friend and explained why books were so important, "By getting the sounds of other languages from books, I can make my work applicable to practically any country in the world.... I want lots of books so as to glean the best teaching methods from each...."

And always he was thinking of his students, those who would be translating the New Testament for some minority group somewhere. "A person can spend hours and hours and hours for day after day, trying to understand a sound. To help such a person with one such sound is worth two books alone."

He used me as an example. While typing his manuscript, I had come to the part about "cerebrals"—sounds which are made with the tongue tip turned upward and back. I paused in the typing long enough to follow instructions and what came out was one of the Mazatec sounds that had been puzzling Florrie and me. Ken was delighted; he wrote Townsend that the manuscript was already bringing results.

Ken wouldn't leave his books even when he was going back to San Miguel; he took some of them to read while there. This time Nida was planning to be with him about a month, and Ken was looking forward to more help on the grammatical analysis of Mixtec.

Everybody was a bit concerned about Gene. Two months after being out among the Tarahumara-speaking people, he had become ill and had had to leave Mexico. He had come back for the linguistic week and everybody hoped he would stay healthy while he was out with Ken.

The train ride to Parián and the day on donkeys to Nochistlán were uneventful. From Nochistlán to Tlaxiaco, they were able to ride in the back of a truck that made the trip about once a week. But the trip by truck was hardly more pleasant than it would have been by donkey.

Even on a road with only gentle curves, Ken had frequently succumbed to motion sickness, and the road between Nochistlán and Tlaxiaco was, for the most part, a winding donkey trail with an occasional detour into the fields wherever the rocks in the road were too big for the wheels to straddle, or for one wheel to climb over. Ken had learned as a child that if he didn't watch the dancing landscape, he was less likely to get motion sickness. He wanted to be ready to work when he reached Tlaxiaco, so he buried his head in his sleeping bag, and in that way rode blindfolded the entire eight hours it took the truck to go the fifty miles.

The strategy was successful. Ken wrote home, "I arrived with stomach in good position and condition"—he had arrived ready to work, that is. (In those years, medicines for controlling motion sickness were not yet available.)

In a little hotel there in Tlaxiaco, Ken and Gene started looking at the Mixtec material again, but after a couple of days, some of the symptoms that Gene had had up in Tarahumara country began to reappear. The plan had been that after working with Ken, Gene would go on to help Walter Miller with the Mixe language, and then Landis Christiansen with Totonac. It was a big disappointment to everybody when Gene had to return to the States again.

Ken went on to San Miguel and his stay there that year, 1937, was easier than it had been the preceding year. There were several very practical reasons why. This time he had Flit (powder and solution) with which to control the fleas. He wrote, "The other night I dusted the bed and myself with Flit and have had wonderful sleep ever since."

Then, too, old Narciso had suggested that Ken move to a house owned by his son Leto and, since the dirt floor in that house did not have the deep cracks that provide such good hiding places for them, there were fewer fleas there.

The air mattress he had brought back also helped. He was delighted with it, "Boy, that sure is a nice invention! This year I have studied with a lot more enthusiasm than I did last. Perhaps the air mattress is one of the reasons."

He was also eating better. The previous year he had eaten with the landlord's family. He wrote, "I get as good grub as they know how to cook."

He described the diet, "They eat beans and corn, mostly. The beans are boiled for hours and then fried in lots of grease. The corn is soaked in lime to soften it, then ground by hand between two stones." The corncakes, that is the tortillas, are baked "over an open fire on top of a flat griddle made of baked clay ... and eaten with salt and chile."

Ken supplemented the food he received at his landlord's by buying fruit in the market, and sometimes he asked the women to cook an egg for him. They did, but since eggs were considered to be expensive, he had to pay extra for them. He said that the eggs were about ten cents a dozen, "So expensive that the Mixtecs export a lot but eat few."

But that year of 1937, Ken was doing most of his own cooking and of course had eggs in one form or another frequently. Sometimes he'd make an omelet and sometimes pancakes. But he varied the menu once in a while by adding a bit of flour to the omelet, or by adding an extra egg to the pancakes. Then he started to experiment. Where was the borderline between a pancake and an omelet? Add an egg, subtract some flour—when did the pancake become an omelet? Add flour, subtract an egg—when did the omelet become a pancake? After studying the situation, he decided that the borderline between the two dishes was indefinite.

Since he used lots of eggs, probably from his neighbors' point of view he was eating a rich man's diet. He wrote, "The Mixteco Indians are friendly and intelligent, but extremely poor."

He knew that the children were undernourished, so he ordered and studied literature on the soybean and gave seeds to Narciso's son, to the director of the school where he had stayed in Chalcatongo, and to schools in several other towns. He hoped that eventually the soybean could provide a milk substitute for the children. (It never happened; the soybeans didn't grow well. Perhaps the seed Ken had bought was the wrong variety.)

One of the indications of the poverty of the town was the fact that a ten-year-old boy, instead of going to school, might be assigned the task of herding the family pigs. He could spend two or more years just to see that three pigs did not wander; then those pigs would be sold for fifteen cents (in U.S. currency) each. Such a waste of human resources appalled Ken.

Of course some of the children of the village were allowed to go to school and Ken became acquainted with them when they discovered that he had blank paper (none was sold in the town). He gave a sheet or two to the first students who asked. The next day others came; he gave them some too. The day after that still more were there, and they said that the teacher had sent them, so Ken offered to sell the paper. But they had no money with them. Then he decided to barter; he'd give them paper if they would teach him a few Mixtec words. They agreed and everybody was happy; the school children had their paper and Ken was able to get on with his language work.

He was glad to be able to work with the students because the men had been busy in their fields and he had not had enough study time with them. It helped when occasionally Narciso, or one of his sons, would come at five o'clock in the morning—before starting their regular work. It was cold that early in the day, however, especially when the wind was whistling in through unchinked cracks in the log wall. Ken wrote, "My fingers now are a bit stiff from the cold, enough to bother typing." (Often the Mixtecs themselves got up at three in the morning and started the fire in order to keep themselves warm.)

When spring came, Ken was surprised by the beauty of the cactus flowers. He wrote, "The cactus plants are beginning to blossom, and I have seldom seen prettier flowers. True, they guard themselves well, so I do not meddle with them."

The warmer weather did have one disadvantage though—June bugs. One evening when he was trying to study, he was disgusted by the number of times they ploughed into his hair. He declared war and killed eleven of them in about an hour.

He found that most anything could cut his desire for work: June bugs, cold weather, fleas, malaria (he had had an attack a few days after arriving back), and clanging church bells. (When there was a fiesta for one of the saints honored in the village church, the bells would clang for two days and nights. Drunks screamed, fireworks exploded, and the village band played.)

No matter what had caused the distraction, every time he took time out, Ken had a guilty conscience. He considered that he was lazy and that he had sinned if he had not worked when there was work to be done—and therewas much that should be done: linguistic books to be read, his Mixtec language notes to be organized, vocabulary to be memorized, letters to be written.

He had been sent by the Lord to translate for the Mixtecs, and when, in his opinion, he had goofed off, he quoted Proverbs 10:26 in reference to himself, "As vinegar to the teeth, and as smoke to the eyes, so is the sluggard to them that send him."

Distressed at laziness that he seemed unable to control, he suddenly discovered one of the advantages of having a director. Townsend, elected by the membership in January, had told him not to work too hard. Ken felt tremendous relief. He wrote, "To take it easy under orders is sure swell." But he still yearned for what he called "positive self-control," the ability to set up priorities and do them.

6 DIALECT SURVEY

(Spring of 1937)

Whenever Ken had occasion to go to Chalcatongo or Tlaxiaco, he asked one of his Mixtec friends to go with him, and their time on the trail together was mutually helpful. Ken took that opportunity to tell the men Bible stories, and on one of those trips he told Nalo about the death of Lazarus. He told how Jesus arrived at the grave four days after Lazarus was dead, but when He called, "Lazarus! Come here!" Lazarus walked out still wrapped up in the grave-clothes (John 11).

Ken wrote that Nalo's eyes just about popped out of his head, and he told Ken, "You pour those stories into my head well."

But sometimes Ken's conduct on the trail distressed the men. There was the matter of Mixtec etiquette. Ken was in the habit of tearing along and if he met a group of people, he'd just call out a general "Hello." That did not do at all. When he did not stop and shake hands with each person and greet each person individually, he had committed a grave social error. The Mixtecs were very outspoken about the matter and sometimes they called to him, "What's the matter? Why didn't you speak to me? Are you angry?"

So Ken's friends began to teach him how to be polite. He memorized his lesson, the average conversation which occurs when two Mixtec men meet on a foot path.

"Good afternoon, Sir."

"Good afternoon, good afternoon, good afternoon." The men usually had packs on their backs, hanging by a woven palm-leaf tumpline from the top of their heads or from across their chests. Even though their load might be heavy, the greetings were not shortened, but their motions were done slowly lest the burden shift. There was a handshake and a low bow. If one was much younger than the other, he might kiss the hand of the older.

"Are you well?"

"Fine. Are you well?"

"I'm fine. Go slowly and carefully, and come back safely, Sir."

"Of course, Sir, and we will talk together again."

"Certainly, Sir. Come to the market Thursday and we will talk together."

"Certainly. I'm going and coming back."

"We will talk together, Sir."

Many times, when Ken thought he was in a hurry, he had to stop and greet each one of a group of people, and then do it again when he met another group, and another. It reminded him of the Lord's instructions in Luke 10:4, "Salute no man by the way." Ken wondered if a herald could spend so much time greeting people that he'd never get his message out. He pondered the idea, but he saw the value of Nalo's lessons when he asked the mayor of Chalcatongo how a new teacher was doing.

The mayor answered, "Oh, he's all right in the classroom, but he doesn't like to talk to folks."

Ken had caught up to the mayor and the inspector of the government boarding schools on the trail as they traveled to Tlaxiaco. He chattered away to the mayor in Mixtec and told some of Narciso's stories both in Mixtec and Spanish. The mayor chuckled and commented that Ken knew more Mixtec than he did, even though he himself had grown up in Chalcatongo.

The inspector was interested in the chapters Ken had written on phonetics, and in the typed-up stories by Narciso. When Nalo saw how well they were received, and heard that Ken had given a copy to President Cárdenas, he got enthused and, much to Ken's delight, he himself told Ken two stories.

The stories were not only useful for language analysis, but they could also be used to entertain a houseful of Mixtec company. Of course the villagers were interested in most anything Ken had. One of the things that really captivated them was a little toy donkey with a clown walking behind him. The donkey had laid down, or had fallen down, under his load, so the clown was pulling on his tail.

When a key was turned, a mechanism inside the toy moved both clown and tail from side to side.

The first time Ken showed it off, he took it to a group of masons who were working on a new school wall. They were fascinated, but he must have stayed just long enough to tantalize them, because later they went to the house followed by big boys, little boys, old boys, and town officials. All of them wanted to see the clown trying to make the donkey get up.

A donkey down under a load was a familiar problem to them. When a donkey falls down or lies down under a heavy load, often he can't stand up again without help. The handiest thing to grab hold of and lift by is the tail. It seems also to have been a problem in another part of the world a long time ago. "If you see someone trying to get an ox or donkey onto its feet when it has slipped beneath its load, don't look the other way. Go and help!" (Deut. 22:4, *Living Bible*).

The children came to wind up the toy by the hour and once four boys stayed all night. They slept on the floor on Ken's straw mat. The excuse for not leaving earlier was the rain, but the rain had stopped while they would still have had time to get home before dark. There was no doubt that the real reason was the donkey. Before settling down for the night they asked Ken to tell them one of Narciso's stories. So he did. Then they said that they needed to be up by five o'clock, so he set the alarm for them. When it went off, they claimed that it was only four, so they rolled over and slept again until the darkness turned grey. Then quietly they left to begin their chores for the day.

Since the Mixtec people were accustomed to beginning their work at the first signs of dawn, it would seem that Nalo should have been able to start on a trip with Ken before the sun was high. But it didn't work out that way even though he had talked it over with Nalo and his family well in advance.

For sometime Ken had wanted to walk to the Pacific. One of the reasons for going was to get material on the Mixtec dialects. He wondered how many dialects there actually were, and he wanted to know a little about the difference in the dialects before deciding how the sound system of San Miguel should be symbolized.

Ken was still limping because of his weak ankle and leg, but he was determined to know more about the Mixtec region. If getting the material was part of his job as a Mixtec translator, then he was also sure that the Lord would take care of him. He got a cane to give support to his leg and asked Nalo to get together the other things that would be needed for the trip.

Narciso insisted that Ken buy some onions (they grew profusely in a town about a day's walk from San Miguel). If Nalo carried a basketful, they could resell them on the coast and that would defray part of the cost of the trip. Ken demurred and Nalo was not enthusiastic, but Narciso, Nalo's father still insisted, and fathers were usually obeyed, even by adult sons. Ken hesitated about refusing to do things Narciso's way. He had learned that if he did refuse to do things the Mixtec way, and they proved to be correct (as they did a good share of the time), then their "I told you so" took the form of "We are not entirely stupid." So Ken said o.k. and they bought about two hundred onions. Ken also had them buy garlic to trade for tortillas on the road, and corn with which to make the forty tortillas they planned to take with them, as well as the corn that was to sustain Nalo's wife while they were gone.

The appointed day came and Ken had wanted to leave by the light of the moon, but the tortillas were not made by then. It was almost noon before they were finished. Then the onions had to have most of their leaves pulled off and be packed in a big basket, sixteen inches wide and sixteen inches deep. The onions filled it to within five inches from the top. Again Ken objected to taking them, and again he was overruled.

Then Nalo tried to pack into that five inches of space the things Ken wanted along: three books on phonetics, a notebook in which to record linguistic data, a few gospels, a diary; a quart of Flit, a flit gun, two cans of flit powder, a flashlight, a mosquito net; extra shirt, underwear, four pairs of heavy socks, slippers, razor, thread, soap, toothbrush; ointment for minor infections, snakebite kit, box of quinine (Ken had had an attack of malaria the previous month and he knew that he might need that quinine again at any time); a quart bottle of water, a dozen small cans of milk, four small cans of sardines, a can opener, a can for boiling coffee, a cup, matches, half dozen oranges, half dozen bananas; the forty tortillas and Nalo's own clothing and blanket.

Then even Narciso could see that they did not want all the onions, so he agreed to take out about fifty, but he objected to the Flit and the books. Ken insisted on having those, but he did consent to leave home a tarpaulin that he had planned to take—Narciso said that they would not meet any rain.

In the early afternoon, April 27, 1937, they were off, the basket piled high and Ken carrying his own blanket and a few other things. In a half an hour, when they had almost reached Nalo's ranch, it started to rain. They dashed for shelter into the little house he had there, and ate their dinner. After an hour the rain had stopped, so they and started on again.

The first few hours they were walking through barren hills, then about dark they crossed a river and climbed a mountain on the other side. In the small village there, a storekeeper gave them permission to sleep on the floor. They bought a little unrefined sugar, made some coffee, and lay down to rest.

The next day even Ken was satisfied when they started out again at about four o'clock in the morning. Immediately the road began to drop steeply and soon the mountainsides were all wooded. There were so many birds that there was never a pause in their singing; there was just one continuous stream of melody.

By noon it was very very hot and Ken had already finished his supply of water. (He hadn't tried to ration it because a fellow traveler had told him that they would soon reach a village where he could refill the bottle.) When they finally reached the tiny place, there was no store, but they managed to buy a couple of stalks of sugar cane about five feet long. They chewed on those and Ken wrote, "Boy, was that good!"

Sometime later they came to a spring. They stopped, boiled water, and made coffee right there instead of putting hopes in the town ahead. It was a good thing they did, because that village didn't have a store either. They did manage, however, to buy a little sugar from the schoolteacher there.

The next morning they were off by moonlight, and this time they were accompanied by two fellows also from San Miguel who were carrying four dozen earthen jars on their backs. They expected to sell them in Pinotepa de Don Luis, the big town ahead.

At last they arrived in a village big enough to have a store. While they were there about a dozen men with machetes and old-fashioned guns stomped in. Immediately they confronted Ken, "We want to know what you are doing!"

"If you wish, I will gladly show you my credentials."

"Very well. Come on!"

So they went to the municipal building. The village men sat, resting the butts of their guns on the floor. Ken sat too, facing two young men behind a desk. He greeted them pleasantly and asked them what he could do for them.

"We want to know with whom we are talking!" roared the one who was mayor. Ken handed him letters from the Mexican Institute of Linguistic Investigations and from the Secretary of Labor. While the man at his left, the secretary, was reading them, Ken prattled on about linguistics, and urged the mayor to plant soybeans for the benefit of his people. Also, interspersed through it all, he asked questions about the town and whether or not the towns nearby talked Mixtec.

After a while the mayor resumed his official voice, "Well, he has shown his papers. I guess we might as well let him go get his supper."

The next day he walked with Ken and his companions to the edge of town and urged him to show his credentials in each town or village through which he passed. (After that Ken made it a point to do so.) The mayor also urged that he get a guard, insisting that there were bandits in the area.

Ken and Nalo kept traveling, staying longest in towns where most of the people spoke Mixtec. The Mixtec of those lowland towns was very different from that of the highlands. Nalo could talk to them enough to buy from them, or get directions to the next town, but he could pick up practically nothing when the people were conversing with each other.

The school teacher in one town asked Ken to speak, in Mixtec, at a small gathering, a program that was to commemorate Mother's Day. Ken did, but he said later that the dialect was so different from his that the people understood nothing.

In six days Ken and Nalo had reached Pinotepa de Don Luis. From there they took a bus to some salt works. It had been built where a low reef cuts a lake off from the ocean in the summer time, but, during the winter, storms cause salt water to go over the reef and fill the lake. When the hot summer sun dries up the water, men scrape up the salt and filter it through sand. That is the salt that is sold throughout the Mixtec region.

That afternoon Ken and Nalo walked a couple of miles further to the Pacific and took a swim. In their few days of travel they had dropped from about eight thousand feet to the ocean itself.

Ken had walked down from San Miguel to have a chance to hear various Mixtec dialects, but it was typical of him that he was interested in everything else along the way. He wanted to see and experience everything new he possibly could even though to do so cost considerable effort.

The men from San Miguel enjoyed traveling with him. They were complimented when he called himself a "resident of San Miguel" when he was speaking with people from another town, and they were almost gleeful when he was the one who climbed a big mango tree to shake down fruit for himself and them.

In most towns they stayed only a few hours, or, sometimes, a day or two, since Ken was always wondering what the dialect in the next town would be like. He took down word lists, sentences and stories. In some towns they said they knew no stories, so he gave them a Spanish translation of one of Narciso's and they told it back to him in their dialect.

They got off to a late start one morning so had a six-hour walk right in the heat of the day. By the time they arrived in Jicayan, Ken's bottle of water was empty. The water in Jicayan was very polluted, so he tried to get boiled water by asking for coffee. Because it wasn't their custom to make coffee in the middle of the day, he had to wait until evening for it. His throat was so dry it was difficult to talk, but of course he did anyway—it would have been impolite not to.

Jicayan was a good place to study Mixtec because the town secretary had found a capable language helper for him. Ken stayed there a week even though the heat in that lowland area gave him a headache. He worked only four hours a day on Mixtec. The rest of the time he put in reading the books he had brought with him. Soon he had finished *American Pronunciation* by Kenyon, and had begun *An Outline of English Phonetics* by Jones.

Then Ken and Nalo started traveling again. They even spent a day in a town where the people spoke Amuzgo, and in another town they found a man who spoke Trique. The man was too drunk to be of much help, and Spanish-speaking folks stood around to listen, comment, and try to be funny. Even so Ken was able to tell that this Trique dialect was different from the one he had heard in the market in Tlaxiaco. He was fascinated with it, as he is with every language that is new to him, and was glad to listen even though it was for only a few hours and under trying circumstances.

Then the time came when they had to start the long climb back up to the highlands which they had left more than three weeks before. According to the map, they had only a short distance to travel that day and the next, but the corkscrew turns of the mountain trail made the distance much longer. It was raining when they stopped to eat their lunch in the shelter of a huge rock. The wet slippery gumbo soil caused both Ken and Nalo to stumble, and several times they went down. Fortunately neither of them was hurt.

By now they had regained enough altitude so that the nights were cold. They slept on the floor of a mountain hut, but were up and under way, traveling by flashlight, by three o'clock in the morning. One of the reasons for the early start was to warm up a bit. Another was that Ken was anxious to get his mail. He hoped there would be a postal money order in it. They had been away twenty-five days and he arrived back in San Miguel with less than a peso in his pocket.

As he thought over the trip, Ken was glad he had gone. He had learned a lot about Mixtec as it was spoken in the lowlands. Then, too, he was rejoicing about Nalo. He had been telling him more gospel stories, and Nalo really seemed to understand and believe. Nalo had even started to read the gospel by himself in Spanish, although he had to ask Ken what some of the words and verses meant.

And somewhere along the way, Ken had thrown away his cane— he didn't need it any more—by the time the trip was over he was walking without a limp.

About four days after he was back in San Miguel he had an attack of malaria. He was so chilly in the morning that, in addition to a wool shirt and sweater, he had had to wrap up in a blanket while he sat typing. In the afternoon he wasn't cold. He was hot in spite of studying in his shirt sleeves, and he wrote, "The malaria had to come back to make me realize that I in myself am not worth a hoot. Only the Lord can keep me in this country, and apparently He has chosen to do so ... in a state of imperfect health. Since the choice is His, that is o.k. with me, but I will take the best precautions I can."

7 STUDYING IN ANN ARBOR

(Summer of 1937)

On June 9, 1937 Ken was twenty-five years old. Somehow the event seemed momentous to him. He had set that date, years before, as a time when adult, productive life must be under way. From then on, he'd really have to work. He wrote in his diary, "If ten years from now something has not been accomplished of good hard work, well done, the future will not be so bright." He wanted very much to accomplish something worthwhile, and he determined to make an all-out effort. In his opinion there was one major hindrance. He put it in writing that day, "I'm just as lazy as ever."

Townsend had plans for Ken's immediate future. He had heard that Edward Sapir would be teaching at the summer session of the Linguistic Society of America, the Linguistic Institute which was to be held that year at the University of Michigan. Since Sapir was one of the best authorities on American Indian languages, Mr Townsend sent Ken to do postgraduate study with him.

Ken had already had some contact with Sapir. Sometime before he had sent him a copy of the first two chapters (a 115-page manuscript) of his *Phonetics: An Introductory Manual*. Sapir had answered, encouraging Ken to go to the University of Michigan and telling him, "We certainly need a scientific study of Mixteco."

Ken didn't have much money when he arrived in Ann Arbor, and he needed a scholarship, but since he arrived on campus the last day of registration, things looked rather hopeless. He filled out an application anyway and along with the data listing "schools attended," he submitted his record book of linguistic research. From his work on Highland Mixtec there were sixty pages of legends, seventy pages with word lists and legends from ten different towns in the Highland Mixtec, a beginning Mixtec-Spanish dictionary of six hundred words, and a discussion of the Mixtec sounds. Also included were twenty pages of word lists and legends of Lowland Mixtec, three pages of numerals and words of Amuzgo, three pages of numerals and words of Trique, a discussion of the sounds of Otomí. Ken also referred to the fact that he had had some contact with the phonetics of Aztec, Totonac, Maya, and Mazatec. Then he included an article, "Likenesses, Differences, and Variations of Phonemes in Mexican Indian Languages" which appeared in *Investigaciones Lingüísticas* 4:134-39 (1937).

Sapir had already recommended a scholarship on the basis of the manuscript on phonetics, but if there were no scholarships available the recommendation would not help.

As a matter of fact, there was no scholarship available. All had been promised to worthy applicants. Then, just before Ken arrived at the office of Professor Charles Fries, director of the Linguistic Institute that summer, the telephone rang. There was a message stating that due to an emergency one of the applicants had had to drop out. The scholarship that was to have been his, Professor Fries passed on to Ken. It was thirty-five dollars, the cost of tuition and fees. With that amount of help Ken was able to stay on at Michigan. ("Thank you, Lord," said Ken. To him it seemed that the Lord Himself had kept the scholarship available for him.)

He immediately took the opportunity to get suggestions on the first chapters of his phonetics book for beginners. Sapir congratulated him on the pedagogy, saying that he had gone into detail about things that other people might have taken for granted. Ken and Sapir had started talking in Sapir's office, had continued at lunch, then gone on to Sapir's room and talked until midnight. Sapir skipped a reception in order to do that. When Ken became aware of it, he apologized. Sapir set him at ease, saying that the reception would have been work, but talking linguistics was restful.

Sapir turned Ken's manuscript over to Bernard Bloch and Morris Swadesh for criticism and suggestions. Bloch at that time was teaching at Brown University; later he became a professor at Yale and editor of the journal *Language*. He criticized the manuscript severely—the orthography, the arrangement, and things not explained clearly. Ken wrote, "So far ... the only thing he has admitted that I am right about is that there is no book, now available, to fill the need I describe to him."

Swadesh had already written several articles on phonology, and he was more positive in his comments. Ken says that Swadesh's articles contributed a great deal to his first understanding of phonemics, and he was anxious to get on with the writing of his book while he was near men who could give him advice. But he was finding that he could not both write and do justice to the linguistic courses he had signed up for. It distressed him that it had to be so. He wrote, "Book, book, book. So it runs in my dreams, almost to haunt me. Desires to get it done, desires to get it done right...."

Ken's family was to hear moans such as this for the next forty years as he undertook (and usually finished) one book after another and one article after another.

Against his will, the courses began to take priority. He was taking two courses from Sapir. The one called "Linguistic Science" included meaning, psychology, and the general make-up of language. It followed pretty much the content of the book *Language* that Sapir himself had written, and also the book *Language* by Bloomfield. Ken found that he was well repaid for the hours he had spent reading linguistics while he was out in San Miguel. He wrote Townsend, "Anybody who 'memorized' Bloomfield's book *Language* would not feel uncomfortable in a single lecture I have heard," and he suggested that the students in Camp Wycliffe be required to read it.

Ken himself had not found that book to be easy. While still out in San Miguel he had written, "I have read parts of it four times to try to remember it all, but still fail miserably." Bloomfield himself was in Ann Arbor, but Ken had no classes with him, and Bloomfield didn't indulge in much chit-chat—not even linguistic chit-chat. Therefore Ken was influenced more by his book, that summer, than he was by personal contact. Later Bloomfield was to be a big encouragement to him (see chapter 9).

Sapir's course "Field Methods in Linguistics" was mainly an analysis of Navaho grammar. Ken found it pretty complicated—most verbs could have five stems; subject and object and tense could be fused together. He wrote, "To add to the difficulty, Sapir throws in important observations with a glance, as it were, and with such extreme rapidity that you cannot record them all at once on paper...." (It wouldn't be many years before Ken's students would be saying similar things about him.) He liked the courses, however. He said, "Little hints here and there bunch up to make a surprising whole."

Ken's third course was "American Dialect Geography," taught by Bernard Bloch. Bloch was one of the workers on the *Linguistic Atlas of the USA* and in class he was giving the history of the work, illustrated by the New England survey. He was also giving the extra sessions of phonetic dictation in order to prepare the students to hear the sounds and variants which might be met in dialect survey work.

Ken wrote, "The classes we have in phonetics put an awful strain on my abilities. In fact, some of the stuff I am pretty well stopped on.... At such times it is a comfort to know that our brains, our times, our lives, and work are all in the hand of God...."

Perhaps knowing that he was in God's hands helped him to make a decision that he now calls one of the most important judgments of his life. He determined never to try to save face by concealing his ignorance—he'd let his ignorance show. Because of that decision he was able to ask questions about anything, and that opened the door for people to teach him. He could talk with people in all walks of life and learn from them. It was not always pleasant to let his ignorance show, of course. "When you do that," he says, "some people think you're a dope."

He was very aware of the fact that in the Navaho class there were two or three students who had an edge on him both in analyzing forms and in phonetics. It helped his courage to know that, "When it comes to teaching folks how to make sounds, I am ready to bow to none." He was getting a payoff for the hours and hours that he had spent the previous summer learning how to pronounce and how to teach the pronunciation of glottalized stops. Now, in Ann Arbor, it took him only ten minutes to teach a fellow student who had just received his Ph.D. degree from Yale. Then he taught several others; one of those was Zellig Harris who was (and is currently) a professor in the University of Pennsylvania. That was especially satisfying to Ken, because as he said, explaining his satisfaction, "He has me beat on linguistic analysis and his ear, in general, is quicker and better trained than mine."

Sapir heard about those ten-minute sessions, and he chuckled and began to call Ken, "Glottal stop Pike."

Ken has said that much of the value of that summer at the University of Michigan was not the things he learned during class hours; rather it was the information he picked up informally outside of class. He especially appreciated the times when, after class, he, and perhaps another student or two, would go some place with Sapir to get a bite to eat. Often they would sit and talk linguistics until nearly midnight.

Ken told Sapir that he had not yet analyzed the tones of Mixtec. He knew that there were pairs of words that differed only by tone, but Sapir told him that tone could not be analyzed by pairs of words only. He suggested that Ken notice the tones that the different words had relative to the tones of the words they preceded or followed.

Thinking about it, Ken could see possibilities and he was anxious to get back to San Miguel and develop the idea.

As the years passed and Ken looked back on that summer of 1937, he always thought of Sapir as one of the great sources of stimulus in his life. He admired his ability to be interested in the work of others—even beginners. And he was wistful as he noticed his gentleness—he wished that he himself were that gentle.

8 HOW THEY SING!

(Fall 1937—Feb. 1938)

In the meantime, while Ken was studying in Ann Arbor, the fourth session of Camp Wycliffe was under way in Arkansas. That year the session was held in Siloam Springs, and those who compared the situation with that of the previous year in Sulphur Springs thought that they were living in luxury. They were renting the summer camp grounds of the Baptist Assembly and it had good cabins, a swimming pool, tennis courts, and classrooms. Students still ran the kitchen—the shopping, cooking, dishwashing, etc.—but under more convenient circumstances than they had before.

There was another difference. The students were studying harder than the students of 1936 had studied. In addition to the courses taught the previous summer, Eugene Nida was teaching general linguistics and also a course in the word structure of the Indian languages he had worked with while in Mexico.

Dr. McCreery had started the phonetics course, but he was able to stay only the first half of the session, so Ken had been asked to supplement the phonetics given by him. The session, with about twelve students, had started July the 19th, and Ken did not get there until near the end of August.

Ken, with great enthusiasm for his subject, tried to teach the students all that he himself had learned the preceding two years: the sounds he had encountered in Mixtec, Mazatec, Otomí, Totonac, Aztec, Zapotec, Mixe, Maya, Amuzgo, Trique, Navaho; the sounds found in the African languages he had read about; the things he had learned about tone, rhythm and vowel length; and the theory he had learned by reading such books as those by Bloomfield, Daniel Jones,

Kenyon, Sweet, Passy, Cummings, Ward, and Palmer, and the articles by Swadesh; and the information he had picked up in his classes that summer in Ann Arbor. He had only one month to get it all across. That was a lot to do in a month, but he was trying.

The way a knowledge of phonetics was able to help in language acquisition had seemed almost like magic to Ken. He knew from personal experience that it could make the difference between failure and success. As he looked at the twelve students who hoped to be learning and translating the New Testament for some little-known language, he wanted to give them all the help he could.

He had the students keep a "trouble list." If there was something they did not understand in his lecture, or, if they muffed a sound in class, they jotted it down, then Ken worked with them privately until the point was understood, or until they could pronounce the sound they had missed.

Ken's days were long; he was spending many hours outside of class, tutoring anyone who was having trouble. He was driving himself hard because he determined to get across the information he knew the future translators would need. With his customary enthusiasm, he affirmed before God that they would learn or he would bear the responsibility—not the students, but he himself. Somehow he would find a way to see that they learned.

The first reaction of the students was one of surprise. Phonetics had been easy under Dr. McCreery, but now they were working their heads off. Surprise too because they had not imagined that there could be so much to learn. Then they began to protest. One student said he'd be more willing to work that hard if he could see what it all had to do with translation.

Then the real blow fell. Townsend went to Ken and told him that some of the students thought he was trying to make them feel inadequate and that that was why he was giving hard assignments. That hurt. In the privacy of his room, Ken wept.

Failed again.

As usual Ken turned to the Scriptures to try to find out what had gone wrong, and years later he told about the lesson he had learned at that time.

He had wanted to serve, and he had given all he had—all his time and all his strength. (He'd worked until midnight often enough so that perhaps his health was in danger.) You might say that for the sake of the students he had "given his body to be burned." But it had all been useless. He said later that he had failed, not because they were not learning, but because they thought he didn't love them. So he stopped telling himself that he'd teach everybody everything; he gave up on somebody once in a while. But he determined, the Lord helping him, to serve with love (I Cor. 13:3).

The immediate effect was that Ken admitted to himself that he could not teach the students in one month everything that he himself knew. Once he had conceded that, the pressure eased both on himself and on the students.

He was still tutoring me by mail. Just a few days before the session was over, he wrote saying that I should become aware of the fact that in some languages some vowels were pronounced faster than others. He told me how to make drills to teach myself to both hear and pronounce vowels with differing time values. Consonants, too, he said, could be both long and short. "Train yourself," he urged.

He also wanted me to be agile in my handling of tone in speech. "Train yourself for three levels of pitch and any kind of glide between.... Start with easy combinations."

Tone, at that time, was Ken's main concern in his relation to the Mixtec language. He was anxious to get back to San Miguel and try out the suggestion Sapir had given him about studying the tone of words in relation to the tone of the preceding and following words.

On his way back to San Miguel he had a demonstration that showed him why the Mixtec men had laughed so heartily at the toy donkey and the clown who was trying to get him up. Ken had hired a man with three donkeys to take his baggage to San Miguel. They had started out all right, but after they were a few hours on the trail, one of the donkeys lay down. They tried to lift him back on to his feet, and the owner tried whipping him. Neither method worked. They had to take his pack off before they could get him up. Then by the time they loaded him up again, the other two donkeys had lain down. No wonder Ken's friends had howled with delight at the frustrated little clown—they knew exactly how he felt.

When they were about half way to San Miguel, they met Narciso, Nalo, and Leto on the trail. (Ken had written asking them to come, but they were arriving about a day late.) The load that was being carried by the lazy donkey was transferred to the men, and then, with his back empty, the donkey tripped along happily the rest of the way.

Part of the load was a phonograph, and the men were enchanted with it. At one time nineteen folks were in Ken's house listening, but usually the groups were smaller. On Christmas Eve, Narciso, Leto, his wife and several strangers stayed until two-thirty in the morning. They played the phonograph, ate candy, competed in games, and listened to Ken as he told them about the birth of Christ.

Ken was having plenty of social contact with the people, but he was finding it hard to get the seated-at-the-desk, pencil-in-hand type of study that he felt was necessary. In order to figure out the tone system, he needed someone who would do the boring job of repeating verb conjugations, and saying lists of words one after another so that he could hear the pitch differences—or so that he could hear that the pitches were the same.

Leto had agreed to work for him, but for reasons Ken never did figure out, he usually didn't show up. Ken asked Nalo to study with him, but he didn't turn up for work either.

Knowing that the Lord controlled all things, Ken was not sure how hard he should insist on having a language helper. He remembered how beneficial it had been to read linguistic books—maybe the Lord wanted him to finish Jesperson's *Language: Its Nature, Development, and Origin* instead of working on Mixtec.

But even while he was reading linguistics, Ken was uneasy. He knew he was going back to the University of Michigan the next summer, and it bothered him to think of facing Sapir, Swadesh, Bloch, or Bloomfield with the tone analysis not done.

Ken realized that the Lord had blessed him in conversational Mixtec, and in his teaching at Camp Wycliffe, but, without the analysis of the Mixtec tone, that was not enough. Ken read the fifth chapter of Luke where Peter told the Lord, "We have toiled all the night, and have taken nothing," and Ken identified with him. That's the way he felt too. He felt that he had toiled all night and had caught nothing, and he longed for the Lord to bless him and fill his net with fish, the way He had filled Peter's.

On the last day of 1937, Ken heard shots in the distance. People told him that there was a border dispute between two towns to the south, so Ken climbed to the roof of the old village church. He thought that perhaps from there he could see what was going on, and actually he did see smoke from one of the burning cabins. Then he looked down and saw Leto in the square below. He had been drinking so much that he was staggering. Ken was discouraged. He had thought that Leto had conquered that habit, but now he knew one of the reasons he had not been showing up for work, and it was a reason that Ken figured could not have been engineered by the Lord. Maybe the other hindrances to his language study program were not the Lord's will either. Ken decided he needed special help from the Lord and he'd have a special time of prayer and ask for it.

The next day, New Year's day, early in the morning, Ken walked up the mountain behind the house. He'd had no breakfast, not even water. He said later that sharp hunger reminded him to keep praying, and when he fell asleep, in a little while it woke him up again. So, off and on all day long out there on the mountain, he read Scripture, told the Lord "thank you" for His goodness to him, and asked for His blessing—and for a language helper. In between times he slept.

At dusk, hungry, thirsty, and tired, Ken went back to his cabin to get something to eat. While he was preparing it, Nalo dropped in. He watched Ken for a while, then told the reason for his coming. He offered to teach Ken Mixtec provided that he could come early and finish while the dew was still on the corn—his sickle didn't cut well after the corn was dry. Ken was delighted, not just because he was about to get help on the language, but because he was sure that Nalo had been sent by God Himself.

The next morning Nalo was there at five o'clock. The wind was blowing in through the cracks of the unchinked log cabin—in January in the early morning at 8,000 feet it is usually cold. Ken could see his breath as he talked and his fingers were so stiff he could hardly write. Nalo sat huddled in his blanket, but in spite of discomfort, he came faithfully and studied two hours every day— sometimes more.

For the next month Ken was making lists of nouns. Each list was alike in its tone pattern and different from the tone pattern of each of the other lists. He had also been working with verbs. Now he wanted to give a final test to the technique he had been using—was he really ready to say how many tones there were in the scale they used in their speech?

He thought he was, but in addition to his need to know the answer for Mixtec, he was concerned for Florrie Hansen and me over with the Mazatec-speaking people, and for Otis and Mary Leal studying one of the Zapotec languages. He wanted the tone solution to help not just him with his Mixtec problem, but he wanted to help his colleagues too. So he took another day out to pray.

He told the Lord, "I'm desperate. It's now 1938 and I've been working here since the fall of 1935 and this language is too much for me. But, Lord, there's no point in solving just this one. Please, Lord, I want an answer, but, please, hold up the answer until when it comes it will serve as a technique for helping with other languages too."

Then the next day, and the day after that, he compared the pitch of the various lists of nouns as they occurred following the same numeral, or following the same adjective, etc. And he compared various lists of verbs as they occurred with the same prefix or suffix. By the end of those four hours with Nalo, he was sure that San Miguel Mixtec used three tones in its speech (high, mid, and low), and that conclusion has stood the test of years.

It had been a long hard struggle; in fact the struggle was still going on, for he had to learn the rules for when and how the different sequences of tones changed. In spite of those difficulties, however, he thought the language was beautiful. He wrote, "Right now a stranger is in my house talking with Narciso. How they sing!"

9 A MARVELOUS JOB!

(Spring and Summer, 1938)

Ken and Nalo hadn't spent all their time with monotonous word lists. Every day they worked awhile with Scripture. There was the day they went through the part that tells about the resurrection of Christ (John 20:1-10). Ken and Nalo talked about each verse, putting the various attempts at a translation on four-by-six-inch slips. Then after they had gone through all ten verses, Nalo told the whole section back without referring to the notes. As he talked, Ken wrote down what he said and the result delighted him, "He did a marvelous job! I only had to prompt him a couple of times."

Ken had been looking for a method that would ensure an idiomatic translation, and he decided that a translation was really good if it read the way Nalo talked as he told back a portion from memory. Of course Ken worked it over afterwards to be sure that everything in the original had been included, and to cut out any additions, but he was satisfied with the result.

As Ken became more sure of the tones of Mixtec, he typed out some of the translated verses and helped Nalo to read them. Two of the first verses were about God's forgiving our sins (I John 1:9), and about how He loves us (John 3:16). Not long after that, whenever they came to an expression such as "the disciple whom Jesus loved," Nalo would explain it as "like He loves me."

The two men enjoyed working together, and in their student-teacher relationship the roles were constantly shifting from one to the other.

There was the day they went out for a walk and Ken saw a sycamore tree. He climbed it and told Nalo the story of Zacchaeus

who climbed a tree so that he could see Jesus (Luke 19:4). Nalo
listened, then taking the role of teacher he told Ken that a something
was growing in the tree that was good to eat. The word he had used
was new to Ken, but he could see a couple of white things hanging
high, way out on the tip of a branch. They were about the size of a
big pear.

With considerable effort, Ken climbed high enough so that he
could dislodge them with a stick. Nalo picked them up and laid them
carefully beside his pack. After Ken was on the ground again, he
went over to get a better look, to see just what kind of fruit he had
harvested. On the outside of one, he saw a small worm. What? Then
Ken understood. Those white things were two big clusters of worms,
but they were so tightly intertwined that he couldn't distinguish the
separate worms even from only a few feet away.

Nalo was gleeful because he had fooled Ken, and he laughed so
hard he could hardly stand up. When they started home, to Ken's
amazement, Nalo carefully gathered up the two ball-like objects.
"He's going to burn them," Ken thought.

No. He was carrying them home because, actually, he had not
been kidding. They were good to eat, and the Mixtecs thought they
were delicious. Nalo's wife toasted them on her clay griddle and
Ken managed to get down a couple. He found them to be not half
bad; they tasted crispy, something like popcorn, he said. But he
hoped he wasn't offered them very often.

Most of the time Ken was doing his own cooking, and usually he
fared pretty well. It was on Thanksgiving day that he decided to
have something a little different. Leto got a chicken for him and
dressed it, but Ken sputtered into his diary that the first panful had
been burned on the outside while raw on the inside. Then he cooked
the rest more slowly and that part was neither raw nor burned.

Pancakes were still his specialty. He not only cooked them for
himself, but he served them to his guests. Sometimes he used them
as a kind of demonstration that he didn't need a wife in order to
have tortillas; he could make his own brand. Look! Taste!

Maybe his friends weren't convinced about the wife part, but
they liked his pancakes. Then one day one of the very important
town elders came to call. He had not only been mayor, but he was
one of the few who were influential in the selection of other mayors.

He had brought his wife with him, and he requested that Ken teach her how to make pancakes. Ken's letter didn't say, but I suspect he taught her with the same flourish he teaches other people other things.

Ken had made it a point to show respect to the town elders. He not only called himself a "resident of San Miguel," but he wanted to fulfill any duties a resident had. Sometimes the men were expected to give their labor. That is, a project was frequently accomplished, not by hiring people who were paid by taxes, but by each man doing his share.

That spring they were building a covered porch, or portico, along the front of the townhall. Each man was supposed to pick up three big rocks out on the mountain and carry them into the town square. Outsiders, schoolteachers, for example, were automatically excused.

Ken didn't want to be looked on as an outsider, so one morning he went out, found a big stone, tied a tumpline around it, threw a blanket over his back for padding, and with it hanging from the top of his head, started off for the center. He wasn't very expert at tying the tumpline and it slipped—fortunately just as he was easing it down onto a bank to rest. He re-tied it and succeeded in carrying it the rest of the way safely.

People were really startled. Perhaps it was the first time they had ever seen an "educated" man with a rock on his back. The mayor thanked him, and then told him solemnly that he lacked two. (A man's allotment was three.) The approval, expressed by the glances the men threw his direction and by their joking remarks, was worth the headache he got from it.

A couple of days later he went back for his second rock and some men were with him. They were very solicitous, helping him choose one that was not too big, helping him tie the tumpline, and easing it up onto his back. On this second trip, it was his ankle that bothered him. He had walked without a limp for almost a year now, but his weak leg protested at the weight of the rock, so, on his next trip, he carried a cane. He felt real satisfaction when the rock thumped down onto the ground at the feet of the mayor. After that the men's way of asserting that Ken had earned the right to be counted as part of the town was to say, "He carried his three rocks."

The Mixtecs had such a hazy idea of the world that it was hard for them to picture where Ken was from. They tried to understand and they asked questions. Typical was, "Is United States in Spain?" To help them, Ken drew a map of Canada, the United States, and Mexico and showed them the approximate location of San Miguel, Mexico City, and Connecticut, the place where he was born.

Nalo became acquainted with a different part of the world when Ken took him with him to Huautla to see Florrie and me. They traveled five days: the first two days walking to Nochistlán, the third on the bus to Parián, the fourth on the train to the station nearest us, and then a half hour by bus, the fifth walking over the mountains to Huautla.

Ken had been thinking of dropping by ever since he had figured out how to hear and write the tones as they occurred in the speech of San Miguel Mixtec. He was sure that I would need help with the tone of Mazatec and the little matter of a five-day trip did not stop him. He brought Nalo with him because he wanted to show us how he had lined up the words in order that they be heard more easily.

Florrie and I were delighted. It was good to talk English with someone besides ourselves, and, yes, we did need help on the language.

The day after they arrived, Ken took out a list of Mixtec words and said one phrase after another, using the same numeral but changing the nouns. For example, "two houses," "two boys," etc. Nalo repeated each one after him. Then Ken went down another list of nouns, but using the same adjective with each. For example, "good dog," "good squash," etc. Using the same numeral, or the same adjective, gave us something with which to compare the tone of the nouns.

Because of previous study, Ken knew what the tones should be and was pronouncing them correctly. Repeating the phrases after him was an easy job for Nalo and he sat relaxed. Very relaxed. Pretty soon his head dropped forward, his eyes closed, and his speech became little more than a mumble. Ken signalled to us to watch how he would wake him up. The next phrase he said was "good corn," but he said it with the wrong sequence of tones. Nalo started to mimic him. Then he sat up wide awake, "No, no! Not like that! It should be..." and he pronounced the phrase correctly.

"O.K.," said Ken. He continued down the list and Nalo relaxed again. With that demonstration Ken showed us that a wrong tone was distressing enough to jerk a man from drowsiness to protesting attention.

The next day, and for several after that, Ken continued to help us to hear tone in Mazatec. We worked with nouns, moved on to adjectives, and then on to verbs—even those with four or five syllables.

Florrie and I were encouraged; we were on the right track. Now all we had to do was sweat away at it for a couple hundred hours or more—checking and memorizing—and we'd know the right tone for all the words in our Mazatec file.

Ken was thrilled. He had been able to apply to Mazatec the same technique he had used to determine the tones of San Miguel Mixtec. He remembered that he had asked the Lord to enable him to help his colleagues with their tone problems. The progress that Florrie and I had made was evidence that the Lord had answered. Ken was grateful.

When Sunday came, we were ready to celebrate the victory. Florrie, an excellent cook, was equal to the occasion. "Pumpkin pie!" was the only entry in Ken's diary for that day, but it was celebration enough when compared with months of pancakes and a try or two at toasted worms.

A week later Ken and Nalo were on their way to the village where the Townsends worked, then Nalo returned to San Miguel, and Ken went to the States. Now that he knew the solution to the Mixtec tone, and had seen that the same technique had worked in solving the problem of the tone of the Huautla Mazatec, he was looking forward to meeting his linguist friends again in Ann Arbor.

When he reached there a couple of months later, it didn't take him long to start talking about the success he had been having in the analysis of Mixtec tone. Probably the first to whom he actually demonstrated the technique was Charles Voegelin, then professor at DePauw University, currently at Indiana University. Voegelin had said that he had not been satisfied with the results he had had when trying to analyze a tonal system. That summer he was working with a man who spoke one of the Sioux languages, so Ken demonstrated with that language how he would go about doing an analysis of tone.

At first Voegelin was impatient—Ken's system did seem to get off to a slow start—but by the end of two hours Voegelin was quite excited about the method and was ready to try it himself.

Among others who showed interest were Harris of Pennsylvania, Sturtevant of Yale, and Bloomfield of Chicago. Professor Fries, the director that summer of the Linguistic Institute of the Linguistic Society of America, asked Ken to give the material at a luncheon conference. Ken spent the next three weeks preparing for the lecture—in addition to the months he had already spent on Mixtec—and when the day came, he spoke for an hour and a half on the topic, "The Problem of Tones in Mexican Indian Languages." For the most part he used Mixtec data, but he also drew from his experience with Mazatec.

The paper was very well received and to this day Ken remembers with gratitude the encouragement the men gave him. Professor Sturtevant said, "There's a lot of work done there," and when Professor Bloomfield had occasion to write to Ken later, he said, "I learned a great deal from your account of Mixtec."

Professor Fries said that it had been equivalent to a doctoral dissertation and he suggested that Ken study for a doctorate. Ken doubted that what he had done would be sufficient because he had just barely begun on the analysis of Mixtec grammar, but Fries replied that he was referring to the method of tone analysis. He said that a problem solved was a better topic for a thesis than the description of a language, and that the problem Ken had solved had been bothering numerous people. Writing the dissertation shouldn't take him long since he had already done the research: all that was left to do now was to look at the literature and see what other people had done on the topic.

Some of the other linguists had showed interest in the SIL project too. The questions they had asked at the luncheon conference were not just on linguistics. For example, they wanted to know, "How do you get someone to study these languages?" So, at their request, Ken told them about the purpose and program of SIL—that some people believed that all people everywhere should have access to the Bible and so young folks were willing to study languages in out-of-the-way places in order to translate the New Testament into little-known languages.

They asked who paid their salaries. That led to a discussion of churches and individuals who, although they did not do the work themselves, gave money to support those who were doing it, and how, somehow, the Lord guided the givers so that the young folks doing the job were taken care of. The men at the conference were amazed.

Probably they wouldn't have been so impressed if they had known that Ken arrived in Siloam Springs, Arkansas, that year, with just seventeen cents in his pocket. Ken's own faith in the Lord's provision never wavered. He had had enough, and then more money had arrived by the time he needed it.

Actually he was thrilled. He had gone to Mexico expecting to tell the unschooled about Jesus Christ. Now, because he had studied the language of some of those unschooled folks, a group of university professors were asking questions that let him tell them too about the Lord.

After the luncheon, Ken considered Fries' advice; however, he thought that he didn't have the time to get a Ph.D. because he had to be in Mexico most of the year, but Fries said that he could take courses in the summers at the Linguistic Institute. Ken still thought it would be impossible because he had to teach at "Camp Wycliffe", the Summer Institute of Linguistics, during the summer. Fries had a solution even for that; he would arrange with the professors to let him get credit in spite of the fact that he had to leave Michigan early that summer.

Ken had only been auditing courses, but Fries persuaded him to register for credit. So he did—the very day that he was leaving for Arkansas where the Summer Institute of Linguistics was being held.

Bloomfield had been teaching both the courses that he had registered for, so he needed to talk to him about requirements. It just happened that they were taking the same train as far as Chicago, so they arranged to sit together. Uppermost in Ken's mind at the time was the analysis of the tone of San Miguel Mixtec. He was so pleased to have learned, not only the number of different tones in the system, but also the rules for the way that the some tones were substituted for one another in a sentence, that he chatted on and on about the system and how he had arrived at the answers.

As they neared Chicago, Bloomfield told him. "Look, Pike, I have to turn in a grade for you, and just in case somebody asks me about it, it would help if you write me a letter about the things you have just been telling me."

So Ken wrote him a twelve-page letter on Mixtec tone, the verb system, and the consonants involved. That constituted his summer's work for 1938.

For the next several years, Ken spent part of each summer studying at Michigan, and except for that year of 1938, he managed to stay through to the end of the sesson. Part of each summer he spent teaching at the Summer Institute of Linguistics. During the other months of the year, he divided most of his time between linguistics (reading, thinking, writing) and the Mixtecs (being friendly, analyzing the language, teaching, translating). Actually the two types of work were intertwined as he studied linguistics while living in the Mixtec-speaking village. In spite of giving time to the Mixtecs as well as to the students of the Summer Institute of Linguistics, he was to have all requirements completed and take the final exam for his Ph.D. degree on August 11, 1941.

In the end, his dissertation was not on tone. When he got around to writing it, his material on tone had become routine to him. His interest by that time was in phonetics, and so phonetics became the subject of his Ph.D. dissertation. His work on tone was to become a separate book, published later.

Ken has said that he might never have made the attempt to get a Ph.D. degree if it had not been for Professor Fries who guided and encouraged him. Ken thinks of Fries as a great shade tree, and that he was privileged to be able to develop academically under his influence.

10 EVELYN

(1938...)

Ken had additional responsibilities at the Summer Institute of Linguistics school that summer of 1938; Mr. Townsend had asked him and Eugene Nida to be co-directors. Also, since Dr. McCreery was unable to attend, he had the entire responsibility for the phonetic course. Nida was in charge of grammar.

Actually, Ken had come to the conclusion that the students needed to know a lot more about phonetics than just how to pronounce and record sounds. By the summer of 1938, he was teaching about phonemes, how a sound in a given language could vary and still be considered the same by the speakers of that language, and he was showing ways of determining whether or not a sound was "the same" or "different." What he taught was a kind of more-easily-understood combination of the theories of Bloomfield, Sapir, and Swadesh.

He told the students to watch for the various positions in which the different sounds occurred in a word, and in a syllable, and to notice what sounds they preceded or followed. The content of what he taught had been more or less outlined in his article that had been published the previous year, "Likenesses, Differences and Variations of Phonemes in Mexican Indian Languages and How to Find Them," *Investigaciones Lingüísticas* 4.134-39 (1937).

The biggest change for Ken, however, in that summer was due to the fact that Evelyn Griset was there.

Ken and Evelyn had met in 1935 when Evelyn was helping her Uncle Cam in the care of his wife, Elvira. (Mr. Townsend and Evelyn's mother are brother and sister.) Aunt Elvira had had tremendous courage, but it was housed in a very frail body. In spite of a heart condition that made her future uncertain, she was willing to leave home and go with Uncle Cam to a small town in Mexico where there were no medical facilities. She didn't have the strength to do much housework, and sometimes she needed special care. Evelyn had taken the 1935-36 season between her Junior and Senior years at the University of California at Los Angeles to go with them to Mexico. She was twenty at the time, and later Ken described her in a letter to one of his brothers as, "tall, weight a hundred and fifteen pounds, blueish-green eyes," but he had been most impressed by the way she had adjusted to life in a little village without modern conveniences.

Evelyn found things to enjoy all around her. There were the donkeys, for example, that brayed loudly at any hour. She wrote her family, "One is going off now; he is our prize—he can go longer, louder, more longingly, pathetically than any other." And she was amused by the way the men drove them, "They run up behind them and push them off the road so that a car can go by—the very same way we have to push our garage door when it is acting its very worst."

She enjoyed her contact with both the Spanish-speaking and the Aztec-speaking people. She used to call on one of their Spanish-speaking neighbors and read to her from the New Testament while the woman helped her with the pronunciation. But Evelyn was learning more than Spanish—she learned, for example, to sit balanced on a bench, six inches high, eight inches long, and three inches wide while she had her lesson. She thought that was quite a feat.

The Aztec-speaking women were dubious about their ability to learn to read, so Evelyn had to encourage them, cheer them on, until they were willing to try. In the cornstalk house of one friend (cornstalk walls, adobe cornerposts, and thatched roof) she sat on the bed made of three boards stretched across two sawhorses. She was delighted when her hostess learned to read the first page of a primer and was willing to try a little more.

Perhaps even more pertinent as far as Ken was concerned was the fact that she didn't let "linguistic talk" get her down even when she and her Aunt Elvira felt like outsiders at their own dinner table.

That fall of 1935, when the young fellows stopped by to see Townsend, they were always talking about the new sounds they had just found in the languages they were studying. Then, worse still, Ken had written something on "What is a Verb." Evelyn's comment to her family was, "Glory be! It's terrible. I can't get the point—but evidently there is one.... He's comparing the verbs of various languages."

Ken also profited by the good training Evelyn had had that year as she watched her Uncle Cam and Aunt Elvira relate to the people of the village, to the university personnel, and to the government officials. Actually Evelyn had been making strangers feel at ease in her home most of her life. Her father, Eugene Griset (a French-speaking Waldensian, born in Italy in 1876), was in the habit of teaching people about Jesus Christ. When he was a young man he had spent part of his free time helping at the YMCA, and he had also taught a boys' Sunday School class—one of his pupils had been Cameron Townsend. Later he had married his pupil's older sister, Lula Townsend (born in Colorado in 1888). In 1941 he focused on the servicemen stationed in the Santa Ana area of California where he had his big farm. After a short chit-chat with them, he often invited them to go home with him for dinner. His wife and their three children (Evelyn, Lorin, and Florence) worked as a team to make the young men feel welcome.)

Perhaps because she had grown up in a home that had been a kind of open house, she seemed to be aware of people's needs and their reactions to a situation. That was one of the benefits Ken acquired when they were married; it wasn't long before he was calling her his "social antenna" or his "social consultant"—he needed a social consultant, because sometimes he himself was completely blind to the way people were feeling.

Evelyn so fitted into the Townsend home too, that when she returned for her senior year at UCLA, Uncle Cam wrote her mother, "She has been an untold blessing to us." Apparently life in the Aztec village had convinced her of the value of working with minority groups, because the summer after she graduated from UCLA (1937), she and a girl friend returned to Mexico to spend the summer in the Townsends' tiny house. In the fall she went to study at the Bible Institute of Los Angeles (Biola), as part of her preparation for more work in Latin America.

Then she was ready for that final step of preparation—courses at the Summer Institute of Linguistics. In Arkansas, Evelyn was studying hard, and Ken undoubtedly was attempting more than anybody could expect to accomplish, but somehow they managed to see each other occasionally and come to the agreement that life together would be just right. Both of them had hoped that their courtship would be inconspicuous, so they felt triumphant when people were surprised at their engagement.

The Legters had invited everyone to a birthday party for their grandson, but, as the favors were passed out, the guests began to realize that there was more afoot than the celebration of a little boy's first birthday. Evelyn, for example, received a little green fish labelled "PIKE." It was Mr. Legters who actually made the announcement, and everyone was very happy about it all. Aunt Elvira wrote the Grisets, "We firmly believe that Evelyn and Ken were made for each other."

Legters remembered that someone had given him a diamond ring to be used for bringing the gospel to the Indians, and he thought that, if Ken would have the stone reset, it would be a nice gift for Evelyn. He urged Ken to take it, reminding him that he had received no salary for his teaching, and that not even his transportation to Arkansas had been reimbursed. It was a fact that Ken had no money with which to buy a diamond. So, with a thank you, he accepted it. Both he and Evelyn considered that the ring, ready and waiting for them, was another indication that the Lord was leading and blessing them.

When should the wedding be, and where? Evelyn would have liked to be married in California with her folks, but there was no money for travel, so letters began to go back and forth with Mrs. Griset offering good advice about dresses, household goods, etc.

The Grisets had never met Ken, so Evelyn tried to clue them in with her letters. She wrote, "I do love Kenneth very much," and in another letter she added the information, "Do you know that Kenneth never ate raw tomatoes until he was in college? Our diets have been as different as our dialects."

Ken had grown up in a small town in Connecticut before it was possible to ship vegetables in from warmer climates. The only vegetables and fruits the Pikes ate in the wintertime were those they had canned, or that they had been able to store in their cellar—cabbages, carrots, potatoes, apples, etc. Besides, he didn't like raw tomatoes. On the other hand, Evelyn had grown up in California, surrounded by a vegetable garden, she sometimes ate raw tomatoes twice a day week after week.

Perhaps because of his New England background, Ken's letters at the time didn't express his feelings very well. It was almost thirty years later, when their daughter Barbara became engaged, that he wrote a poem for the occasion, and it contained the essence of the way his own life had been with Evelyn. (The poem was later published in *Stir-Change-Create,* 1967, p. 145.)

BELOVÉD

Alone—no longer.
Two, is one—
Meets need
    of both.

Soul longs
To tell, and ear
to hear you
    Speak!

In that summer of 1938 when Ken and Evelyn became engaged, Evelyn had been tutoring some of the students who were having trouble with phonetics. In spite of her success with the students, however, she felt that Ken was far out ahead of her as far as linguistics was concerned. She wrote home, "I hope I'll be able to keep up with his vocabulary just a little anyway."

She had already seen Ken help her Uncle Cam with Aztec, me with Mazatec, and another colleague with Totonac. She had insight enough to know that in the future Ken would travel still more in order to help others. She determined to study linguistics so that she could go with him as an assistant and know that she was pulling her weight academically.

She succeeded.

She later carried a full load as linguistic consultant when they went to workshops in Peru, Ecuador, Australia, New Guinea, Nepal, India, and later in South America and Africa. Sometimes she felt that the task would overwhelm her, "but if I stopped doing things that frighten me, I guess I wouldn't do much."

At the Summer Institute of Linguistics school at Norman, Oklahoma, she has taught in each of the three departments, phonetics, phonology, and grammar, and much of the time she has been head of the department where she was teaching. She has also taught in the Summer Institute of Linguistics schools in Australia and England.

In their work as a team, Ken says that Evelyn is the pedagogue, while he is the one lining up the theory. When it came time to write *Phonemics: A Technique for Reducing Languages to Writing* (published in 1947), she wanted a book of problems with a discussion of the answers; she thought the students would learn better that way. She convinced Ken, and that is the style in which it was written. Then, in 1954, Evelyn and her staff made a 140-page *Laboratory Manual* to supplement the *Phonemics* book.

This dual life of housewife and linguist has not always been easy, especially when the children were small. Evelyn wrote her folks, "I find it most distressing to switch from keeping house and taking care of a family, to working on a linguistic problem as consultant for someone. I get absorbed in one and the next time I come to—woe is me—my other job is being woefully neglected—but I don't think Stephen was late to school this noon."

When the children were older, Evelyn registered for classes at the University of Michigan and, in 1963, she received her masters degree in linguistics. Throughout the years she had been doing some writing and had co-authored descriptive articles with several of her colleagues that she had been helping. She also wrote an article on her own theoretical developments in grammar. In 1977 *Grammatical Analysis* was published, a book which she co-authored with Ken— they had been working on it for some time.

In 1976, when Ken was both chairman of the linguistic department at the University of Michigan, and director of the English Language Institute there, the Dean looked for a way to lighten his load. His answer was to have Evie teach the course on grammar that had usually been taught by Ken.

Of course, in spite of Evelyn's linguistic achievements, she couldn't travel with Ken all the time, and he sent the following poem back to her while he was on a trip to Australia.

ANOTHER HOLE IN MY POCKET

Poor pocket's
    so Neglected—
Gone's the change
    I expected.

11 TOGETHER

(Fall of 1938)

Since going to Mexico in 1935, Ken had started his letters to Townsend in a number of ways, depending upon what he was writing about. Usually they began, "Dear Mr. Townsend," but some were "Prof. Townsend," some "Prof.," several "Boss," and a couple even "Cam." Now that his wedding to Evelyn Griset, Mr. Townsend's niece, was about to take place, he added a new one to the list—"Uncle Cam." This familiar name soon became a habit with him. The habit spread and in a few years Townsend was Uncle Cam to most of the SIL members.

Ken and Evie were back in Mexico City by October 15th, and plans for the wedding and life among the Mixtecs went full steam ahead. First they went to get the engagement ring reset, and then to buy groceries, kitchen utensils, etc. There was a friendly wholesale grocer in town, and Ken and Evie made it a point to do their ordering far enough ahead so that it could be boxed and expressed to Parián, in time to be there ahead of them. A little delay in train service was expected.

Ken was buying tools, too, to use in building a house. There was no real store in San Miguel, and they wouldn't be able to buy even a nail out there.

Ken was also going around with Uncle Cam to see the linguists of the area. There was to be a linguistic week organized by the Mexican Institute of Linguistic Investigations, in conjunction with the Federal Ministry of Education, the Department of Indigenous Affairs, the Academy of Aztec and Otomí Languages, and the Summer Institute of Linguistics. It was to be from November 7th through the 12th. About half of the papers would be given by members of SIL and the rest by Mexican linguists. Ken's was to be the second paper on the program, and in addition to getting his own ready, he was advising all the rest of us on ours.

Ken had written an additional paper, "Phonemic Work Sheet," and he wanted to get it into print—his colleagues and others could profit from it. By using small type, a summary of procedures for determining the units of a sound system could be printed on one side of an eight-and-a-half by eleven inch sheet of paper. The other side was to be a chart labelled with the various components of sounds. Then space was provided where the actual sounds of a specific language could be written in. There were the usual delays and hitches of one kind or another, and Ken went to the printshop almost every day for a month before it was finally done. It turned out to be extremely useful in spite of its unpretentious size.

Evelyn was going out to Pátzcuaro to be with Max and Elisabeth Lathrop until time for the wedding—November 13th. But before she went, arrangements had to be made for the civil ceremony. Everybody told them that there were often delays, and Reverend McKean, the pastor who would perform the religious ceremony, advised them to have it a week or two in advance. In Mexico the only legal wedding is the civil one.

So, one afternoon a day or two before Evelyn was to leave, they asked three friends to go with them down to the judge's office to see about getting the papers started. Everything went smoothly. The paper work was completed easily and the judge had the time and inclination to see the marriage through that day. So. Surprise! Ken and Evelyn left the office as Mr. and Mrs. Kenneth L. Pike. They were thankful to have one more step behind them, one less thing to worry about as they looked forward to November 13th.

But that was not Uncle Cam's reaction. He was very disappointed and therefore very upset. He had been hoping that the civil wedding would be a big to-do with lots of government officials present. Maybe there could be a sermon in connection with the wedding and that would provide an opportunity to tell them about Christ. Just maybe the wedding could be on the President's lawn! But now that the knot had already been tied, all those dreams had come to nothing. Uncle Cam had had such confidence in his dreams that he was sure that Ken and Evelyn had been willfully disobedient to the Lord.

They didn't feel that way about it at all. Both were in the habit of praying that the Lord guide them, and they figured that the civil ceremony could not have been completed in one afternoon without the Lord's special help. They couldn't think of anything to feel guilty about.

Uncle Cam spoke very sharply about the matter. He said that it was apparent that they did not respect the Mexican law because they considered the church ceremony to be the pertinent one. Therefore he felt disgraced in the eyes of the Mexican officials, and he himself would not attend the religious ceremony. Furthermore he felt that Ken and Evie had deliberately deceived him—they should have told him that they were planning to be married that day.

It is true that Ken and Evie had known that Uncle Cam would have liked to invite government officials, but Evelyn didn't want it that way. It seemed inappropriate to her to have people at her wedding that she did not know. She preferred to have only her own colleagues and friends there. But she and Ken had not tried to deceive Uncle Cam; he had known that they were going to start proceedings that day, but neither he nor they had had any idea that the civil ceremony could be arranged for and completed all in one afternoon.

Mrs. Griset tried to be a peacemaker. She wrote Uncle Cam, her brother, that Ken and Evie were the principal parties to the contract, and that they should be allowed to make decisions about their own wedding. She also wrote Evie telling her to try to be considerate of the people who were helping her.

Ken and Evie were trying to be considerate, and they had not intended to distress Uncle Cam. Immediately they began looking for ways to rectify the situation. Since his big objection had been that the Mexican law was, in his opinion, being disrespected, Evelyn suggested that he talk with Rev. McKean about the wording of the religious ceremony. Instead of pronouncing them husband and wife, he might say something to the effect that since they had already been married by the state, he recognized that act and solemnized it before God. When the pastor assured Uncle Cam that the ceremony would be performed in that way, he decided that he could go to the church wedding after all. (Eight years later, after Aunt Elvira died, Uncle Cam married Elaine Mielke. Lázaro Cárdenas, a former president of Mexico, was the best man, and his wife, Amalia, was matron of honor at the wedding. In that way Uncle Cam's big dream did eventually come true.)

So harmony between Uncle Cam, his niece, and nephew-in-law was restored, but there was a difference for Ken. Previously he had almost automatically responded to Uncle Cam's every wish. He was grateful to him for letting him work with him in Mexico, for the opportunity to translate the New Testament for the Mixtec-speaking people, and he admired his leadership. Now, however, both he and Evie had seen that their thoughts and feelings could differ from those of Uncle Cam. Specifically, they had not tried to deceive him, and they were still convinced that the Lord had guided in the timing of the civil ceremony.

To Ken it was a very graphic lesson from the Lord that he needed to use his own judgment, that he should not always depend on Uncle Cam to make the decisions. That change in Ken's point of view was to have an impact in the years to come as the Summer Institute of Linguistics and Wycliffe Bible Translator organizations grew and policies were determined.

In the meantime friends and colleagues rallied around to make the wedding a happy time. There was a shower with the traditional jokes and practical gifts: a gasoline iron, a wool blanket, baking dishes, meat grinder, a wall-type can opener, a six-quart pressure cooker, two canvas chairs, etc.

The church was decorated, and when the organ started playing at five o'clock that Sunday afternoon, everything was beautiful. A quartette sang "O Love That Wilt Not Let Me Go" and "O Perfect Love." There was a solo "Because," and then Uncle Cam and Aunt Elvira, as the relatives closest to the bride, were escorted to the front pew.

The organist began playing for the bridal procession and the matron of honor walked down the aisle. A flower girl followed. Then Evie came wearing an exquisite white satin dress with a cathedral-length train. Up front waiting were the pastor, the best man, and Ken. When Evie had almost arrived, Ken came down from the chancel and met her at the foot of the steps. He took her hand, put it on his arm, and they went up the steps together. As Evie said later, "It all seemed very natural."

During the reception, the organist played a medley of hymns on the piano and Evie cut a three-tiered white cake. The quartette sang again and Uncle Cam led in prayer. There were more pictures, more chit-chat, and then the bride and groom made their get-away—but they didn't go far!

They could go only as far as the Paseo de la Reforma where Ken had reserved a little apartment on the top floor. The reason for such a short journey was that, at the last minute, the Linguistic Week had been postponed. It was now to begin on November 14th—the day after Ken and Evie's wedding.

Ken and Evie had not wanted to postpone the wedding—the invitations had already been mailed out. On the other hand, Ken thought he would be negligent in his duty if he cut the linguistic meetings—and his colleagues would feel orphaned. The answer seemed to be to change the plans for the honeymoon. Actually the little apartment on Reforma was a nice little place, and it was on the prettiest street in Mexico. When they went a few steps up to the roof, they could see out over much of the city.

So, the day after their wedding, Ken and Evie were present for the opening of the linguistic week. They were there when the Rector of the National University made the opening remarks, and when the subsecretary of the Department of Education greeted the people at the conference.

Ken's was the second linguistic paper, and it was on "Analysis and Charting of Phonetics, Phonemics, and Tonemics." Apparently he did well, but the thing that really delighted him was later when he saw Evie pick up a broom and start sweeping in their little apartment. That touched his heart and he wrote that she looked almost as pretty and intriguing as she had in her wedding dress. It was nice he felt that way because she would soon be trying to turn a humble Indian hut into a home out in the village of San Miguel.

They were leaving by train from Mexico City on the 25th of November, but Ken kept finding more colleagues to consult with and more languages to listen to. Accompanied by a group of well-wishers, they managed to make it to the train about two minutes before it pulled out. Ken couldn't bear to waste those two minutes, so he leaned out the window and gave final linguistic advice on somebody's paper until the train was actually moving.

Two of their colleagues, Otis and Mary Leal, were on the train too, on their way to continue their work among the Zapotec-speaking people. They were going to the city of Oaxaca, and they urged Ken and Evie to go on with them. They could do a little sightseeing as part of their honeymoon.

That sounded intriguing, but Ken and Evie thought it about time they got out to San Miguel, and they didn't want to delay just in order to sightsee. They had taken considerable pains to express their baggage on ahead, and they expected it to be at the station waiting for them. Of course they knew that delay was possible, so they decided that when the train stopped in Parián, Ken would check on the baggage. If it was already in the station, Evie would get off too, and they would go right on to San Miguel. If the baggage had not yet arrived, Ken would get back on the train, and they would go spend a few days in Oaxaca City.

The next morning when the train stopped in Parián, Ken immediately stepped off. Evie and the Leals waited expectantly. After a bit Ken came back and without a word took his seat beside Evie. Otis immediately asked, "Has your baggage arrived yet?"

"I don't know," Ken answered quietly.

"You don't know!" They couldn't say any more. They just looked at him.

As the train got underway, Ken explained. The station had burned down the night before, and the station agent couldn't remember whether or not the Pike baggage had already arrived, but he sort of thought that it had. If so, it had burned along with everything else.

So Ken and Evie went to spend a few days in Oaxaca City.

None of the letters tell how they felt at that moment, but maybe Ken remembered what he had said before, "It sure is great to know that God is just as big, just as strong, just as wonderful, when things seem to be all mixed up, as when they give a person joy."

Anyway, in Oaxaca City they didn't let the thought of burned baggage spoil their fun. Walt and Vera Miller met them at the train and took them all out to see the tombs at Monte Albán that had been built centuries ago by the Zapotec-speaking and the Mixtec-speaking people. Ken had a big time crawling through a tunnel that wandered around under one structure. The tunnel finally got too narrow for him to go any further, and it took him so long to get back that Evie up on top began to wonder if he was stuck there.

The next day the Millers took them to the town of Mitla to see the ancient ruins that still give indication of the glories of the old Zapotec kingdom.

Then once more it was time to be on the way to San Miguel. They took the train back to Parián, and their baggage was waiting for them there. All 1,580 pounds of it. It had arrived after the fire, and so their groceries, household equipment, and wedding presents had not been burned. The Lord had saved their things for them by letting them be held up awhile.

In Parián two fellows who worked in connection with an antimony mine were on their way to Nochistlán in a truck, and they let Ken and Evie ride along. From there they got a ride on to Tlaxiaco in still another truck, a new one. It bounced and groaned up this mountain, and down the next, scraping the mountain on one side to avoid a fall-off on the other. The usual speed was about five miles an hour, and only occasionally did they reach twenty. Evie wrote that now she knew that a truck could go just absolutely anywhere.

But apparently it couldn't, because for the rest of the way, from Tlaxiaco to San Miguel, the animals had to take over. Eight donkeys carried the baggage. Evie had a horse, but she walked part of the time, and Ken walked most of the time. They left about six o'clock in the morning, and after they had been on the road four hours, they stopped to rest. The Mixtecs who were with them built a fire and heated up some water, while Evie hurried from tree to tree picking the orchids growing on them. They ate their sandwiches, drank hot tea, and started out again. The horse got tired, too, and Evie found it to be quite a chore just to keep him moving. They arrived about four-thirty in the afternoon.

Ken's old friends gathered around to welcome them. They looked at Evie with admiration and asked Ken how much he had had to pay for her—they had to pay for their brides. When he answered, "Nothing," they were amazed. A good wife like that was worth a fortune.

12 HOUSE BUILDING

(Spring of 1939)

Even before they had left Mexico City, Ken had sent copies of his two-page "Phonemic Work Sheet" to friends he had met in Ann Arbor and to other linguists. It was well received: Bloch (then of Brown University) wrote that it was "well thought out"; Bloomfield (then of Chicago) thanked him for the list of instructions and said that they seemed "simple when you write them out"; Harris (of Pennsylvania) wrote, "The points on the back are really excellent"; Voegelin (then of DePauw) said that he planned to try the article out on his phonemics class. Such a response was very encouraging to Ken and spurred him on to more reading of linguistics and gave him confidence as he continued writing about phonetics.

Evie caught some of his enthusiasm and almost every evening they read a few pages of Bloomfield's *Language* together, discussed it, and tried to apply it to Mixtec, Spanish, etc. Years later when Evelyn was asked if it was true that they had had evening chit-chats about Bloomfield, she answered, "Yes! It was fun, and that was when I really began to learn linguistics."

Evie was determined to learn to talk Mixtec too, and she and Ken had agreed before she set foot in the area that she would not talk Spanish there. That took self-control, especially when she was with the Spanish-speaking school teachers—she had majored in Spanish in UCLA and had conversed in Spanish the whole year she had been in Mexico with the Townsends.

Ken told the people that she understood Spanish but that he had told her not to talk it. In spite of what he had said, they assumed that she didn't understand it either. A time or two she was amused as she heard Nalo explaining her actions to an outsider. For example, one day he told a stranger that she and Ken read or wrote all day long, just like the people of San Miguel plowed or planted their cornfields all day long—of course if the people of San Miguel studied that much, they'd get a headache. He agreed that when the Mrs. wrote, her letters looked nice; that was because she had been making them all her life. She didn't do much else, really; she just cooked their meals, baked their bread, and things like that.

Of course it wasn't long before Evie started saying a few things in Mixtec and that was very satisfying. Everybody wanted to see pictures of her family and they listened with delight as she told them which ones were her father, her mother, and her brother and sister. They were especially delighted when she showed them a picture of her uncle's truck.

Ken and Evie had visitors every day and much of the day, partly because the house they were renting was right on the town square across from the school. It had only one room, but it was the best house in town. It had a hard-packed clay floor instead of the usual dusty floor that the fleas found so congenial. The roof was made of rough hand-hewn shingles each about three feet long and six inches wide. The roof of their house was tight, but those of many of their neighbors had holes, and the birds slipped in and ate the grain stored in the loft.

Everybody's house had log walls, but Ken and Evie stuffed excelsior in the cracks of theirs to keep out the cold wind. (During the winter months the inside of the house might be below freezing at night, and even at noon it was sometimes pretty cold.)

There was no window and just one door. The landlady didn't want a window cut in the wall because she was afraid of thieves, so the only way for light to come in was through the open door—that let flies in too. Ken made a big door with shiny silver screen and that kept out most of the flies. It was the first such door in the area and people looked at it with wonder. Then, when they thought no one was noticing, they would come up and softly touch it.

In the kitchen corner of the house, Ken built shelves for the dishes, and Evie hung her kettles on the wall near the stove. She had a big table that she used as a work table and drainboard. It was put in a spot where the uneven places in the floor matched the length of the table legs. They had a kerosene stove, but fuel had to be brought in twenty miles from Tlaxiaco, so Ken made a charcoal burner out of an old kerosene can. Evie heated water on it, and that saved on the hard-to-get fuel. Water had to be carried, of course, and again the five-gallon kerosene cans came in handy.

The bed, short and narrow for "tall" Americans, was in a corner across the room from the kitchen, and in another corner Ken had a table that he used for his desk. Probably his was the only typewriter in town and the mayor asked him to serve as scribe—he typed all their official documents for them.

The men enjoyed seeing all the new-fangled things—the typewriter, the oven that Evie would place on top of the charcoal burner, the tools that Ken had used when he made the burner and the book shelves. One noontime nine men stood around watching while they ate their dinner—probably they themselves had never eaten with a fork.

On the other hand, Ken and Evie were interested in watching them in their daily lives. One day Ken happened to stop by a neighbor's homes while a man sat daubing mud on his ten-year-old daughter. The top of the girl's head was already piled high with dried mud, and one eye was almost covered with it. Her face was streaked, and Ken watched the man as he continued to dip his fingers into an earthenware pitcher, lift out a glob of mud, and draw lines on her arms in the shape of a cross—supposedly representing the cross of Christ.

"What are you doing?" Ken asked.

"I'm trying to get her soul back," her father replied. The girl had fallen on the mountainside and according to him an angry ground spirit had snatched her soul at that time. Her father was trying to appease the ground spirit so that it would let loose of her soul. If the spirit wasn't appeased, the child might get sick and die, he said.

That man was trying to prevent illness. Sometimes they tried to cure an illness by appeasing the spirit of a steambath house. When the witchdoctor said that it was the spirit of the steambath house that had caused the severe illness, friends of the patient dug a hole at the mouth of the little house and buried an offering of food there. Then they carefully swept out the chamber with branches of a special tree (a "steambath" tree), and built a fire in the stone fireplace on one side of the little room. When the rocks were hot, they switched the patient briskly with branches of the special tree, carried him inside the chamber, and threw water on the hot rocks. Steam enveloped the patient and he was left there for fifteen or twenty minutes. Hopefully, the spirit appeased, the sick one would soon be better, but it happened with many of them that their fever became worse.

When the failure was apparent, the witchdoctor tried to make another diagnosis. He stirred a hen's egg in with certain herbs, and a turkey egg with other herbs. Then he smeared the concoction over the upper half of the sick one's body. Somehow that was supposed to tell him what he had been turned in to. Sometimes he had become a coyote, sometimes a fox, or maybe even a thunder storm.

Such customs distressed Ken and Evie. They looked forward to the time when the people of San Miguel could read the New Testament in their own Mixtec language—a belief in Jesus Christ would deliver them from fear of the spirits.

The ability to read was important, not just so that they could benefit by the New Testament, but so that they could be integrated with the rest of Mexico. The director of the San Miguel school and Ken had at least one common goal—that the children learn to read, so, when the director saw in a Oaxaca paper something about the article of Ken's on Mixtec, the director asked him to help teach reading. So Ken did—several hours a day.

He had more than forty beginners, ages five to fourteen, who didn't know enough Spanish to respond when the teacher asked them to shut the door. They were an undisciplined crowd, jumping, fighting, eating during classtime. Even though he talked in Mixtec, Ken found that he needed more variety than just a Mixtec primer to hold their attention for two hours a day, so he used flashcards too. Evie was busy half the day copying new lessons and making more flashcards. She was also teaching the beginning lessons to the girl who came to help her with the housework.

In spite of their all-out effort, Ken came to the conclusion that for the average student to learn well enough to read the New Testament would take some months of study—unless God granted a miracle.

Ken also worked a couple of weeks with students who were already in fifth and sixth grade, and that was more encouraging. After a few hours of good hard practice, they were reading well.

In addition to the classes at school, Ken was spending an hour each day teaching the workmen who were building their new house, and the workmen were making better progress than the school-children did.

Ken and Evie had started their new house soon after arriving back in San Miguel. At first they had thought that they would buy a house and remodel it, but that didn't work out, so they decided to build. Ken told Evie that she could draft plans to have the house any way she'd like it, but with one restriction. The longest log (that would determine the length of the house) could be no longer than the longest cabin in the village. (The length of the cabins in the village had probably been set by the height of the tallest trees.) That was about thirty feet, so they planned that their house would be thirty by twenty feet.

They'd have two floors. Downstairs would have two rooms. Two-thirds of the space would be for a kind of people-room, arranged with their friends in mind—they wanted them to feel at home there. The rest would be the kitchen—they were especially anxious to have the Mixtec women feel at home. Upstairs there would be a gable room at each end, and in the middle a dormer window for a small study.

For the first two months Ken had spent most of his time and energy on the project. He had gone out to the mountain with Nalo to mark the trees that would be used for logs. Everybody told him that it took about three weeks for the lumber to dry, and, since it all had to be split up into logs and planed by hand, it would take another month to get it down to the village. To save a little time, they bought a small house so they could use the dry logs right away for flooring.

Ken found that building the house took a lot of thought on his part. For example, he spent hours figuring out how wide to make the steps in the stairs to the second floor, and, not wanting to bump their heads on the ceiling, how much of a slant the staircase should have.

It took time to make contracts with one person to cut and deliver shingles, with another for boards, another for logs, someone else for windows, etc. Usually the men underestimated the time it would take them to do what they had bargained for, and sometimes the planks and logs, when delivered, were crooked.

The cost of the various jobs was also underestimated, and Ken found himself running out of money. He had men working for him full time on the house in addition to all those who were doing contract work. Of course they had to be paid, so Ken hiked the twenty miles to Tlaxiaco and telegraphed for money. (That was one of the few things Evie admitted to being unhappy about; she didn't like it when he had to go off and leave her like that.)

There was one part of the house building that she found to be very special. Every Saturday evening, the men who had been working on the house stayed for supper. They loved it. Evie filled her six-quart pressure cooker full of beans and meat, had a mixing bowl heaped with potatoes, a big frying pan full of gravy, and there was plenty of chili. The men brought their own tortillas, but the time came when they didn't bother to eat any of them—then Evie was really complimented, because no amount of food was supposed to satisfy unless a person had three or four tortillas as well.

After supper they played games, and, perhaps because the Mixtec people had never really learned how to play, they had a wonderful time. Sometimes the fun went on until one o'clock in the morning, with a little time out while Nalo read a bit to everybody from the New Testament.

One evening they played ball with a balloon, another time Ken taught them how to make paper airplanes. He tossed a few at Evie, so she got a rubber band and shot paper wads back at him. The men thought that was great. Then they changed to musical chairs, and other parlor games. With so much activity, a cloud of dust rose from the clay floor—a reminder that it would be nice when Ken and Evie had their own home with a wooden floor in it.

During those four months, work on the house had gone ahead slowly. The foundation had been laid, and because the house was on a hillside, it had to be about three feet above the ground in front, and six inches in back, By the first of May the walls were up, the ground floor was in, the stringers were up for the second floor, and one side of the roof was finished—they needed more shingles before they could do the other side. There were two front windows, and one of the kitchen cupboards was done—complete with doors.

They were having trouble getting more boards, and it was a great day when a man arrived carrying two dozen long ones. (Ken had found that a carpenter could plane one side of about eight boards in a day.) It was apparent that the house would not be finished before they had to leave for Mexico City. If they wanted a house to come back to in the fall, the work would have to go on during the summer.

They had come to know the workmen pretty well, and some seemed to be especially trustworthy. They made arrangements with them to go on working throughout the summer: Nalo, his cousin, and one of the best carpenters.

Ken and Evie also wanted to come back to a pretty yard, so Ken had the men clean up around the house, digging and fertilizing a portion. Then he planted cosmos, zinnias, gladiolus, morning glories, and a couple of other things.

All too quickly the final day came, and picturing in their minds how beautiful the house would be when they came back, they left for Mexico City.

In Mexico City, the second week in May, there was a meeting representing a number of organizations. Among them were: the Department of Indigenous Affairs, the National Institute of Anthropology and History, the Panamerican Institute of Geography and History, and the Summer Institute of Linguistics. One of the purposes of the meeting was to come to an agreement on the alphabets to be used when writing the different Indian languages of Mexico.

Two linguists with Ph.D. degrees were there from the States and their choice of symbols was, many times, made to agree with the symbol used by the International Phonetic Association. Uncle Cam, Ken, and the rest of the SILers, on the other hand, wanted symbols to correspond as much as possible with those used in the Spanish alphabet. It became apparent that the opinions of those with Ph.D. degrees carried more weight with the Mexican officials than that of the SILers who had analyzed some of the languages and had lived in the villages with the people who spoke those languages, but had no degree.

That week, as the discussions continued, Ken became acutely aware of the fact that it would be a definite advantage to the SIL program for him to have academic credentials. The credentials were needed, not just when teaching courses in the SIL school, but also when talking with government officials and educators. Knowing the degree was vital to Bible translation, Ken headed back to Michigan more determined than ever to really work at getting it.

13 PHONETICS

(Summer of 1939 - Spring of 1941)

After a quick visit in California with Evie's folks, Ken and Evie left for Ann Arbor, Michigan. Professor Fries had a scholarship waiting for Ken that paid his tuition, and that left them with enough money on hand so that Evie could register for classes too. She enjoyed the classes, but the "money on hand" didn't last very long.

For one thing, three men were still working on their house in San Miguel—Ken and Evie hoped to be able to move into it when they returned in the fall. And the men were doing very well. By November the downstairs was finished, including lots of cupboards, ironing board, and windows. The upstairs still lacked partitions, but the wood had been cut and planed. It needed to dry a little more before it could be used.

But life in the university, and house-building down in Mexico, left them very short of funds. One day all the cash they had between them was seven cents. Ken got down on his knees and thanked the Lord that He had promised to take care of them, and that He always would—and then he tried not to worry.

A little later that day the mail came, and in it was a check for five dollars. An engineer in Massachusetts believed that the Mixtecs of Mexico should have the New Testament in their own language, and he wanted to help provide it. He wrote the check for Ken on the third of July, but because he had sent the letter to the Mexico address, it hadn't reached him until the 24th—the very day that Ken's capital had consisted of seven cents. When it arrived, that five dollar check looked like a million to Ken.

Uncle Cam wrote and asked how he was getting along financially, and Ken answered that the Lord was taking care of them, though "rather spectacularly." That is, on three occasions within less than a month they had not had enough money for the next day, then, just in time, the Lord had graciously sent cash. So the Lord was proving to them that He had His eye on them, but it would have been easier on the nerves if His care had been a little less spectacular.

Due to their lack of spare cash, they had to manage their resources carefully, but that fact didn't keep either one of them from having a good time. One of the things Ken enjoyed most was talking with people who were interested in linguistics. He missed Professor Sapir who had died that winter, and he remembered him with gratitude. In Ken's opinion, Sapir's linguistic knowledge had already helped in spreading the Gospel to the Mixtecs, and in time it would be used in helping the speakers of many other little-known languages.

With the Linguistic Society of America meeting in Ann Arbor again that summer, lots of other people were providing stimulus of course. There was the day Ken was walking across the campus with Professors Fries and Trager. George Trager (a leading young theoretician of that time) was teaching the course in phonetics, and he told Fries that he had never learned how to make the "implosive" sounds. Those were the sounds that had taken Ken a year to learn and which he had taught numerous students at the Summer Institute of Linguistics school in Arkansas with no trouble at all.

Ken was sure that Trager would like to learn, and he was completely confident that he could teach him, so, feeling rather brash, he offered. Trager thanked him for the offer and invited him up to his office.

Part of the reason that Ken was confident that he could teach Trager quickly was because he knew that there were glottalized stops in Taos, the language Trager had been studying. A glottalized stop also used the closed larynx, but it pushed the air outward instead of drawing it in. Ken figured that it would be very easy to show Trager the difference.

So, the first thing he did as he sat facing the professor was to tell him to make a glottalized stop. Trager responded, but to Ken's horror, he didn't make the kind of sound that Ken called a glottalized stop. It was a sound sort of halfway between a glottalized stop and an implosive—the larynx was closed but it was not moving either up or down. There was no way for Ken to turn back. The only thing he could do was to go ahead and tell this teacher of phonetics that he wasn't making a glottalized stop either.

Trager listened, willing to receive help, and followed Ken's instructions. In a very short time he was making both glottalized stops and implosives. He thanked Ken and asked him to present his ideas to the phonetics class.

In getting ready for the class presentation, Ken lined up the material more carefully. He talked about the number of places the airstream was closed off as each sound was made—the number of "closures," and what caused the airstream to move—the "mechanism," and whether or not the airstream was moving inward or outward—"ingressive" versus "egressive." Then he saw that he had a system in which all sounds of the human voice could be classified (except for whistles and trills).

Charles F. Hockett, a young man who had received his Ph.D. just a couple of years before, sat in on the lecture. (Since then Professor Hockett has become a prolific author on linguistic topics. He has been at Cornell University since 1946.) He had been planning to write a book on phonetics, so he asked Ken to give him a copy of the lecture. He would like to use some of the material in his book. Ken said, "Sure."

That request to have the material in writing, the satisfaction of seeing the neat system as he presented it in Trager's class, and the desire to help his SIL colleagues, all served as stimuli that kept Ken working on the theory of phonetics, even after he and Evie were back again among the Mixtecs. The ideas kept expanding and developing.

Each week Ken expected to finish the project—but he kept on. One of the ideas that developed was "segmentation," a technique to determine when one sound begins and another leaves off, that is, a means of chopping a sound continuum into chunks. He set up his definition of a "segment" in terms of muscle movement—the closest point toward closure (especially for consonants), and the most open point (especially for vowels).

It excited Ken to think of helping his colleagues to pronounce sounds from any part of the world. (Thirty years later, when SILers were studying more than five hundred languages, it seemed to Ken that there were only a few important additions that needed to be made to his old theory.)

Actually Ken had helped not only his SIL colleagues, but others as well. Trager, when he reviewed Ken's book *Phonetics,* said, "Phonetics is so young a branch of science that it is still true that most phoneticians are self-taught. Pike, however, has taught himself so well that from now on the rest of us can go to him for the basic knowledge we need." *Studies in Linguistics* 2:1.16 (1943).

In Hockett's article, "A System of Descriptive Phonology," *Language* 18.5, footnote 4 (1942), he said that most of the phonetic material presented in that article was taken from Ken's dissertation. He was able to refer to it before it was published in 1943 because he had read a typed copy.

Professor Bloomfield had also read a typed copy of the book, and on June 24, 1940, he wrote to Ken that the "...theory strikes me as a big thing.... You have certainly given the background or perspective for ordinary phonetics of speech."

The book had its real beginning in 1936 when Ken began the struggle that lasted a year as he tried to learn to help one of his SIL colleagues to pronounce the implosive sounds of the Cakchiquel language. He took another step in 1939 when he helped Trager to pronounce those same sounds. Years later, thinking about that very difficult beginning, Ken told his class, "If you face something that is holding you back, instead of it being just a burden to you, it can become a starting point for something that will help the rest of you."

But Ken's book *Phonetics* was just getting under way that summer of 1939, and it wasn't finished until 1941. He remembers how he had expected to write up that lecture for Hockett in just an hour or two. Sometimes he consoles his students for their seemingly slow rate of progress by telling them how the lecture on phonetics developed into a book that took two years to write.

14 TREASURE

(Fall of 1939 - Spring of 1940)

In the meantime, that fall of 1939, Ken and Evie started back to be with the Mixtecs in San Miguel. All went well during the train ride and even on the bumpy truck ride through the mountains. Then in Tlaxiaco, the town where even trucks had to stop, Evie began to feel weak and nauseated, and she kept on feeling that way.

They didn't know how much progress the men had made on their house, and Ken wanted to be sure that there would be a good place waiting for Evie in the village, so, on the fourth of November, he half-walked, half-ran the twenty miles to San Miguel. Evie stayed behind in the hotel in Tlaxiaco. Neither of them liked it that way, but that seemed to be the best they could do—they were glad that the owners of the hotel were friendly.

Arriving in San Miguel, Ken found that their new house wasn't habitable yet, so he sent one of the men back with a note to Evie— he'd come for her in a couple of days, he hoped. Well, he was gone a week—a long week for Evie waiting, and a long week for Ken working.

To make the place warmer, Ken had the men put mud between the logs of the upstairs walls and glass in the windows. He even set up a wood-burning heater. He cleaned the kerosene cook stove and put it upstairs, making a temporary kitchen that would be nearer to Evie.

Then, when he had done enough so that he figured Evie could be warm and fed, he hired seven of his Mixtec friends to go back with him. They carried Evie to San Miguel on a litter made of two poles with gunnysacks stretched between. The seven men—plus Ken—

worked as two crews; one crew would carry a while, and then the other would take over. Evie traveled beautifully, but Ken arrived exhausted.

They had hoped that Evie would regain strength in a few days, but soon it became apparent that she was expecting a little one, and the weakness, the nausea, and the vomiting continued. She did pretty well as long as she rested in bed, but for weeks she could be on her feet only for a very short space of time. Actually it was the third week in January before she was able to eat a meal out of bed and keep it.

In the meantime Ken had his hands full. Five or more men were still working on the house and Ken was supervising and helping them. They put in cupboards, a closet under the stairs, finished the porch, and chinked the walls both outside and in.

Evie loved the wide pineboard floors (beautifully polished with linseed oil), and the way the house was becoming more and more convenient. There was even running water both upstairs and down. It came in from a fifty-gallon tank that had been put on the bank behind the house. The workmen kept the tank filled by carrying water in two five-gallon cans hanging from a stick balanced across one shoulder. They carried it up from the center of town or down from a little spring on the mountain.

The carpenters were building furniture, or putting in closets, etc., but there were also everyday chores that needed to be done. Chenta, a twelve-year-old girl, was hired to be the dishwasher and to help with the meals as much as she could. The wife of one of the carpenters did the laundry.

But hiring people didn't solve all the problems; they had to be taught and guided. Evie did much of that from her bed, and after a while Chenta was preparing most of the noon meals. Ken did breakfast, and except when Chenta left something already prepared, he also cooked supper. With Evie's guidance, he had gone beyond pancakes. For example, one evening he fried three eggs hard, chopped them up, and put them in white sauce; he even heated up some rice to go with it.

Visitors enjoyed watching, and one of them saw Ken put wood in the heater, then he saw him move across the room and fry an egg on the kerosene stove. The visitor became very puzzled and he asked

Ken how it happened that he could put wood in the stove in one part of the room but cook in a different part.

It also fell to Ken to teach Chenta how to starch the clothes—not to get them too stiff, to get them stiff enough, not to put something white in starch that had been colored by dark clothing. "Poor Ken," wrote Evie, "it is like he is running a three-ring circus.... Really though the clothes came out very well—I was pleasantly surprised." (There were no "permanent press" clothes in those days.)

The school teachers were helpful and friendly. One family sent over some chicken soup, and another a plateful of chicken and fried bananas. Evie, now that she was doing pretty well in Mixtec, had started to talk with them in Spanish, so they enjoyed visiting together.

In fact, the whole town had made them feel welcome, from the little boys who stopped by with some maguey thorns they hoped to use as needles in the phonograph, to the town officials who were delighted with the cuckoo clock that Ken and Evie had given them. And, in spite of all the difficulties, they enjoyed the people and they decided to have a big celebration on Christmas day.

They invited all the workers and their families, not just for dinner, but for fun before and after dinner too. Ken and Evie provided the turkey, fruit, and candy, while the guests provided the tortillas and *mole* (the hot sauce). The carpenters came early to kill and clean the turkeys and women arrived soon after to put them on to cook. They did it in their usual way, in a pot over a fire on the floor of a little house just across the yard from Ken and Evie. Part of the fun, of course, was the chit-chatty time the women had working together.

The men and boys had a rollicking good time playing pick-up-sticks until dinner was ready at two o'clock. They ate upstairs so that Ken and Evie could be together, and the women ate, according to their custom, in the little house where they had done the cooking. Each person had a small bowl with meat in the bottom and *mole* poured over the top. Hot tortillas were placed at strategic points so that they were within reach of everyone. The tortillas not only provided a substantial part of the meal, but they were also used as silverware. Second and third helpings were routine and everyone ate until completely satisfied.

After dinner the women went upstairs to hear a Bible story and to sing choruses and hymns in Mixtec. Then Ken started them off on a peanut hunt. Chenta had helped him hide the peanuts, and she was so thrilled that she could hardly keep from telling where they were.

Then they played a kind of volleyball with balloons. After the volleyball game they gathered around to break a traditional *piñata*, a pottery jar filled with goodies. It was hung in the middle of the yard, and one by one the guests were blindfolded and given a stick with the opportunity to whack at the jar. By means of a rope and pulley, the master of ceremonies tried to keep it out of reach. Eventually the stick connected and then the goodies fell; everyone dived for them and scooped up as much as they could get their hands on. It made for a very satisfactory screaming and squealling time.

By five-thirty the women were tired out and ready to go home. The men stayed on for Bible study and to sing some more, and that was when Ken and Evie took the wraps off their own Christmas present—a new portable organ. Evie was the pianist of the family, but she wasn't playing much just then. Ken could make the organ roar by plunking down eight fingers and two thumbs, or he could pick out a tune with one finger. The carpenters liked it best when it roared, but they also liked to sing accompanied by the one finger. After that they wanted to stay and sing every evening—and usually they did.

The end of carpentry work on the house was in sight. The men had enjoyed working on it, and of course they had made good use of the salary they had received. Ken didn't want to lay anybody off, so he was delighted when he thought of asking Lesiu to write out a translation of some simple stories. Before Lesiu actually sat down and picked up a pencil, Ken called over Nalo and first Ken and then Nalo prayed aloud asking the Lord to help Lesiu to do a good job. Then Ken started him off with the story of Joseph as taken from the last few chapters of Genesis. Lesiu's translation was not perfect, but he came up with a lot of new words, and as a beginning it was much better than nothing.

Ken was encouraged about Lesiu, but he was getting more and more concerned for Evie. A little after Christmas she had had an especially bad day. Even with plenty of blankets, she had been cold until Ken heated some rocks and put them in the bed with her. She threw up several times that night instead of just during the day. She was some better in the morning, but Ken yearned for her to be really better, and he was trying to figure out a way to get help for her.

He wrote to a doctor in Mexico City for advice, but the doctor didn't answer. They invited me to San Miguel, but I was running a fever and was told that I might do more· harm than good. Evie's mother asked the family doctor in California, and he and Dad in Connecticut agreed that transporting her on that bumping, jouncing truck might be worse than just letting her stay in bed where she was. Dad mailed some food supplements (liver, iron, and vitamins) from Connecticut, and I sent some out from Mexico City.

Still the idea of going to Mexico City kept coming back. But suppose they managed to get her there, then what? Where would they stay? In those years SIL didn't have a headquarters in Mexico City—they would have had to live in a hotel and eat in restaurants. That would have taken more money than they had.

Actually in their nice new house, with girls to help with the work, living in San Miguel was ideal. The men walked to a town an hour and a half away and bought vegetables and meat for them, so they had good food. Ken had the opportunity to buy some honey and he got the whole batch—thirty-one pounds of it!

Ken and Evie were agreed that San Miguel was the place for them at that time, but Ken kept thinking, wondering—was there something else he could do to help her? He was also getting more and more frustrated because two months had passed and he had accomplished nothing academically. Perhaps it was those two things added together that made him so irritable that he could hardly stand himself. Evie's judgment was, "He's a dear," but he felt helpless about his crabbiness. It reminded him of how dependent he was on God. He wrote, "We need to let the Lord run our lives, and to trust Him for strength to keep from sinning."

In hope of tying into that strength, he went without food and water until noon one day while he prayed and read the Bible. He was not satisfied; he was still very much aware of a need for God's power. So the next day he went without food and water until sundown while he prayed and read some good devotional books. And again the third day. Yes, then he felt blessed. The easiest way to see it was that his disposition improved a bit. And he actually sat down at his desk and started to work.

He chose to begin by writing up that lecture on phonetics that he had promised Hockett. After he was once under way, he became excited about it. His ideas developed and expanded as he followed out the implications of this and that. He worked hard on the details and soon he saw that he was coming out with a new phonetic theory. He also saw that the ideas would be useful in the SIL school to serve as a basis for the phonetics course there. His work should help in the teaching of the more difficult sounds and in making a distinction between phonetics and phonemics.

He kept doggedly following on with his phonetic ideas in spite of the fact that, come June, he was supposed to appear in Ann Arbor with his dissertation written on tone. But he had solved the problem of tone the previous year and working on it no longer excited him. Now it was the classification of vocal sounds that held his attention.

He sat working at his desk while Lesiu was some place else in the house translating the Gospel of John. He was doing so well that Ken thought he'd try Felix too, another carpenter. Felix didn't understand as much Spanish as Lesiu did, and he asked so many questions that Ken had him put his desk right beside his own. That way Felix didn't have to get up and go looking for Ken, instead he could just speak up whenever he needed to. Lesiu took up another spot in the same room.

Then Ken asked Nalo to begin work on the Gospel of Mark. Nalo felt that he was rather slow, so he told Ken about two other fellows. He thought that Angel, especially, had a better head than his own; he was sure that he'd do a better job. So Angel came and started working on the book of Acts, and Richard began the Gospel of Matthew.

So there Ken sat surrounded by five Mixtec translators. One minute he was thinking about phonetics and the next he was explaining the meaning of some hard word from the New Testament. He had supplied the men with a dictionary, but that didn't help much because the dictionary definitions had hard words too.

Sometimes when they asked for help, Ken would go over the entire passage giving them a rough translation. Then he would tell them, "Now you hunt for good words and fit them in."

The men wrote each verse on a different three-by-five slip of paper. That way Ken could add other words and ideas, without getting them confused with the man's original. The men worked hard, sitting there eight or ten hours a day, studying the Spanish New Testament. They would take time off only for a little while when they went to do some small job around the house. Ken was very pleased with them. He wrote Uncle Cam, "Building the house served excellently as a means of finding faithful and diligent men." By the time Ken and Evie left for the States that spring, Lesiu had finished the Gospel of John, Felix had finished Luke, Nalo had done five chapters of Mark and five of Ephesians, Angel had finished Acts, and Richard had done nine chapters of Matthew.

Even while Ken was thrilled by what the men were doing, he was asking himself about the value of the work. The narrative parts, because the men understood them better, were the most valuable, but there was also an advantage in discovering which were the difficult parts, so that Ken could begin pondering them early.

To a certain extent the amount of Spanish the men understood depended upon the number of years they had been in school. Angel had had the most schooling with six years in primary school. One of the other men had had five years, and the rest had had three years or less.

Nalo had been right in his judgment of Angel; his work turned out to be much better than the others, and Ken had hopes that he would be a great translator. He said of him, "Angel may, indeed, prove to be like his name—a messenger of the Lord." (Actually the work of the other men did not turn out to be too useful. Most of it was eventually thrown away.)

Nalo himself was learning more about the Bible, and at last he had the courage to believe that there was only one real God. The people of the area, on the other hand, considered that each town had at least two major gods, and many minor ones. Miguel was the patron and official god of San Miguel and, except for those times when he was carried in a parade, he resided in the big church in the center of town. But even though he was the official god of the town, the people didn't consider him to be very important.

The most important god was the "Old Man," and one day Nalo took Ken to see him. They went up the mountain overlooking the village and stopped before an outcropping of rock that was more or less in the shape of a man. There were bumps for knees, stomach, and head. There were holes for eyes and ears. According to the people of San Miguel, the Old Man had created that region. He had made the earth, flowers, grass, and even the people. Other towns of the area also had Old Men who had created their regions, but unfortunately the Old Man of San Miguel had been something of a rake, and he had given away the good streams and springs of the town as presents to his illicit lovers. That had left San Miguel short of water.

The Old Man died, but somehow, according to the people of San Miguel, he still knew when people were disrespectful, and he still had power to kill such people, or to harm them in some way. The people didn't take chances. Whenever they went up to see the Old Man, they brought flowers to lay beside him, and they knelt and put their faces against the rock, or kissed it. They also asked for favors. They believed that it could answer prayers for health or for good crops.

Nalo told Ken that it had been a long time since he himself had been up to see the rock because he hadn't wanted to honor it, and he had been afraid not to.

The day that Ken and Nalo sat near the Old Man, they read how the people of Thessalonica had "turned to God from idols, to serve a living and true God, and to wait for his Son from heaven..." (I Thes. 1:9a-10b RSV).

Nalo was thrilled to know about the one real God, and he frequently told someone else about Him. He also talked about the privately owned saints, the patron saints of the different villages, and the Old Men. Thinking of Psalm 115, he'd point out that they had mouths, but didn't talk; they had eyes, but didn't see; they had ears, but didn't hear; they had feet, but couldn't walk. Especially, when he talked about, "They have feet, but they can't walk," his friends nodded in agreement—they themselves had helped carry a saint from one place to another.

Nalo appreciated the Bible and he wanted others to have it too, but he realized that not everyone could afford one. He knew that a tenth of his income, in some special way, belonged to the Lord. He thought about it awhile and then asked Ken if it would be all right if he spent that money buying Bibles for some of the other fellows since he was making a bigger salary than they were. Ken, of course, was delighted with the idea.

Nalo kept telling his friends about the Lord, and sometimes he brought them to the Saturday evening supper at Ken and Evie's house. Everybody had a good time while they were eating, and afterwards they enjoyed singing hymns in Mixtec. They studied the Bible awhile as a group and then finished off with games. The people who came to those Saturday evening get-togethers were the handful of people who, in later years, Ken was to call his "treasure"—they were so valuable that Christ died to win them. Ken, the scholar who prizes academic achievements, says, "I wouldn't swap that treasure for a book on phonetics, or tone, or intonation or...."

By the end of February the men were working almost exclusively on translation. The house for the most part was finished and the men did carpentry only as relaxation from desk work. One of the little jobs they did was to make a rocking chair for Evie. Looking forward to a little Pike, Ken thought it would be especially nice for her. The men had never seen a rocking chair, so Ken and Evie had to describe it to them carefully. The chair part wasn't difficult, but the rockers were. Neither Ken nor Evie could remember how much of a curve a rocker had. They and their Mixtec friends figured it by studying one as it was pictured in the Montgomery Ward catalog. According to Evie, that catalog served many times as an encyclopedia.

Evie was feeling much better; the pills with liver, iron, and vitamins had undoubtedly helped. She was still not strong, but she was able to keep her food down and could be up and around much of the day. She had even started cooking breakfast!

Evie was especially pleased with Easter Sunday, because that was the day the women, not just the men, came to hear about Christ's resurrection. The men had asked to be told about Christ's resurrection, but of course they wanted to sing too—every Mixtec hymn several times. Then they wanted to pray. Evie wrote that they hadn't planned to have anything quite so "churchy" but, by responding to the men's requests, that was just the way it worked out.

After Easter, Ken and Evie's stay in San Miguel for that season was drawing to a close. They knew they had to leave, but where should they go? They discussed and weighed the pros and cons of various places. Should Evie have the baby in Mexico? in Connecticut? in California? At last they came to the conclusion that California was the answer.

But how would they get from San Miguel to Mexico City? For the first day of the journey, to Tlaxiaco, Evie traveled the way she had come in, by litter—except that Ken wasn't one of the carriers this time. For the worst part of the truck ride, from Tlaxiaco to Nochistlán, they blew up an air mattress and Evie rode stretched out on top of the antimony ore. The air mattress absorbed the shock of the bumps, but April is the hottest month of the year and the sun beating down on the back of the truck was pretty bad. They rested that night in Nochistlán, and the next day Evie rode in the cab of a truck to Parián. The following morning they climbed aboard the Pullman car for Mexico City. A few days in Mexico City, and then on to California and home—to the Griset family. At that time there was no place in the world that Evie would rather have been, and, yes, Ken felt that way too.

15 THE PH.D. DEGREE

(Spring 1940 - Summer 1941)

In California, in spite of the beautiful situation in which they found themselves, Ken was depressed and feeling worthless. He knew he shouldn't feel depressed and so he thought that maybe he was failing the Lord somehow. That made him feel worse than ever. Again Mrs. Griset was a source of strength. She told Evie, "That's not a spiritual problem. We all know that Ken wants the Lord's will more than anything else. See that he gets to the doctor; there must be something physically wrong."

So Ken went to the doctor, and Mrs. Griset had been right.

The doctor ordered a gamut of tests and found that Ken's basal metabolism was considerably below normal. He said that the low basal metabolism could account for the way Ken tired easily, and he prescribed thyroid medication to be taken twice a day. That was a surprise since people usually associate the lack of thyroid with someone who is chubby and lethargic—Ken was thin and tense. But the thyroid medicine helped.

Ken became more cheerful and better able to concentrate on his writing. Actually, if he forgot to take the medicine for two or three days, Evie noticed the difference in the way he acted and would ask, "Have you been taking your thyroid medicine lately?" Well, no, he had forgotten. Years later, the doctors at the University of Michigan suggested that he substitute vitamin B complex for the thyroid medicine. He did and that also worked well, but for that decade in the 1940s the help from the thyroid medicine had been crucial.

Every day Ken went down to the town library where he could work without interruption. He continued writing on phonetics and revising what he had already written. Then one of the big advantages of being in California became apparent, Evie's second cousin, Mildred Lukens, was there. She typed the manuscript for him and he was able to send a copy of the sixty pages to Professor Fries in Michigan before leaving for Arkansas where the courses of the Summer Institute of Linguistics were to be held that year.

Evie stayed in California—their baby was expected sometime in June or July—but Ken went to Arkansas a week before the classes were to start. He arrived early so that he could help me get ready to drill the students in hearing and pronouncing sounds.

About fifty students enrolled that year, and the first week of classes Ken taught phonetics and phonemics five hours a day. The phonetics he taught was based on the air mechanism theory that he had just finished writing up, and he was delighted when he found that it really did help the students to mimic and identify the sounds they heard. That first week Ken had the students for all their class hours. Gene Nida waited until Ken had left for Michigan before beginning his grammar lectures; that was when I began too, giving the students practice in hearing and producing sounds. Ken returned two weeks before the end of the session and for several hours a day he taught the students more phonetic and phonemic theory.

When he arrived back on the University of Michigan campus, Ken was uneasy because he wasn't carrying a finished dissertation on tone languages. Tone languages was the topic that had been approved, but he had become so interested in phonetics that that was where he had put his energy.

When Professor Fries met him and asked him what he had been doing, Ken felt terrible because the dissertation wasn't done, but he went rattling on about his research on phonetics. Since Fries was in charge of a seminar that summer, he suggested that Ken talk at it. Those attending were: Leonard Bloomfield of Yale University; Bernard Bloch then of Brown University, later of Yale; Edgar H. Sturtevant of Yale; C. F. Voegelin then of DePauw University, later of Indiana; J. Milton Cowan, then of the University of Iowa, later of Cornell University; Charles F. Hockett later professor at Cornell University. That was it. Those were all who attended the seminar.

The first day Ken talked about ingressive and egressive sounds. Fries asked him if that summarized his research. When Ken said no,

Fries suggested that he take the seminar the next week as well. That time Ken talked about how to divide a stream of speech into segments. Again Fries asked him if he had finished. When he said no, Fries suggested that he take the third seminar. That time he talked on the difference between vowels and consonants.

It was after he had given the seminars that Fries told Ken that he could do his dissertation on phonetics if he wanted to, but he added that Sturtevant (for many years the chairman of the department of linguistics at Yale) thought that Ken should add bibliographical references. Sturtevant explained that to be fair to the reader, Ken needed to say which parts of the material were his own contribution.

Ken didn't want to take the time to go through the literature, but if he was going to use his research on phonetics for his dissertation, he had to. So he started to read and became interested in what others had written. He says, "That's when I got hooked on bibliography," and he has been a bear on it ever since. When he is interested in a topic, he wants to know what the literature says about it.

After a while he found a way of working through the bibliography fairly rapidly. He'd keep in mind the several things he was interested in, then check to see what each book said on those topics. There were about a half dozen books that he felt he needed to read more carefully, and those he took with him to Mexico.

He stopped a couple of weeks in Arkansas at the SIL school, and then went on to California. The time in California was very special because that was when he first saw his daughter, Judith Lee Pike, who had been born that summer.

Actually it was the thirtieth of November before Ken, Evie, and Judith were making their way from Tlaxiaco back to the Mixtec-speaking people in San Miguel. Ken was on a horse, Evie on a mule, and Judith was lying contentedly in a basket that was tied to one side of a donkey's back. She and her basket were balanced by brooms, a washtub, and a suitcase tied to the other side of the donkey.

The men with the donkeys moved ahead at a faster pace than Evie's mule, but Evie didn't want Ken to make him speed up. Whenever Ken did give the mule a crack or two, his gallop gave Evie such a jouncing that she was glad when he slowed to a walk again. Besides, she was afraid she'd fall off. The donkeys got farther

and farther ahead, until they were out of sight. Then Evie thought of
her baby up there with only the men, and she let Ken give her mule
another whack. They managed to catch up after about an hour, but
staying near was a struggle all day long. (The trip took eleven
hours.) About half way up the last big hill, Judith began to cry, so
Ken took her out of the basket and carried her. That made her
happy again.

The donkeys recognized the fact that they were getting into home
territory, so they began to walk faster, but Evie's mule became even
lazier until it took a lot of whacking and clucking to make him go at
all. The men went on ahead and arrived at Ken and Evie's house
about an hour before they did. When their old friends, Angel, Felix,
and Lesiu knew they were coming, they ran down the trail to meet
them. It was a heart-warming welcome. Besides, with them there,
Evie could just sit on her mule. The men almost automatically began
to hiss the language a mule understands and with them walking
behind him, he moved right along.

Nalo and Narciso were waiting at the house. They had swept the
floors, carried the baggage inside, and started a fire in the wood
stove. It was good to be home.

A couple of days later Evie went to the center of town and
everyone flocked around to see the baby. They were delighted with
her, but when they put their fingers into their mouths and then tried
to touch Judith's face with their wet fingers, Evie wasn't delighted.
Somehow she managed to keep her out of their reach. Actually the
women were being kind; the teachers told Evie later that the people
of that town believed that if a person looked straight at a baby, the
"evil eye" might make him sick. A wet finger to the cheeks,
forehead, or lips was the charm that was supposed to protect him.

It was only strangers who tried to apply the charm to Judith; the
people who had been around very much soon learned that they were
welcome to watch Evie care for her, but fingers from their tongues
to her face were not part of the routine. Sometimes half a dozen or
more women would gather to see her bathed and fed. Afterwards
Evie, or Modesta (Nalo's wife) would tell them a Bible story and
they'd all sing a hymn or two.

They loved the hymns, and Ken taught the men how to put
Mixtec words to some of the tunes frequently sung by Spanish-

speaking believers in Mexico. One day he hummed for them the first line of "What a Friend We Have in Jesus," gave them a rough translation, and asked them to suggest Mixtec words. At first they balked at the idea, so Ken sang his own words and with delight they joined him. He started on the second line, and Nalo offered a suggestion, then Lesiu had another. Over and over the song they went, changing a word here and there until everybody was satisfied and all knew it by heart. Tucked away in their hearts, it became one of the things that gave them courage when someone called them "donkeys" for not offering flowers to hilltop crosses.

Their courage encouraged Ken and Evie and made minor inconveniences seem very minor. For example, there was the difficulty with which groceries were received from Mexico City. They were almost out of nonlocal food one day, when Nalo brought in a donkey load that had arrived in Tlaxiaco for them. It was eleven o'clock, time to start dinner when he arrived, and Evie knew that she had ordered some canned tuna fish. As Nalo lifted the first box off the donkey's back, Evie ripped it open looking for some tuna to fix for lunch. Nalo said, "She's going after those things like a buzzard goes after a dead animal."

There was none in that box, but the second one that Nalo lifted down from the donkey was torn enough so that Evie could see a can of tuna inside. She didn't bother to open the box properly, she just tore the hole a little larger and pulled out the can. "There she goes," said Nalo. "She's even getting at it just like a buzzard picks the eyes out of a carcass."

As time passed Ken and Evie were enjoying the fellowship with the people of San Miguel more and more. They liked to bundle Judith up and go off to visit with them in their homes. Judith rode in a blanket on Ken's back, keeping time with his stride by kicking him in the back with her toes. She entertained herself by pulling on his ears and hair until she became so sleepy that she no longer found them intriguing. Then Evie rearranged her position in the blanket so that she could stretch out and sleep awhile.

Almost every Sunday they went somewhere for a Bible study with a half dozen or more men. One of the men would choose a section to be studied, and usually there was something in it that he did not understand. They'd talk about that part, each man contributing an explanation if he wanted to. Ken took his turn right along with the others. Little by little the men's knowledge of the Lord was growing.

As usual when Ken was in San Miguel, he divided his time between people and linguistic research. Under time spent with "people," he included helping them to improve their water supply. It was a great satisfaction to him to ease their life even if only a little bit.

One of their springs had produced about two gallons a day, but the morning after Ken had showed them how to dig it out deeper, one of the men lifted out forty-five gallons—and the spring soon refilled. In another section of town, a few sheep were bunched around a stagnant pool. Ken and the men dug into the stratified rock of a cliff there and found a beautiful little stream. They made a trough about a foot deep and several feet long, wide enough for the women to dip a gourd into it. Then they made a place to catch the overflow where the sheep could drink.

Ken tried to do an especially nice job on one of the seven springs he helped them with. Around that one he built a little springhouse. At first that was fine, but the water level must have lowered and although it had been flowing rapidly, later the water dried up. The people figured that the sacred snake that guarded the spring must have been offended, so they tore the structure down.

In the meantime, Ken's linguistic research was going well. He was writing a review of the literature on phonetics. He studied carefully the phonetics of the half dozen books he had brought with him, and he was writing comments on the other linguistic books that he had read before.

That spring of 1941, it also became apparent that his family was going to need a greater share of his time. Evie had come down with hepatitis, or "jaundice" as it was often called in those days. So, once more Ken began to cook some of the meals. Two of the Mixtec women did the laundry and kept the house clean, but he began taking more responsibility for Judith.

Mrs. Griset wrote suggesting that it might save Evie's strength if the baby were weaned. Judith was given a bottle and Ken was often the one who held her while she drank. He observed that the tug on the nipple was strong, and almost steady. That startled him. If the mechanism was the same as that used when some African languages make clicks, he would have expected a series of tugs on the nipple. He wondered what Judith's tongue was doing—why was the pull on the nipple steady? He waited until she was sucking vigorously, then he jerked the nipple out, and looked into her open mouth. For a short time before she howled with rage, her tongue kept on working, but instead of going back in one sharp movement as it does when a click is made, there was a little hump on the front part of her tongue, and it worked its way backward in a kind of a ripple. So Judith, at less than a year of age, contributed to a sentence on page 93 in Ken's book *Phonetics,* "A nursing baby uses a type of ingressive oral mechanism, but with certain peristaltic modifications in tongue movement which are not pertinent to sound production."

Evie took Judith to California to be with her grandparents for the summer, and Ken went on to Ann Arbor, Michigan. It was six weeks until the SIL classes were to begin in Arkansas and Ken was determined to get his dissertation finished and turned in before then. He was working long hours and the first three weeks he revised Part I which was an analysis of the literature on phonetics. The next three weeks he completely rewrote Part II, in which he presented his phonetic classification of all oral sounds. He finished the revision, and a steno typed it, but there were multitudinous square brackets and some phonetic symbols that had to be drawn in by hand. He hired a couple of students to put them in for him, and he made his deadline. That is, it was turned in before Fries, the chairman of his doctoral committee, left for Europe. (The dissertation was revised a bit then published as *Phonetics: a Critical Analysis of Phonetic Theory and a Technic for the Practical Description of Sounds.* Ann Arbor: University of Michigan Press, 1943.)

The seventy dollars that he spent for the brackets, however, depleted the money he had been saving for his train fare to Arkansas. He'd have to wait in Ann Arbor until more money arrived. In the meantime, classes were due to start in Arkansas, so he sent me a telegram and asked me to take over until he got there.

I was to teach four hours the next day, both phonetics and phonemics. I had never taught phonemics before, and had taught phonetics just one summer, but, except for Gene Nida who was in charge of the grammar course, I had had more experience than the rest of staff. So I taught. Teaching phonetics was easy, and of course I had sat in on Ken's phonemics classes the previous year, so I had an idea of what to do.

When Ken arrived a couple of days later, he was surprised at how well the classes were going, and he thought he noted that I had more prestige with the students that summer than I'd had before. He decided that it was because I had taught the two courses on the first day, and that I would not have had that much prestige if he had started, and I had taken over a week later.

He thought it was good for the school if the students had confidence in all their teachers, so after that he tried to make sure that even beginning teachers met their classes the first day. And, as the school grew, he saw to it that staff members had definite responsibilities, and that students knew they had those responsibilities. It was part of his program to develop the potiential of his staff and build up their prestige. Some of his technique he learned from Uncle Cam, who, Ken says, is a master at the art of putting his associates into the limelight.

Evie started teaching phonetics that year, and both of us assisted Ken in teaching phonemics.

The date for Ken's oral exam for his doctorate had been set for August the eleventh. He was going to Ann Arbor for it, of course, but there wasn't enough money for Evie's train fare. The SIL students thought she ought to be there, so very quietly someone began to take in donations. It wasn't long before they had enough to buy a round trip ticket. Then, "Surprise!" they presented it to her.

Evie was delighted, and instead of lesson plans for phonemics, she began to think about what the well-dressed wife wears to her husband's doctoral exam.

Everything went well and Ken received his Ph.D. degree (granted officially in the spring of 1942), but the more important thing was that SIL had its first member with a Ph.D. In later years many more would follow in his footsteps.

Kirk Franklin

Ken in the office, 1979.

Dave Duncan

Ken with his sister, Eunice, 1981.

The Pike children. Ken is next to the youngest.

Ernest and May Graniss Pike, Ken's parents.

Ken and Evie shortly after their marriage.

Recovering from the broken leg that pushed Ken to start writing phonetics, 1936.

Barbara rides to Tlaxiaco carried by a Mixtec friend, 1947.

The log cabin, chinked with clay, that Ken built.

Old Narciso and his little friend listen to Pikes' record player.

A traveling merchant and family rest on the Pikes' porch.

Ken studying with three of his Mixtec friends, 1941. Narciso is on the far right and Angel is beside him.

Angel teaches his wife, 1944.

Ken waiting for the airplane in Las Casas, 1947.

Barbara and Judith try out Ken's horse just before he leaves for Jungle Camp.

Ken on his way to Jungle Camp, 1947. His family stayed in San Miguel.

Ken and Evelyn with little Judith, 1942.

Judith, Evelyn, Ken, Barbara, and Stephen, 1956.

Ken with a new friend while conducting a workshop in Papua New Guinea, 1962.

Ken with Graham Scott saying goodbye for a Fore leader in Papua New Guinea, 1962.

Ken in Peru with one of his Aguaruna friends, 1955. (While studying this language Ken developed the theory of rhythm groups larger than the syllable.)

Mrs. Anna Hawk teaches Ken some Cheyenne at the University of Oklahoma.

Frank Robbins, Sarah Gudschinsky, and Ken discuss a linguistic point.

Uncle Cam and Ken chat together at SIL-Norman.

Kirk Franklin

Ken and Evelyn, 1979.

Professor Martinet congratulates Ken on receiving his honorary doctorate at the Sorbonne in Paris, 1978.

Ken and Evie consult with Dr. Desai on tagmemic analysis of Gujarati while Dr. Sharma listens.

Surprise! After 47 years, Ken finds himself with Evie in Beijing, China's palace museum.

16 LANGUAGE LEARNING BY GESTURE

Dr. House, the chairman of the Modern Language Department at the University of Oklahoma had told Miss Della Brunsteter (now Mrs. George Owl), an assistant professor of French, to prepare herself to study the Indian languages of that state. So, in 1940, as part of that preparation, Miss Brunsteter went to the University of Michigan to take the linguistic courses held there that summer. While at Michigan, she became acquainted with Eugene Nida, and it seemed to her that informal conversation with him about language was more helpful than her formal classes were.

When she found out that he and Ken taught linguistics in Arkansas, she begged for the privilege of attending. Probably they thought that she would change her mind if they explained the situation to her. For example, the students were expected to give an hour's work a day—she insisted that she would not mind washing her share of the dishes, or doing any other kind of work. All the other students were studying linguistics in order to be able to translate the New Testament, or to tell about Christ in a little-known language—perhaps she would feel out of place. She insisted that she could relate to them. Actually she believed in Christ too, and she admired people who were willing to give their time to teach about Him.

So Gene and Ken agreed to let her attend, and, in 1941, she took the classes in Arkansas. She finished that summer more convinced than ever that the courses were valuable, and she thought it would be advantageous to both the University of Oklahoma and to SIL if they were held on the University campus.

The first step in that direction was to provide opportunity for the university personnel to meet Gene and Ken. She persuaded her colleagues to ask Ken to give a demonstration showing how a person could begin learning a language even though he had no interpreter, no dictionary, and, when he started, no words in the other man's language.

Ken first did such a demonstration in 1936 when one of his students told him that she was worried—suppose she found herself some place where there were no bilinguals. His purpose was to show her and the other students that they could write down the language as soon as they heard it, and that they could learn the meanings of words and expressions by noticing when the different words were used and the people's reaction to them. That was the way he had learned Mixtec.

His demonstration was comforting—yes, language could be learned without an interpreter. The demonstration was also a convincing presentation of the value of linguistics, and watching him "smash the language barrier" as *The Charlotte Observer* put it (August 1, 1975, p. 18A), is always a good show.

Throughout the years Ken has interested audiences with his monolingual demonstration many times in many countries. Watching one is something like watching a high diver in Acapulco, Mexico, as he dives from the cliffs there into the ocean below. It's beautiful, and you know he's an expert, so you don't expect trouble, but there is always the chance that he might end up on the rocks instead of in the ocean. That possibility makes you watch all the more intently.

As Ken stands on stage surrounded by a half dozen blackboards and faces a speaker of some language—any language, you expect him to be able to write down what the stranger says. You expect him to put meanings to the noises the stranger makes, but—will he fail this time?

When he begins a demonstration, Ken never knows where the stranger is from, nor the language he will be talking, since someone else has made the necessary arrangements for the stranger to be there. He himself talks in Mixtec, using that language as a kind of verbal gesture, confident that no one chosen for the demonstration will understand him. Ken usually carries a couple of big sticks, little sticks, a big and a little leaf, and other small items. They are conversation pieces, things to talk about with the minimum chance of ambiguity. They are also chosen because, presumably, every language has a word for 'leaf', etc.

After seeing one demonstration, you are sure that Ken will soon learn the difference between 'one stick' versus 'two sticks', 'a big leaf' versus 'a little leaf', etc. He'll probably get a verb or two, for example, 'I sit down' versus 'he sits down', and even 'I am hitting you' versus 'you are hitting me'. Possessed nouns, verb conjugations, etc, appear to be easy, but Ken doesn't stop there. He goes on to clauses with subjects, objects, and maybe even an indirect object. These last few years he has sometimes been able to build up to sentences with both dependent and independent clauses.

The audience comes expecting Ken to write the language and to figure out grammatical constructions, but the speed with which he does it is always amazing, and it is fun to watch the reaction of the stranger helping him. It is apparent that he is enjoying the encounter. When Ken, reading from his scrawls on the blackboard, manages to make up and say his first sentence, the stranger is surprised and delighted. The audience is delighted too and they clap in appreciation.

Ken often starts out the demonstration by telling the audience that what he is about to do is not a stunt, but that language learning by gesture is often a part of the job of translators who go into an area where there are no interpreters. He expects his students to be successful at it.

A number of his colleagues have given very successful demonstrations to their classes, to university gatherings, and to church groups. Some of them have turned the demonstration around. For example, Ron Snell once pretended to be a speaker from the jungles of Peru who knew only the Machiguenga language, and who was trying to learn English.

He talked to the person helping him only in Machiguenga and wrote the English responses in phonetic script on the blackboard. Some of the problems of language learning became vivid to the audience, as they saw Ron appear to be confused. At first he thought that "orange" meant "fruit," then, as he learned more, he decided that he had been mistaken and that the meaning of "orange" was actually a color. The audience was following him, empathizing with him, all the way through his demonstration.

But even after years of experience, there is still the chance that Ken, or one of his colleagues, will fail. Ken tells about the time in Australia when he was in front of a crowd of two thousand people. The aboriginese man who walked out on the stage to meet him just stood there. He didn't say one word. Ken greeted him in Mixtec. No answer. He held out a leaf and talked about it in Mixtec. No comment. If the man didn't talk, Ken would have nothing with which to demonstrate his linguistic techniques. He continued chattering, trying to elicit a response, and the crowd waited breathlessly. Finally, after more than five minutes, the man burst out with a rumble of protest. Ken wrote it down on the blackboard and said it back to him. The man answered something. Ken wrote that down too. Then little by little the man began to respond to gestures about the leaves, and sticks, and other things.

By the time forty minutes had passed (the time Ken usually allots for eliciting data), he had learned words, most of the sound system, and a few points about the grammar. But those five minutes had seemed very long to him. Later someone gave him a possible explanation of the man's behavior. In some of the aboriginal cultures of Australia, there are no greetings. Instead, a stranger simply walks into camp and sits there awhile before he starts to talk; that is what the man working with Ken had done that day.

He is still getting requests for monolingual demonstrations. In fact, the University of Michigan Television Center thought that many more people would be interested. They filmed one in three-quarter inch color television video cassette and made it available for rent or sale. The demonstration they filmed was one in which the unknown person was a speaker of Indonesian. Watching Ken interact with him, then write on the studio blackboard and analyze his findings is really very impressive.

Impressive, but not perfect, some people say. For example, as part of the SIL course at the University of Oklahoma, Ken has been doing the demonstration once almost every year for more than thirty years. Therefore some of the students who take the second year course saw the demonstration the previous summer. I am told that a second year student may advise those in the first year, "Be sure you go to the monolingual demonstration; it is good for your morale. You may end up feeling that you are smarter than Pike."

That is, if they sit up front and listen carefully, they may disagree with the way he records a sound or two. Their conclusion: they heard better than Pike. Wow! No matter who was right, the fact that they knew enough to pick out a sound that might have been recorded differently is a triumph for students who have had phonetics for less than two months—a triumph for their instructors too.

17 AT THE UNIVERSITY OF OKLAHOMA

(1942...)

In 1942, for the first time, the courses of the Summer Institute of Linguistics were held on the University of Oklahoma campus. The Department of Modern Languages, as part of the regular university curriculum, gave credit for the courses taught by the SIL staff. In 1943 and 1944, because the US navy was training recruits there, there was no room for SIL at the university. For that reason SIL moved to Bacone College near Muskogee, Okla., but except for those two years, SIL has held classes at the University each summer since 1942.

Ken was delighted by the move to the university campus. It not only provided the needed academic credentials, but being in an academic environment helped the students to study linguistics with enthusiasm while working toward the translation of the Bible into little-known languages. In his chapel talks to students, Ken would occasionally emphasize Luke 10:27, "Thou shalt love the Lord thy God with all thy ... mind...." And with reference to Luke 21:1-4, he told at least one group of students, "Take your academic mite, the little bit you can do, work as hard as you can, and drop it into God's collection box."

Working right along with Ken was Eugene Nida. Nida received his Ph.D. from the University of Michigan in 1943. The topic of his dissertation had been "A Synopsis of English Syntax," and those first years he carried the responsibility for the grammar courses taught at SIL. He was a tremendous teacher and his lectures were very popular.

Ken and Gene made a good team. As part of that teamwork they would start the summer off by analyzing an American Indian language together in front of the class. As the Indian spoke, Ken wrote the utterance on the board, while Nida made comments on the grammatical constructions they found. Then Ken talked about points of interest in the phonology.

Nida was a good administrator, and during those years he was the one who took care of most of the public relations with the university. When he left in 1953 to work full time with the American Bible Society, Ken missed him. He wrote, "...it makes things look a bit lonely like—it is more difficult for one poor old stick to burn as brightly by itself as it can when two are together."

But he wasn't the only stick very long. Turner Blount began to help him with administration and Ken was soon appreciative, both of his willingness to take on work, and of his judgment. Others took up some of the linguistic load. William Wonderly had received a Ph.D. in 1947 from the University of Michigan; he taught field methods. In the decade of the 50's, eight members of SIL received Ph.D. degrees. They were: Richard Pittman, 1953, Robert Longacre, 1955, and Sarah Gudschinsky, 1958, from the University of Pennsylvania; Benjamin Elson, 1956, and Howard McKaughan, 1956, from Cornell University; Viola Waterhouse, 1958, and Velma Pickett, 1959, from the University of Michigan, and John T. Bendor-Samuel, 1958, from the University of London.

That first year, 1942, when SIL transferred to the University campus, the number of students more than doubled in size, that is, one hundred and twenty-three enrolled that year. (By 1975 SIL was holding classes in five universities in USA.) With the enlarged student body, more teachers were needed. Ken didn't seem to regret the constant demand for new assistants, since he recognized it as a means for their growth; the new staff members gained in confidence and ability as they acquired experience. There was no doubt that their services would be needed as SIL continued to expand.

Especially in the phonetic classes, the students learned faster if sections were small, and soon the policy developed that no more than ten students should be in a phonetics lab section, and no more than twenty should be in a phonology or grammar lab section.

The teaching assistants did well even their first year since the department heads provided a lesson plan for each day, and gave suggestions on how it should be presented. In the phonology course it was Evie who got the briefing sessions started. She had made lesson plans for herself, and when her fellow staff members saw them, they asked for copies. It wasn't long before it was the accepted practice for a department head to brief the staff daily. In phonetics, for a number of years, it was my lesson plans the staff used.

Probably the students were glad that Ken himself didn't teach all the lab sections—the assistants weren't so frightening. Ken's dramatic presentation got the point across, but most students were glad when his attention was directed at someone else. And Ken was glad for the assistants, not just to keep the sections small, but because he wanted to be free to put his time on other things.

Even in 1942 Ken's driving interest had changed from phonetics to intonation. That spring Professor Fries, founder and director of the English Language Institute at Michigan, had asked him to help prepare materials for use there. The native speakers of Spanish and Portugese were having difficulty using English intonation even after they had learned the correct pronunciation of single words. To help them, Ken set out to analyze the intonation. He made good progress. The staff at the English Language Institute began using his materials, and the Latin American students began to sound more American in their speech. His intonation theory and lesson plans were published as *Pronunciation,* Vol. I of *An Intensive Course in English for Latin-American Students,* 1942.

Copies of the mimeographed edition arrived in Oklahoma that summer, and Ken immediately started to use it, not to teach Latin Americans how to pronounce English, but to help English-speaking students to learn to pronounce a tone language. He reasoned that speakers of English would be better able to speak a tone language if they became aware of the intonational system of their own language.

To help them hear it, using a slide whistle, he played the sentence tunes of several stories while the students watched the words. They were delighted. Then he lectured awhile, restricting himself to the intonation that people usually use when listing things; he changed and lectured with the intonation used when someone was being very formal; he changed again to the intonation used when a person is signalling that he is doubtful about a matter. The students reacted—amazed that intonation could be controlled that way. Then he began teaching them how to do it. He designated a certain intonation and called on one student after another to read a sentence while controlling the intonation in that specified way. It was tricky but soon a number succeeded.

By the end of the summer they had learned an amazing amount of linguistics, and they had a chance to try it out the last two weeks, analyzing a language they had never previously studied.

An increasing number of those trained at SIL were beginning to publish the results of their field investigations. At that time many of the papers were coming from the seminar that Ken had started in 1944 to help SIL members analyze the minority languages they were studying. One of the goals of the seminar was to help them write publishable papers. Of course he spent many hours with individuals in addition to the time in class.

The SIL courses were good, but Ken wanted to be sure that the staff members themselves kept on learning. He urged them to attend the meetings of the Linguistic Society of America, and because he had been stimulated by informal contact with other linguists, he suggested that the SIL young folks sit with non-SIL people. He told them, "Think of the man who knows the field as an elaborate index; he can give you hunches, tell you bibliography, etc. In informal talks he is indexed to your problem. Formally, in class, he is not indexed to you." He urged them on with, "Everyone can tell you something that you would like to know, if you know enough to ask the right question."

He wanted them, too, to contribute to others, so he suggested that even before they left for the meeting they think up a one-minute answer to the question, "What are you working on now?" Or, a thirty-second lead such as, "I'm studying Aztec right now, and I have one problem...." (In the 1940's most of the SIL staff spent the winter months working with an Indian language of the USA or Mexico.)

Every summer a half dozen or more went up to attend the meetings, and Ken recommended that some of them give papers presenting the results of their research. At the summer session of

1947, six of the twenty-two papers were given by SIL members. That was the session at which the Linguistic Society of America passed a resolution commending the work of SIL. They said:

> RESOLVED, that the members of the Linguistic Society present at the Summer Meeting having heard a report by Professor Kenneth Pike on the teaching in practical phonemics carried on at the Summer Institute of Linguistics at Norman, Oklahoma, and on the impressive series of publications appearing from the pens of its staff members, it is the sense of this group that the work being done by the Summer Institute, as exemplified also by the papers presented by its students at this meeting, should be strongly commended by our Society and welcomed as one of the most promising developments in applied linguistics in this country.

All of SIL was proud that day. SIL was proud too when Ken was made President of the Linguistic Society of America for the year 1961. Somehow even the young SIL members knew that the honor was partly theirs—and that the Lord was helping them all. For years Ken had said that any worthwhile thing he had ever done came about because he had been trying to help a colleague or somebody.

Of course he did some things just for fun. Ventriloquism for example. In 1946, one of the fellows who came to SIL to take the courses in linguistics had been earning his way through college by being a magician. He used to carry a dummy with him, and sometimes he used ventriloquism as part of his act. One day, while Ken was lecturing, the fellow started answering in ventriloquial voice from the audience. Ken pretended that it was coming from outside the window, and together they fooled the students.

Fascinated by something else to learn about vocal noises, Ken asked questions, practiced, and soon was able to control both "near" and "distant" ventriloquial voice. The fellow loaned him his dummy and Ken took it to the 1946 summer session of the Linguistic Society of America. Professor Fries was chairman of the meeting in which Ken was scheduled to give a talk on "The Phonetic Basis of Ventriloquism," and they had a prearranged hand signal which let Ken know that it was time for his paper. So Ken, using distant voice, called, "Let me out! Let me out!" pretending that the voice was coming from the closet beside the podium. People began to look puzzled and concerned, so then Ken went to the closet, picked up the dummy, and changing to near voice, pretended that the dummy was carrying on a conversation with him.

One of the things he had the dummy say was, "I can do something that Professor Kurath can't do." At that point Ken swiveled the dummy's head around in a complete circle and back to the starting point. The crowd shouted and clapped with approval. Then Ken went on to give a phonetic description of the way a ventriloquial voice is produced. People didn't forget that talk, and years later someone who had been there, or someone who had heard it about it from someone else, would mention it to Ken.

18   TO PERU

(1943)

In July of 1943, Uncle Cam wrote a letter to the SIL staff, to the Board of Directors, and to the Executive Committee of the Mexico Branch urging them to make preparations for an advance into countries other than USA and Mexico. As an important part of the preparation he said that, in order to see where they should begin, either the Pikes or the Townsends should make a trip to South America "as soon as the Lord clearly indicates that it is His time."

One of the things that was holding them back was lack of money. Then in August Ken received a letter from Mr. North of the American Bible Society asking him to undertake some consultant work for them in Ecuador, Peru, and Bolivia. A translation of the New Testament into one of the dialects of Quechua was just being finished. The speakers of Quechua covered a wide area, and certain modifications in the translation needed to be made so that it would be usable by the greatest number of people. Various solutions, each with ardent advocates, had been suggested.

Mr. North asked Ken to spend a couple of months on the field assessing the situation, and then return to New York and give them his judgment. They would pay the expenses for the trip and give him an honorarium in addition.

Ken was delighted with the opportunity. It seemed both to him, and to Uncle Cam, that the Lord was showing them that the time for advance had come.

The previous year, 1942, the University of Michigan had appointed Ken to be a half-time Research Associate for the English Language Institute, so Ken called Professor Fries and told him that he was planning on a trip to South America. Fries suggested that he pass by Ann Arbor on the way. Even though Ken was calling from Mexico City (he had gone to Mexico to help Evie get settled in Tetelcingo), he did pass by Ann Arbor.

Those years—during the second world war—were tense ones everywhere. First Ken had to get permission from the U.S. Selective Service to leave the country. Then he had to get a U.S. passport, but they weren't given very freely those days. Before a person could get a passport to Latin America, he had to be okayed by the Division of Cultural Relations. Fries wrote a letter to that department telling them that Ken was the specialist who had been responsible for the pronunciation materials in the English Language Institute book for Latin American students. He said that he was going to Ecuador, Peru, and Bolivia to do some studies for the American Bible Society, but that he would also visit some people in each country in the interest of the English Language Institute.

When Ken got to Washington, he showed the letter at the Cultural Relations office. The man behind the desk asked, "You're Pike?"

"Yes."

"You helped Fries write the book on pronunciation?" "Yes."

The man turned around, and reached for a book on the shelf behind him. It was the English Language Institute book on pronunciation. He opened to the preface, and found where it said that Ken was the one responsible. He closed the book, turned to Ken and said, "Your passport has to come across my desk. When it does, I'll okay it."

Ken was thrilled. From his point of view, this was part of the evidence that God Himself was coordinating things.

He went up to New York to see Mr. North at the American Bible Society, but he wasn't feeling very well organized. (He left his briefcase in the Wanamaker's store—but the salesman caught him. Then he left his raincoat in a taxicab—but the driver called him back.) "I need you!" he wrote Evie.

While he was waiting for his passport to arrive, he went home to Connecticut to spend a week with Mother and Dad, then to Florida to catch a flight to South America. But now things were not going quite so smoothly. The flight on which he had expected to travel was cancelled, and he was off-loaded from the next flight by priority passengers. Other flights were cancelled because of the weather. He had time to study, but he couldn't seem to get at it. He tried to go deep-sea fishing, but not enough people bought tickets, so the boat didn't go out. He did take a sight-seeing boat up the river to a Seminole village where he noticed that the children and women were talking only Seminole—no English.

Actually he was delayed in Miami for a whole week.

In Ecuador at last, he immediately got to work, consulting with the missionaries and listening to Quechua as it was spoken in various places. Then on to Bolivia and more Quechua dialects and more missionaries with different opinions. He became very tired and he missed Evie—and Judith too, so much so he thought he might even enjoy having her mess up his writing.

But even while he wanted to chitchat with Evie, he remembered that he was in a Spanish-speaking country, and that he should be talking the language of the country. He bought a Spanish grammar, a dictionary, a New Testament, and from then on, as long as he was in South America, he wrote Evie in Spanish. Actually it didn't slow him down very much. Both the facts and his mood came across. Sometimes when he didn't know the Spanish word, he inserted an English one. For example, delighted with Evie's letter, he wrote, "*Tu carta me* thrill-ó." Another time when things had been going well, but he was apprehensive about the future, he wrote, "*A ver si viene la* bump." The letter Ken wrote the day he arrived back in New York was still in Spanish, but in his next he was using all English again.

While Ken had been working for the Bible Society in Ecuador, Bolivia, and Peru, he also took time to contact the people that Fries of the English Language Institute was interested in. Now his job for them and for the Bible Society was almost finished. He was in Lima, Peru, and he was about to return to the United States. There were just two days left which he could spend on making contact with government people for SIL.

He felt young and incompetent. He was not a public relations man. He was a linguist, a Bible translator. But here it was up to him to contact government officials and try to make arrangements with them that would allow SIL personnel to come into Peru to translate the New Testament for the little-known peoples of the jungle.

It was a job he knew he had to tackle, but first he read I Timothy 2:1-3 that tells us to pray for all who are in authority. (It wasn't until years later that he noticed that the verses, one through three, that tell us to pray for those in authority are tied in with God's desire, expressed in verses four and five, to have everybody come to know the truth about Himself and Christ.)

Ken prayed for the government officials of Peru that day, but he still felt incompetent. He wondered. Perhaps it would have been better if Uncle Cam could have come. Uncle Cam was the one who was the champion public relations man; he was the one who had had a series of successful contacts with government officials. But God had put Ken in Peru—in that place at that time.

Then Ken remembered the story of Elijah and Elisha of II Kings. Elijah struck the water with his cloak; the Jordan river parted and he and Elisha crossed on dry land (II Kings 2:8). After Elijah had been taken up to heaven (II Kings 2:11), his duties fell on his young follower Elisha. Would Elisha be able to carry on? Would God help him as He had helped Elijah? Elisha picked up Elijah's cloak, called out, "Where is the Lord God of Elijah?" and struck the water with it. Again the river parted and Elisha passed on to the other side (II Kings 2:14).

Ken was trying to follow in the footsteps of Uncle Cam. Would the Lord help him to make arrangements with a government that would allow SIL personnel to translate the Scripture in that country? If God could help Uncle Cam, He could help Ken too.

As Ken prayed, he remembered Elisha's shout, "Where is the God of Elijah?" and he thought, "We'll slap the waters and see what happens."

He went to see the Minister of Education. The Minister had studied at Columbia University and looked with interest at the copy of *Phonetics* that Ken gave him. (In a way, that book was Ken's credentials.) Ken explained how SIL in Mexico tried to do a good scientific linguistic job of analyzing languages and dictionaries; how they made themselves useful by doing such things as preparing literacy materials, doing simple medical work, and helping the people with agriculture; how they hoped to translate the New Testament and help their Indian friends to understand its message.

The minister asked, "Why don't you do that here?"

Ken answered, "We haven't been invited."

After checking a few more details, the Minister invited SIL to Peru, and courteously added, "If there is anything we can do to help, let us know."

With a prayer in his heart, Ken told him that if he'd put the invitation into writing, the SIL members would probably have an easier time getting visas. The Minister did.

Ken rejoiced and was very thankful. He had seen that God could work through someone who was young and inexperienced and not very competent in the area of public relations. Years later he was still telling students, "It was by the hand of God that we were permitted to enter Peru—the hand of God who is Maker of heaven and earth."

19 INTONATION

Ken had started analyzing the intonation of American English in the spring of 1942. He was at it again in the spring of 1943, giving lectures to some Latin Americans, showing them how to teach the pronunciation of English, and doing some demonstration teaching himself to be sure the theory worked.

He was very much encouraged by Bloomfield's reaction to the mimeographed edition on pronunciation that had come out in 1942. Bloomfield (the outstanding linguistic scholar of the country at that time) wrote him, "The book is beautiful and is the first thing on intonation that I have read with any interest or profit. It seems to me to constitute a tremendous advance in phonetics."

After the mimeographed edition came out, Ken re-examined the theory and revised here and there as he prepared to expand it into the book, *The Intonation of American English*. It was an investigation of the way the "tone of the voice" affects meaning, and the way an alphabet of the pitch (written with numbers beside the syllables, or lines drawn over the words) can be used to help a person learn to talk a language with a better "accent."

Ken kept thinking of things to add, until the book when published was 200 pages long. It included a summary of the work that others had done on the analysis of English intonation. It had a section on the theory of intonation showing how various factors— not just pitch—worked together to make up the intonation contour. In addition to the long section on pitch, there were several short ones on stress, rhythm, pause, etc., that were part of the various intonation contours. There was a little about how the speed with

145

which vowels or consonants are pronounced can signal the attitude of the speaker. There were about forty pages describing the specific pitch contours with their meanings, and another forty pages of stories and illustrative sentences on which the intonation had been marked.

Ken had been working hard, but he hadn't finished when it was time to leave for the summer session of SIL at Oklahoma. Actually, all that was left to do was the proofreading of the manuscript, but he wanted to do that before leaving Ann Arbor. He thought about the amount of strength he had—could he do it?

One of his regrets for sometime had been that he was never able to study long hours on successive days. When he tried to do it, he became ill and then had to spend time recuperating. But he had learned that, in an emergency, he could put in more hours than usual if he rested afterwards. So he looked at the job to be done and remembered that he would be traveling by train from Ann Arbor to Oklahoma—a good sleeping time.

Then he went all out. He sat down and proofread for a straight twenty-three and a half hours—no time off. He says he could work that long only because proofreading was a mechanical-type job. Well, he finished. Then he climbed on the train and slept all the way to Oklahoma.

Ken's book on intonation was less widely accepted than his book on phonetics had been. Some linguists, Dwight L. Bolinger for example, worked with pitch contours as basic, while Ken posited four basic pitches (Bolinger, 1951, "Intonation: Levels versus Configuration" Word 7.199-210). George L. Trager and H.L. Smith Jr. (and many others) in addition to four basic pitches, worked with four degrees of stress (Trager and Smith, 1951).

The book, however, did receive some interesting reviews which noted, with appreciation, the work he had done. Professor Eli Fischer-Jørgensen a well known phonetician of Denmark wrote, "Intonation problems certainly are among the most complicated and intricate linguistic problems.... And I want to emphasize that Pike's book is a most valuable and interesting and very stimulating contribution to the discussion of these problems." Eli Fischer-Jørgensen, "Kenneth L. Pike's Analysis of American English Intonation," *Lingua* 2.1.13, (1949).

Pedagogical problems were, as always, of interest to Ken, and he was curious to see how speech teachers and English teachers would react to the book.

In 1946 he was invited to give a paper on intonation at the December meetings of the Speech Association of America. He gave a summary of the theory and demonstrated different intonation contours to the audience. Then he suggested that such an analysis of intonation might make a valuable contribution to the speech department. He said that if a teacher would mark a play for a high school student in such a way that he could see the pitch of the voice to be used, that the student could then be taught to read the material with the expression the teacher wanted; the audience would then think that the student felt in such and such a way whether he actually felt that way or not.

The reaction of the crowd at the Speech Association meeting was a spontaneous gasp of horror. In the discussion that followed it was apparent that many there felt that the students needed to empathize with the character they were portraying. Two of those attending, however, defended Ken's position and told how they themselves had used similar techniques when coaching some of their students.

In a letter Ken wrote later, he said that he had known that he was stepping into a hornets' nest when he recommended writing the pitch on materials the students were to act out, but he had done it deliberately, partly for the fun of it, but also because he was convinced that his analysis of intonation would be of real value to the teachers if they understood the theory and were willing to give it a try.

Howard R. Martin in the speech department of the University of Iowa is one who has given it a try and has found it to be useful. Instead of talking vaguely about "feeling," he is able to show the students specifically how two readings differ. In 1975 Martin and Ken co-authored the article, "Analysis of the Vocal Performance of a Poem: A classification of Intonational Features," *Language and Style* 7:209-18.

Ken thought it would be especially good if a poet would write pitch lines on his poetry. In Ken's opinion, a poet ought to be allowed to say what he means, and since part of the meaning is carried by intonation, he needs to write pitch. If someone reads the poetry with a different pitch than the one intended by the author, then he is not portraying the intended meaning.

Of course some people object to that idea. They say that they want to put their own interpretation on the poem—that is, they don't want any restrictions put on the intonation. Even some poets object because they may want to read the poem two different ways. Ken's answer to that is that, under those circumstances, the poem should be written two ways. But people don't seem to be taking up the idea very fast.

Ken himself started marking pitch and stress on some of his own poetry, and occasionally on parts of his letters to Evie. It is an additional beam with which to carry the message.

(Published in Kenneth L. Pike, 1967, *Stir-Change-Create*, p. 70.)

Since the intonation contours convey the attitude of the speaker using them, could a person's attitude toward life be diagnosed by his intonation patterns? In 1947, Charles Fries, M.D. (one of Professor Fries' sons) was interning in a mental hospital. He invited his father and Ken over to the hospital to listen to phonograph recordings that had been made while some of the patients were being interviewed.

Could linguistics give a clue as to the type of insanity the individual patients had?

Professor Fries and Ken listened to the recordings for a while and then Dr. Fries brought in two patients so that they could interview them. He said that they both had schizophrenia. Ken and Professor Fries protested. They insisted that the two patients were different in their intonation patterns. Becoming more specific, Dr. Fries agreed that they had two different kinds of schizophrenia. That spurred Ken and Professor Fries on, and they settled down to listen to more recordings.

They noticed that some of the paranoid patients used a kind of monotone that Ken had never heard before. Also, they noticed that a manic depressive used a great number of glides. Then, as they listened to one recording after another, they began guessing what the diagnosis had been—Dr. Fries told them whether or not they had guessed correctly.

After listening to one of the recordings, Ken and Professor Fries said that the patient was not paranoid—but his hospital record said that he was. Ken and Professor Fries insisted that he was not like the others, so Dr. Fries checked further and found that the man had had a lobotomy by the time that particular recording had been made. After the lobotomy the man's attitude had changed, and, therefore, so had his intonation.

It had been a fascinating evening for Ken, and he summarized their conclusions as: (1) Intonation patterns indicate what a person's attitude is at the moment. (2) In the recordings of the people in the hospital, the intonation patterns of the people were "normal"; the thing that had been abnormal had been their attitude. When for some reason the attitude changed, their intonation reverted to the more usual patterns. (3) Part of the insanity of some people might consist of the fact that they retain the same attitude over a long period of time. Question: Would it be possible, through the study of intonation, to recognize the attitude on which a patient had become fixed before there is a violent outbreak or some other manifestation of abnormal mental health?

Ken didn't carry on with the project, but he was delighted to find still another tie-in between the study of linguistics and the behavior of people.

In the meantime Evie had become interested in the connection between intonation and little people—babies. How did babies acquire intonation?

She had noticed that when Mixtec babies said their first couple of words, the second syllable had a lower pitch than the first—that corresponded with the way the adults had used those particular words. Why did the first few words of an American baby usually have an upgliding pitch? Why was there a difference between the American babies and the Mixtec babies?

Evie assumed that it was because when American parents were talking to a young child, and they said words like "baby" or "dog", that they were implying, "Can you say 'baby'?" or "Do you know what a 'dog' is?" Because that was the attitude of the parent, they finished the word with an upgliding pitch and that was the model the child heard most frequently.

Some years later, when Barbara, Ken and Evie's second child, was about ready to talk, they were living in an Aztec-speaking village. Ken was away, Judith was at school, and there were no other English-speakers around. Evie determined to take the opportunity to control her own intonation when she spoke to Barbara and see if Barbara's first words would have a falling pitch. So when she talked to her and said "baby" or "dog", she implied, "Here is a baby." or "This is a dog." and she used a falling pitch.

To Evie's delight when Barbara started to talk she didn't use a rising intonation at all. She sounded amazingly adult with her soft falling "baby." When Ken came home, Evie told him what she had been doing and had him join the experiment. With Ken in an adjacent room, where Barbara could not see him, Evelyn called, "Daddy". Her first syllable was long with extra high pitch, while the second was somewhat long and on a lower pitch. Ken responded with "Hello". Presently Barbara herself called, "Daddy", mimicking Evelyn's pitch—in that way Barbara learned her second intonation pattern.

Ken and Evelyn didn't continue the experiment very long, but even in that short space of time Evie had become convinced that children mimic pitch very early in life, and that the intonation patterns which they learn first are those which their parents use when speaking directly to them.

Ken was interested in the outcome and urged Evie to write an article about what had happened. She did. (Evelyn G. Pike, 1949. "Controlled Infant Intonation," *Language Learning* 2.1.21-24.)

20   THE NEW TESTAMENT IN SAN MIGUEL MIXTEC

(1941—1951)

Ken had taken time out to write a book on phonetics and one on the intonation of American English. He had taken time to go to Peru to contact government officials so that SIL members could begin work there. He helped me and other colleagues in the analysis of the languages they were studying. But all the while, the top priority for him was still the translation of the New Testament into the language of the San Miguel Mixtecs. So even while he was working on those other projects, he and Evelyn kept returning to San Miguel.

When they went back in the fall of 1941, Don and Ruth Stark went with them to help with San Miguel Mixtec as a step of preparation for translating for a still different language. They all took the train together to Parián, and then rode with one of the mining company trucks to Nochistlán. In Nochistlán they went to a hotel to wait for the groceries they had bought in Mexico City. The wholesale dealer had said he'd get them on the same train with them, but they hadn't arrived. A merchant in Parián said he'd pick them up when they came in and send them on to them. So in Nochistlán they waited.

While they waited, Ken and Don took trips out to the nearby Mixtec villages. They'd talk with the people and write down lists of words, trying to estimate the relationship between the dialects those villagers spoke and that of San Miguel. Some of the easiest words to get were those such as hair, hand, foot, ear, etc., so they asked for them in all the towns. Then, in return, they'd tell how the people of San Miguel said them. In one town when Ken pointed to his nose and said the San Miguel word for it, the people shouted with delight.

In that town, the way the San Miguel people said "nose" meant "snout." The people thought it hilarious when Ken pointed to his nose and called it, "my snout".

When one of the men saw how much fun it was showing off the outsiders, he insisted on taking them from house to house throughout the village. He'd introduce them and tell his friends, "Talk to them in Mixtec!" (All outsiders, of course, were expected to speak only Spanish.) Then he'd enjoy the amazement of his friends when Ken answered them in Mixtec.

That was during the first week of November, the All Saints season. Everybody was in a holiday mood and had goodies ready to serve any guests who happened by. They were given a bit of honey and bread in this house, or an orange in that one. At the last house they visited, the people asked Ken and Don to sing for them in English. So they did. Then Ken asked them if they would like to hear a story about honey (they were eating some). They did, so he told them about Jesus who died, but came to life again and proved it by eating honeycomb (Luke 24:42). When the man who had been taking Ken and Don from house to house found out that the story was in the Bible, he wanted one, and he walked over to Nochistlán the next day to buy a copy.

In the meantime Evie had been busy looking after little Judith. Judith was a year and a half at the time and she had a smile and wave for most everybody in Nochistlán. They loved it and responded by giving her candy and anything else they thought she might like. Evie wanted to keep Judith's germ intake down to a reasonable amount, and sometimes it was a problem to know how to handle the situation.

Judith loved to get outdoors and into the mud (it had been raining), and Evie found that she had to wash for her every day. Under the circumstances in which they found themselves (in a hotel with no washing machine and no hot water), that took considerable time.

Judith-watching was one of Evie's favorite occupations, but she couldn't get much else done while she was doing it. Ken was very anxious to have her write down some of the ideas she had for his next book. It was to be a book with exercises, teaching students how to analize phonological systems. Evie had been sitting in on

Ken's classes that summer and she thought she had seen what went over well, and what did not. She thought it was important to have the theory presented in the way it would be the most easily understood. Ken wanted her to write up her hunches, and to give her time to do it, he did the washing a couple of days. He, writing home in a jocular mood, said that he had survived, "but with considerable injury to my dignity." But it helped his pride; he loved it when Evie took an active part in linguistics. Actually those suggestions, written up while Ken was scrubbing Judith's dirty clothes, had considerable influence on the way he lined up the material in his book *Phonemics* (1947).

In the meantime, they were still waiting for their groceries and other things to arrive from Parián. Finally Ken decided to go back to Parián and get them. It was good he did because the merchant who had said he would send them on had forgotten all about it. Ken picked them up and started back on a truck. When they had covered about half the distance, it began to rain again and the truck got stuck. Ken left the baggage and went on to Nochistlán on horseback. So they still had to wait several days more before the baggage finally arrived.

After having been in Nochistlán for what seemed like a very long three weeks, they were able to be on their way to Tlaxiaco. They traveled again by truck, and it wasn't an easy ride. The truck jounced and lurched, and the passengers banged against the side of the truck and each other. The ride was scary too—the road was narrow with a steep mountain on one side and a sharp drop-off on the other. All in all, they were very glad for an uneventful trip, and it had been easier than a trip by horse would have been—that would have taken a day and a half.

After a day in Tlaxiaco to rest and to find someone who could rent them mules, they went on to San Miguel. Judith spent most of the time on a pillow riding in front of Ken. Before leaving Tlaxiaco, Evie had sewed the seat of Judith's coveralls into the middle of a big shawl. Ken tied the ends of the shawl around himself, and in that way he didn't have to worry about her falling. Judith took the trip well, laughing and singing whenever she wasn't sleeping. The adults especially were glad to arrive. Ken and Evie were delighted to see old friends, and Don and Ruth began right away to make new ones.

The people loved to hear Ruth play the organ, and the principal of the school asked her to play for a celebration when the students and townspeople were all together. Then she was asked to go to a neighboring town and play for them too. She certainly could make that little portable organ sound great.

Life in the village was never routine, but they slipped into as near a routine life as they could. Evie made the women of the village feel at home with them; Ken started going through the gospels and Acts with Angel; Don and Ruth started learning to talk Mixtec—one of the things Ken had done while they waited in Nochistlán was to make up some language lessons for them.

As Christmas Day approached, everybody knew that they were ready for some fun. Evie invited six people for supper, but by the time it was ready, twenty more than that had arrived—so everybody ate. Then Ken told them the Christmas story; they all enjoyed that, and they just loved the games that followed. They couldn't be persuaded to stop until two-thirty in the morning. By then it was too late to go home, of course, so they all stretched out on straw mats and slept on the floor. They were up early in the morning, having fun again as they all had coffee together.

New Year's Day was another important day. That was when the old town officials turned over their authority to the new ones taking office for the coming year. The mayor who was finishing his term, invited all his subordinates over for breakfast, and he invited Ken and Don too. Then, after everybody had eaten, he asked Ken to tell a Bible story. Of course Ken was delighted to do so.

Ken and Evie carried those happy memories with them for a long time because that spring (1942), again in the fall, and in the spring of 1943 they went to the University of Michigan, Ann Arbor, where Ken worked with Professor Fries on teaching the pronunciation of English to Latin Americans. In the fall of 1943, Evie stayed in Tetelcingo while Ken went to South America at the request of the American Bible Society to give them his opinion about an alphabet problem that had to do with the writing of the Quechua language. Then, early in 1944, he was back in Ann Arbor again.

As they had been doing, and would continue to do, they spent the June through August months teaching at the Summer Institute of Linguistics. Therefore, it wasn't until the fall of 1944 that they were able to be with the Mixtec people again and work once more on the translation.

Evie was expecting another little Pike, so while she stayed in Tetelcingo, the Aztec-speaking village where the Townsends had been working, Ken went out to San Miguel to see if some of their Mixtec-speaking friends would be willing to come with him and work for them in Tetelcingo.

He walked the trail from Tlaxiaco to San Miguel with seven Mixtecs who just happened to be going at that time, and they had a lot of fun along the way. Ken was there several days, and when he came back, Angel and his wife Modesta with their two children, and Patricio and his wife Victoria, were all with him.

Angel spent most of his time working with Ken on translation, or studying ahead by himself. Patricio and Victoria made Evie's life easier; Patricio sometimes worked on the translation, and sometimes served as a kind of handy man, doing jobs around the house. Victoria helped Evie with chores like the washing and preparing meals. Judith liked playing with the two little Mixtec children. So, there together in Tetelcingo, everybody was having a busy, happy time.

Around the first of February, Evie went in to Mexico City so that she would be within easy reach of the hospital whenever the next little Pike should decide to put in appearance.

Before she left, Ken and Evie divided up their money, Evie taking what they figured she would absolutely need in Mexico City, and Ken keeping the rest for use in Tetelcingo. He would have to pay for food and the salaries of the four adult Mixtecs. The first week he had enough, but, by the second, he knew he was in trouble. Unless money came in by Saturday, he wouldn't have enough to pay the salaries of the four people working for him.

The money didn't come in. Ken was very disturbed. He had worked under the principle that he shouldn't go into debt, so he didn't want to borrow, neither did he want to be late in paying. He believed with all his heart that God would supply his every need, and if He didn't, then something was wrong with him—Ken. Perhaps he had sinned, or perhaps he was trying to do the wrong thing in the wrong place. Maybe he should resign from Wycliffe!

Thud. Just the thought of resigning made him feel sick. What would he do? Should he get a job in a university some place? That seemed hollow in comparison with working on a team that was translating the New Testament for minority groups. Besides, any good idea he had ever had about linguistics was based on studying Mixtec. He remembered that it was only after special prayer for his colleagues that the Lord had given him the necessary ideas for works such as the phonetics book and the analysis of tone languages. He wondered, if he moved out of his present job, would he ever get any more acceptable advance ideas? He wanted to do things that would make a difference in heaven—forever!

There was no sense in jumping the fence. He knew he had more pleasure, more chance to give service when he was in the Wycliffe organization than he would ever have any other place, but he was definitely disturbed by not being able to meet his debts. It hurt his pride because he had talked so much about faith—running out of money made him look silly. Worse than that, he had banked on God's being able to take care of him. What had happened? Ken had been thinking that maybe a hundred young folks should go into the jungles of South America, but if his faith wasn't strong enough for God to give the money he needed right there in Tetelcingo, how could he expect God to take care of others in more difficult circumstances. Maybe he should quit.

Sunday morning he remembered about how people who start to plough and then turn back aren't worth much (Luke 9:62). So he decided he wouldn't quit. But he told God that if, by noon, he didn't have the money with which to pay that bill, he would figure that God had definitely let him down.

Well, after church—noon—he told the men that he didn't have the money with which to pay them; he would try to go to the city the next day and bring it back to them. It made him feel sick. It had actually happened. God had let him down.

But wait! Ten minutes later, one of the neighbors came up and handed Ken an envelope. Inside, there was just enough money to pay the men their wages. (Actually there was one peso left over.) So God had not let him down after all.

Later Ken learned where the money had come from. Evie, up in Mexico City, going through an old purse, had come across some money that she had forgotten about; it had been given her some months before. She thought of Ken down in Tetelcingo, knew that he was responsible for Judith and the four Mixtecs, and figured that he might need it more than she did. Saturday she gave it to a colleague who was on his way down, and he gave it to the neighbor to give to Ken. The neighbor did—but not until Sunday.

So the crisis was over, but Ken still felt very strongly that if God did not supply his need, then somehow, he, Ken, was at fault. That inflexible attitude bothered Otis Leal who was translating for some Zapotec-speaking people, and he urged Ken to reconsider. We are told in Scripture that Job, for example, had all kinds of problems while he was living the way God wanted, and it seemed to Otis that, in this day and age, someone could run out of money while he was still living the way God wanted. Otis was very persuasive and Ken granted him the point.

A week or so after Ken's financial crisis, he and Judith went to Mexico City to join Evie, and about two weeks after that, February 23, 1945, Barbara Alice Pike was born. Evie chuckled about the way Ken bragged about her; he thought she was just right.

They all went down to Tetelcingo again, and a few weeks later a letter came from Professor Fries offering Ken a postdoctoral fellowship to work on Mixtec grammar and the intonation book. So, not long after that, Ken was off to Ann Arbor, while Evie and the Mixtecs stayed on in Tetelcingo.

When he returned in the fall of 1945, they were together in Tetelcingo again, and as a part of Ken's research program, he not only worked on Mixtec, but also on several other Indian languages as well. He didn't confine his advice to the analysis of language systems; he'd share his opinions about translation too. His letter to one colleague is worth quoting because it tells us the goal Ken himself had in his own translation. He wrote in 1947, "Remember that a good translation is intelligible or it is not a faithful translation. Over-literalism is not faithfulness but inaccuracy."

Ken liked being in Tetelcingo because it made him more available when his colleagues wanted to consult with him. Also, he and Evie did not spend as much time with the local people there as they would have with the people of San Miguel if they had been in that village. It must have worked out, because Ken's bibliography of items written during 1945-46 when he had a postdoctoral fellowship included six articles as well as the revision and expansion of three books.

By January of 1946, Don and Ruth Stark had joined them in Tetelcingo. Rough drafts of the Gospels, Acts, and several of the Pauline epistles had been done, and now Ken started on Ephesians, and Don on Revelation. They made good progress with other materials too, and were able to take to the printers a collection of Bible stories in Mixtec and some Mixtec legends. The legends were to be fun, something to intrigue the people into reading so that they would take on harder things later.

In the fall of 1946, Uncle Cam wanted Ken and Evie to be relieved even of the responsibilities of the village of Tetelcingo, so the Pikes and the Starks, with Angel and his family, all went to California to work on the translation there. Of course they didn't really want to isolate themselves completely from their surroundings; Evie, for example, soon found herself teaching phonetics one evening each week at Biola. But they were making good progress on the translation.

Angel learned to type, which was a tremendous help; soon he was making final copy of the translated books. Although he typed slowly, he was accurate, and understanding the language, he could almost proofread as he went.

Angel's ability to work amazed everybody. He worked with Ken in the morning, Don in the afternoon, and typed in any free moment and in the evenings. He wore down both Ken and Don and begged for more. He was also developing spiritual understanding as he worked with the Scriptures, and was drinking in any report about the Gospel spreading in other parts of the world. Modesta, his wife, was encouraging him on, delighted to see the completion of one part of the New Testament after another. They were both especially encouraged when the Gospel of Mark, published by the American Bible Society came off the press while they were there.

Ken used to work with Angel in the mornings, but the mail arrived in the morning too. Ken found that when he read the mail, his thoughts became so involved in SIL administrative problems that he couldn't stop thinking about them enough to concentrate on the Mixtec translation. He resolved the problem by letting the mail sit unopened until noon. He tried to spend only two hours each after-noon on SIL business, and then do some linguistic writing, but he found that the linguistics was getting left out.

There was one bit scheduled under "linguistics," however, that he would not push aside. He felt a strong conviction that he should write an article challenging the then-current doctrine that phonemics could be completed without reference to grammar. Somehow he felt such an urgency that, in spite of the priority that the Mixtec translation seemed to have, he took time to write "Grammatical Prerequisites to Phonemic Analysis" and sent it off to an editor.

He really must have felt extreme urgency about that article or he never would have done it at that time. Pressure was building up to get that stage of the translation done. A good draft needed to be finished in a matter of weeks or sooner.

Speed was called for because word had come that Mr. and Mrs. Townsend had been injured in an airplane crash. They were in Jungle Camp (see the next chapter) at the time, and Mr. Townsend wrote asking that Ken go down to Chiapas, Mexico, to be there for the rest of the season. Ken delayed almost a month until they had finished that draft of the entire New Testament and had revised sizeable sections. Two days later, in March 1947, he was on his way to Chiapas, Mexico, taking Angel and his family as far as Mexico City with him.

That summer, while Ken and Evie were teaching at the Summer Institute of Linguistics in Norman, Oklahoma, Don was working hard on the New Testament, revising, polishing, proofing, and Ruth was typing it as fast as he turned it out.

In the fall Ken was scheduled to go to Jungle Camp again, but he was feeling the need of a vacation before then. He and Evie thought that the best place for it was out in San Miguel among their friends there. The roads in that part of the country had been getting better, so one of their colleagues was able to drive them all the way to Tlaxiaco in a car with high clearance and big wheels. The horse trip from Tlaxiaco to San Miguel went well, and Judith and Barbara seemed to think it fun. Soon after they arrived, Modesta came hurrying over with eggs and corn on the cob. It was good to be home.

One of Ken's main projects while he was there that month was to get the Gospel of Mark into circulation, and to help the people to read in Mixtec. So he became a salesman. On market day he went to the town hall and gathered some statistics; then he went to the school and the inspector there gave him news about the surrounding towns. After that, he borrowed a table, and, out in the marketplace with all the people around, he typed the news on a stencil. Again, with the people watching, he ran it off on his new little Rex-o-graph duplicator.

Then he offered it for sale. People didn't hurry about buying, but one by one, about thirty were sold that day, and later a few went to the house to buy. While in the market, Ken read about the death and resurrection of Jesus. A number of people wanted the book that had that story in it, so that first day he sold seventeen Bible story books and two Gospels of Mark. Six people bought books with the Mixtec legends. Selling in the marketplace was all very natural, because that was what most everybody did; Ken joined them there every week. He also walked around, selling from door to door, stopping in homes all over town. He went both to the homes of the elite and of the humble. Everywhere people listened as he read from the Gospel of Mark, and many thanked him again and again for coming.

Evie kept busy too. People would stop in when Ken was out, and then she was the one who read to them. They'd sit and listen awhile and the next day come back for more. School girls came for a reading lesson, and when Evie read to them about Noah and the flood, they were especially pleased to hear about the rainbow.

A group of teachers came and asked Ken to make them copies of the report of their teachers' convention, and to tell Bible stories at the school. He did, and the Bible story time went on for about an hour and a half. Angel was especially pleased. He had been rather blue, because, while he was up in California helping with the translation, his best friend had cheated him out of about five hundred pesos. Angel had asked him to look after his land and house for him while he was gone. What the friend had done was to take the grinding stone and other household and farming utensils, sell off the corn and keep the money. After Angel saw the people buying the Gospel of Mark, he said that the loss of his corn and household goods was worth it, if the people of San Miguel would read and believe the Bible.

Mr. Griset, Evie's father, had come to admire Angel (he had known him when he was in California) and he wanted to help him, so he gave him some money so that Angel could buy a piece of land. It was agreed that in exchange for the land, Angel would spend time teaching the Mixtecs to read and in selling the Mixtec books. Some people were complaining about Angel, they said he wasn't as patient with folks as he ought to be. Ken's comment when he heard it was that probably Angel had done too good a job of understudying him—he, too, was impatient with folks.

The month Ken could be in San Miguel passed and it was time he left to spend a month in jungle camp. Evie and the children would stay on, but before Ken left, Cora Mak arrived and she would be living with Evie and the children. She was already speaking Mixtec because she had been in San Miguel the previous year. (Later Cora and her partner, Ruth Mary Alexander, translated the New Testament into two other Mixtec dialects.) The few weeks they were there together, Evie and Cora worked as a team in helping the people with their medical needs, teaching them to read and to sing new hymns. One of the new hymns they taught had been made up by Angel—Evie was especially pleased about that.

Cora took care of the school children who had made it a habit to run over for a few minutes every noon. At other times of the day, Cora and Evie usually took turns making the people feel at home and helping them in any way they could. Judith spent most of each morning doing school work—reading, arithmetic, and writing; Barbara, according to Evie, was most content when watching lizards, turkeys, sheep, goats, or children. Barbara did cause Evie a few days of concern when she developed a sore throat and fever, and Evie wished that Ken were there.

But everybody, not just Evie, was looking forward to the day when Ken would be back. Actually he was due back on Christmas Eve, and his San Miguel friends planned a big dinner for Christmas Day. They determined that this time it would be at one of their homes, instead of at Ken and Evie's, so they had it down at Angel's place. As usual they all had a happy time, and as usual, Ken was doing more things in a day than anyone could guess possible.

Somehow, before he, Evie, and the children left for Ann Arbor and the University of Michigan about two weeks later (January, 1948), Ken had managed to apprentice himself to a limemaker and learn the steps necessary for making lime.

It was good that he was able to make use of each day, because almost three years would go by before Ken and his family could be back in San Miguel again. During the interim, Ken not only would do a stint at the University of Michigan, and at jungle camp, but he would also go to Australia and set up classes for a branch of the Summer Institute of Linguistics there.

Thus it wasn't until November, 1950, that Ken and Evie were on their way back to San Miguel. Not only did Judith and Barbara go with them, but Stephen Bernard Pike, born November 27, 1948, was along too. Ken and Evie gave him "Bernard" as a middle name because Ken considered his San Miguel friend, Bernardo Merecías (usually called "Nalo"), to have been one of the greatest people he had ever known. After he began to trust Christ thoroughly, he taught other people to trust him too.

In fact, for a half a dozen years until Nalo died, most of the believers in San Miguel had been brought to the Lord by him. It wasn't until a few years later that a number of others began to believe too. Ken was especially pleased with the "fourth generation Christians" who turned up to study Scripture. The lineage went like this: the first generation had been Nalo, taught by Ken himself; the second generation was Angel, taught by Nalo; the third generation was Philip, taught by Angel; and the fourth generation was John, taught by Philip.

There was only a handful of believers, but that handful was vigorous, and they continued to persuade others to trust Christ. Of course some backslid and stopped studying Scriptures, but there were some new strong believers.

Their children were better off, too, when the men tried to please Christ. Nalo said, "We call our babies 'bread' babies because they have big fat arms. These other babies are 'liquor' babies, because their arms are skinny."

Studying the Bible had given the men courage and moral fiber. They had stopped drinking the local brew and, because of that, their children had benefited.

Some of those who were determined to follow Christ well had been going to Ken's house almost every day for more than a year to study with Anne Dyk and Helen Ashdown. Anne and Helen were colleagues who had joined the San Miguel team in the task of getting the Scriptures to the Mixtec-speaking people—those in San Miguel, and hopefully, those in other towns too.

Perhaps because it is hard to teach the same people every day for a year using only the Gospel of Mark, Anne had typed and duplicated a few copies of parts of the Mixtec Scriptures, namely: the Gospel of John, Acts, I and II Corinthians, Galations, Ephesians, I and II Thessalonians, I and II Peter, I, II, and III John. Then, because she had spent so much time teaching the handful of believers from the translation, she was able to give Ken some good suggestions about it.

The four colleagues, Ken, Evie, Anne, and Helen, were all in San Miguel during November and December of 1950. They were working together, making an all-out-effort to give the Mixtec New Testament its final polish before turning it in for publication. Their goal was to have it finished by mid January, the time when Ken and Evie had to leave again for Ann Arbor, Michigan.

Ken, working with Angel, started at the beginning of the New Testament and checked through each verse, making sure that it said what it was supposed to say. Anne, in addition to proofreading, worked on the headings of the sections; Helen double-checked all the names and taught the school children who came in almost every afternoon; Evie kept everybody on the job by getting the meals and taking care of visitors—that included doing the medical work. The men who came wanting to study Scripture sat with Ken and Angel and were taught as part of the normal process of checking the translation.

The team made their goal. Ken finished the final pages of Revelation, and it was agreed that Anne would give the whole New Testament one more proofing and check innumerable other details after Ken and Evie were gone. But what about publication?

Ken assumed that the American Bible Society would publish the New Testament for the San Miguel Mixtecs. He had been looking forward to the time when the believers would have their "textbook." He was sure that they would grow spiritually with the help of the New Testament, and that their growth would be stunted without it. Therefore he had been very disappointed when the American Bible Society wrote that they could not publish the New Testament, because there were too few Mixtecs who were believers and too few who knew how to read.

Ken didn't give up. With Uncle Cam's encouragement, he began to look for a less expensive way to publish than by letterpress. The answer he came up with was to have the New Testament lithoprinted.

A Canadian who was delighted to help provide the New Testament for a group of people who had not had it before would pay the printing costs. Typing would have been difficult for someone not familiar with the language, and it would have made the printing job much more expensive, so Ken agreed to give the printer photo-ready copy.

Then Ken had another chance to see what a great team the Mixtec workers were. Cora Mak, Ruth Mary Alexander, Anne Dyk, and Helen Ashdown all went in to Mexico City where a good electric typewriter was available. There they typed the final copy and then proofread it still one more time. They worked hard and fast and had the photo-ready copy finished and off to the printers by the middle of April, 1951. The printers got right to work on the job, and, by the end of June, there were bound copies of the New Testament in the language of the San Miguel Mixtecs.

Ken was very thankful and he sent copies to Angel and his other friends—with a special copy for the mayor. He hoped the believers would use the New Testament while teaching others about Christ, and that belief in Christ would spread throughout the area.

One of the San Miguel men usually read to friends first from the Spanish New Testament. Then he'd pick up the Mixtec New Testament and say, "This says the same as the Spanish does, but we understand it better in our own language." Then he'd read to them from the Mixtec. Was that worth the years and years of work that the New Testament had cost? From Ken's point of view, yes!

21 JUNGLE CAMP

(1947—1948)

Back in 1934 when the first session of Camp Wycliffe was held, it was not only Townsend's intention to teach the students linguistics and anthropology, but he also wanted them to be trained for pioneer living. As long as the Summer Institute of Linguistics sessions were held in Arkansas, the conditions were rustic and the students had practice in getting along without some of the so-called necessities. When SIL was moved to the University of Oklahoma campus, however, one of the things that disappointed Uncle Cam was that the accomodations were so convenient that they did not give training for life among an aboriginal people. When making plans for SIL to serve the peoples in the jungles of Peru, Townsend also made plans to set up a training camp where the young folk involved could learn how to survive in the jungle.

In the fall of 1945, Uncle Cam took a few of the young folks down to Chiapas, Mexico, to a clearing on the edge of the jungle and gave them some practical experience in jungle living. Then, in 1946, Dr. Paul Culley was in charge. He had been a medical missionary in the Philippines for twelve years and had much valuable information to impart. In spite of this, for some reason the young folks, "the campers" as they were usually called, were dissatisfied. The WBT Board of Directors was considering giving up the idea of a jungle training camp, thinking that perhaps that 1946-47 session should be the last. Uncle Cam said that the sessions could be changed, but not dropped—he felt them to be essential if Wycliffe was to continue expanding into areas beyond the reach of modern civilization.

Uncle Cam, with his wife Elaine and their baby daughter Grace, had been down in Peru contacting government officials and helping the young folks to begin their work there. Then in February the Townsends started back to Mexico City, but on the way they stopped off in jungle camp. They had a busy week, then they climbed into a local chartered plane for a flight from the jungle area to Tuxtla where they could transfer to one of the large airlines. The plane crashed on takeoff. Elaine had a dislocated ankle and numerous cuts and bruises, Uncle Cam had a broken leg, but little Grace was not even scratched. The pilot was in serious condition, unconscious most of the time for several days.

Everyone was thankful that Dr. Culley was still there. He and his wife had intended leaving earlier, but stayed on to be with the Townsends. Now the Culleys put aside their own plans and cared for the injured. Without Dr. Culley's help, the pilot probably would not have survived.

Uncle Cam was immobilized because of his broken leg, but that did not stop him from making plans, and dictating letters to facilitate those plans.

One of his first letters was to Ken, asking him to go down to Chiapas, Mexico, to finish out the session with the campers there. Ken had never been considered an outdoor man (not even Uncle Cam looked at him in that light), but Uncle Cam seemed to think of him as a pinch hitter, a person who would come through in an emergency, and he thought of the jungle camp situation as an emergency. He didn't want the program abandoned, and he was afraid that it would be, unless someone was able to organize it.

For his part, Ken was committed to taking the New Testament to minority groups who as yet did not have it, therefore he was ready to tackle anything necessaary to get the job done, even something that did not seem to be in his line. So he wrote back to Uncle Cam that it would be a privilege to have a part in the program, if things worked out so that he could.

Actually, it was not the easiest thing to go to jungle camp right then. Ken, with Evie, the Starks, and a Mixtec family, were all in California at the time (as described in the preceding chapter), trying to finish one more stage in the translation of the Mixtec New Testament. They succeeded, so a couple of weeks after receiving

Uncle Cam's letter, Ken was on his way back to Mexico. (Evie and the children stayed on in California and met Ken in Oklahoma in June.)

Ken was delayed in Mexico City with the flu, but a few days later he left for Chiapas. From Tuxtla, Jim Truxton of the Missionary Aviation Fellowship flew him to jungle camp. The flight took about an hour and twenty minutes (it would have taken about eight days to go by mule). Ken slept most of the way—his remedy for airsickness, but every once in a while he'd peek out at the mountain ranges below, most of them covered with pine trees. He looked out again as they were circling to land on the narrow green strip below. They rolled to a stop near a hanger with a thatched roof. About fifty yards away on a little knoll was a cluster of other buildings with thatched roofs and wattle walls made of parallel poles chinked with twigs and mud. That was where the campers lived. Then on the other side of a little hill was the river.

The month or so Ken was at jungle camp was filled with new sights and experiences for him. For example: walking over roots so tightly intertwined that his feet didn't touch the ground, walking through a tunnel of bamboo—the tops closing in over his head, vines fifty to eighty feet long hanging down from tree branches—often a dozen to a tree, the barking of monkeys (he thought that they sounded like dogs with sore throats), gum trees tapped by the chicle (chewing gum) hunters, gum liquid boiling in great big pots, canoes hewn from mahogany logs, travel on a swift river, a mahogany log so big that the drivers were using eight teams of oxen to haul it to the river.

But his most memorable experience was his trip with Dave Amram, a man who had been running mahogany camps for ten years—he really knew the jungle. He offered to show Ken some old Mayan ruins that the chicle hunters had stumbled on about a year previously. They had found a small temple, and inside it pictures of Mayan life. The Missionary Aviation Fellowship pilot, Jim Truxton, and Phil Mendenhall, thought it would be fun to see the old ruins too, so they all went together.

Phil was a believer in "living off the land," so he said they would not need to take along food. Dave figured that the chicle hunters and the Làcandón Indians would feed them. They knew that they would have to walk for a number of hours, so they were all glad not to have the extra weight to carry.

The first stage was a short flight to a small strip that had been made by the chicle hunters, the men harvesting gum liquid. After eating a lunch of rice, fish, beans, and coffee that the crew gave them, Ken and the others walked about two hours into the woods with a Lacandón Indian as their guide.

They had guessed wrong about living off the land—all they had for supper that night was a couple of tortillas and a few boiled snails. Ken says that you shake the snails hard to get the snail out of the shell, bite off and spit out the little trap door of the shell, and then chew the remainder. The taste wasn't bad, but as a meal it wasn't very filling.

None of the men slept well because cockroaches and fleas by the score climbed into their hammocks. Ken hadn't known that bugs could get into hammocks, so he hadn't used enough insect repellent.

In the morning after a breakfast of two tortillas, they walked four hours, arriving tired and hungry at the ruins. They looked at the temple—old enough that trees several inches in diameter were growing out of the top. Ken couldn't figure out why the temple had not disintegrated.

They didn't stay at the ruins very long because it was another four-hour walk back to the place where they had spent the night. The only food they had was a little dried corn dough mixed in cold water.

In the morning, after a breakfast of two tortillas, they walked two hours back to the airstrip at the chicle camp. From there they flew home to the junglecamp clearing.

The trip had been valuable in that it had taught Ken to really appreciate a clean base to work out from, and to recuperate in. He never forgot how uncomfortable it was to be hungry. Years later he'd talk about having been so hungry that his bones ached.

His experience may have helped the campers in that it made Ken very conscious of the need for preparedness. He didn't try to teach the campers to be "tough," instead he emphasized "comfort consistent with goals." The object was not to rough it, but to be comfortable if possible while getting the job done. He put that attitude into practice back at the clearing, advocating continuing improvement that would make life there more efficient and comfortable.

But Ken didn't forget linguistics during that time at jungle camp. For a couple of months that spring, I had been out in Yatzachi el Bajo, Oaxaca, helping Otis and Mary Leal in the analysis of the tone of the Yatzachi dialect of Zapotec. It was the first time I had served as tone consultant, so Ken figured that I might need some help. After his stay at jungle camp, on his way back to Mexico City, he broke his journey at Oaxaca City, took a truck for half a day, then walked another day, and joined me in Yatzachi. From early in the morning until late in the afternoon we listened to a man pronouncing the Zapotec words and phrases we requested. After a couple of days Ken okayed my analysis; that gave a big boost to my self-confidence.

As usual Ken spent the summer at the University of Oklahoma as a teacher and co-director of the SIL program there. Then he and Evie went out to San Miguel to be with their Mixtec friends.

Ken was appointed director of jungle camp for the fall sessions of 1947 and 1948. He was to set up the program the first month and perhaps return later. Ambrose McMahon was to be his assistant that first year and Earl Adams the second. So, in the middle of November, 1947, Ken left San Miguel and headed for Chiapas.

After a long (about twelve hours), dusty, bumpy ride beyond Oaxaca City, he arrived in Juchitán where Velma Pickett and Marj MacMillan were studying the Juchitán dialect of Zapotec. He worked with them all day, helping them with the tone analysis, but he needed more time at it. He didn't think he should delay his arrival in jungle camp, but he was spending more time than necessary in travel; he was making the trip by second class bus. The girls paid the difference in price between the bus trip and air travel so that he could stay on an extra day and work some more on the tone analysis.

Linguistics was the focus of his attention those two days, but a little surprise item came up. Marj, who everybody knows is an extremely good cook, became overwhelmed with the difficulty of making bread. For some reason, she just couldn't get it to come out right. Ken became aware of the problem and, building on the experience he had those days out in San Miguel when Evie had to stay in bed, he taught Marj how to make bread. Then he continued on his way with a chuckle. Ken loves helping people, but he had not expected to be able to help in the cooking line—expertise in the kitchen is not his bag.

But, down in jungle camp, food and the kitchen took a good bit of his attention. Part of his program was to emphasize "improvision," and that included making appetizing meals out of local materials. The campers went on an experimental spree; they were delighted, for example, when they succeeded in making delicious cereal with toasted ground corn. More unusual was the snail chowder. "Marvelous stuff," Ken said, "once a person is over the psychological hurdle."

Ken emphasized that after arriving where a minority group is living, a person spends most of the time for the next some years in that same small clearing in the jungle. Little by little he improves his living conditions as he learns how to use native materials and succeeds in improvising the necessary furnishings.

Because the 1947 session was the third group of young folks to be at jungle camp, they were able to use some things left by the two previous groups. One of Ken's first assignments, therefore, was to have the campers seek out and describe the dozens of little improvised items that earlier campers had left behind. Then they themselves were supposed to improvise a way of providing something that was still lacking.

Ken intended that the campers should have a research attitude during their time spent in the jungle or some other almost inaccessible place. They should study, recognize the problems, experiment, and write down the results. For example, the campers needed to find a way to preserve meat. Because they raised and slaughtered their own pigs, they either had a whole pig or no meat at all. They decided to try to keep it by smoking it.

Ken and the campers built a smoke house, put the pork inside, and smoked it. It spoiled. Earl Adams remembers that he was impressed when it was apparent that Ken considered the project to be a success, because they now knew that their smoke house would not work. Ken's comment was, "Just charge it up to education." (Actually that is what our Dad used to say when we kids blew something and he had to pay the bill.)

Then they tried a brine cure and dug a cave in the side of a hill to make a cool place where the meat could be kept. That time it didn't spoil.

A research attitude helped in learning outdoor cooking, simple carpentry, maintenance of a generator, etc. Studying things found in the jungle also made life more interesting. One of the things Ken did while there was to collect fish for one of his University of Michigan friends who had asked him what varieties of fish were found in that part of the world. Ken's fish project demonstrated to the campers that he thought they should be willing to contribute to science by helping anyway they could in the part of the world in which they found themselves.

The extreme isolation of the jungle camp area caused tensions to build up in some people. Just to know that they were a seven or eight days' walk from the nearest bus line could cause nervous strain. Sometimes having a lively interest in their surroundings, and a research attitude, helped to keep the tensions from building. Another way of lessening the strain, it seemed to Ken, was to show the campers, soon after they arrived, how to travel in the jungle. He got them out for a hike every day—at first within easy return to the clearing. Earl tells how Ken himself often set the pace. Sometimes he'd put on his big Mexican hat and sing loudly as he strode ahead. The campers enjoyed the hikes although they found it a challenge to keep up with him, and one of those walks eventually became known as "the Pike Hike." Undoubtedly his years of swimming with the Flounders Club (see the next chapter) at the University of Michigan, and tramping the hills of Oaxaca, had helped put Ken in good condition, until, as Betty Adams says, "He was deceptively rugged on the trail."

One of the walks was along the river through thick woods, where for part of the distance, they had to use machetes to hack their way through.

And then they tried the river itself. They used canoes that people of the area had shaped out of mahogany logs. Going up the river, they'd have to get out and pull the canoe over the shallow spots. The canoes were so heavy that dragging them was quite a job. The water was very swift and sometimes difficult to stand against. After going upstream for an hour or two, they turned around and came down again. It was fun going that direction, but a bit scary to shoot the rapids—once in a while getting swamped. A little experience on the rivers was important for those who might some day be on the larger rivers of Peru.

So life at jungle camp could be scary, but it could also be thrilling, like the time Ken had the trainees take a nine-day trek off into an unchartered valley, traveling with a party of lumber men.

Ken told the campers that they were the ones who would have to convince the Board of Directors that the training was worthwhile; he had them write a weekly paper about their experiences, funny happenings, etc. The Board was persuaded, and eventually all new members of Wycliffe Bible Translators were sent for a session at jungle camp, not just those on their way to Peru.

The 1948-49 session was the last time Ken had direct involvment with jungle camp, but Earl Adams, who became director when Ken left, continued to look on him as an advisor. And Ken continued enthusiastic about the program, especially about the campers themselves. He wrote Uncle Cam, "They could not possibly have been more cooperative. They try extremely hard, until we have to be careful not to let them overdo. They do not balk at anything; girls as well as the fellows have helped dig, mix, and slap mud on houses. They're a great gang."

22 ENCOURAGEMENT AT THE UNIVERSITY OF MICHIGAN

(1942—1977)

Ken appreciated very much the opportunity to be at the University of Michigan. More than thirty years ago he wrote his brother, "Every time I meet the top boys in the field, I tend to get excited about something and crossbreed it with ideas of my own." He also liked the stimulus of having the graduate students criticize those ideas, and he, in turn, stimulated them.

Fries told him that he needed to be at Michigan if he were to continue to help his SIL colleagues with their publications. He insisted that Ken could not stop research without stagnation and big loss to SIL. It also became apparent that Ken's connection with Michigan gave SIL prestige in the eyes of the public. It not only helped potential students to decide to study at SIL, but it let governments worldwide know that SIL was academically sound. Those were some of the advantages, but as Ken's letter had also said, he enjoyed it, "I love the chitter-chatter of technical stuff—but am afraid I will die from social chatter if I ever need any."

Ken received his Ph.D. from the University of Michigan in 1942; then he was Research Associate, English Language Institute, for the spring term of 1942; during 1945-46 he had a Lloyd Postdoctoral Fellowship.

When he turned in his summary of what had been accomplished while he had that postdoctoral fellowship, it included: two articles on Mixtec, one on Maya, an article on English vowels, an article on Mazatec written in collaboration with me, one on Otomi in collaboration with Donald Sinclair, the revision and expansion of *The Intonation of American English* (1942 mimeographed, 1945), the revision and expansion of *Phonemics: A Technique for Reducing Languages to Writing* (1947), revision and expansion of *Tone Languages: A Technique for Determining the Number and Type of Pitch Contrasts in a Language, with Studies in Tonemic Substitution and Fusion* (1943 mimeographed, 1948).

And so, when he became Associate Professor in 1948, he already had four books in print.

In *Phonetics* (1943) he had attempted to describe all the sounds of all the languages of all the world. In his book he included all the sounds that he had been able to find descriptions of. Also, he had experimented with his own pronunciation, deliberately making sounds he had never made before. His book included a description of any new sound, grunt, or groan that he had succeeded in making. (That is, everything except whistles and trills—his techniques did not handle them well.) The hope was that he could teach students how to be ready for any speech sound they might happen to meet anywhere (see chapter 13).

In *Phonemics* (1947) he attempted to teach about sounds as they relate to the language system of which they are a part, and how to distinguish the important sounds of that system from the non-important—the important ones help signal contrasts between different words. It teaches how to write those sounds in a practical way for a language which has had no prior alphabet, dictionary, or written grammar.

In *The Intonation of American English* (1942 mimeographed, 1945) he showed how the tone of the voice affects meaning. He gives a list of meanings and shows how they are signalled that way in American English (see chapter 19).

In *Tone Languages* (1943 mimeographed, 1948) he shows how the tone of the voice distinguishes words in some languages (e.g., Chinese). He shows how alphabets can be formed to indicate this important difference.

The arrangement with the University when he became Associate Professor was that he spend only one semester a year there. During the summer he taught at an SIL school, during the other semester he helped SIL members to analyze languages in South America, Nepal, Papua New Guinea, or wherever they were located. (Later the arrangement was changed to two academic years at Michigan and one abroad with the summer still at Oklahoma.)

In 1948 he wanted a change from phonetics, phonemics, tone, and so he began to focus his research on grammar and syntax. By 1954, Part I of his huge (762 pages) *Language in Relation to a Unified Theory of the Structure of Human Behavior* was in print (see chapter 23).

In 1955, with his bibliography constantly getting longer, Ken became a full professor. He continued being responsible for only one semester at the university, but in 1961 arrangements were made whereby Ken would be there both the spring and fall semesters for two consecutive years. Then he had leave the third year.

The last two years before Ken retired in May of 1977, he was made chairman of the Department of Linguistics, and the last year he was also the director of the English Language Institute where he had been a research associate thirty-five years before.

In 1966 Ken was one of five men to receive the Distinguished Faculty Achievement Award for that year. At the convocation at which the awards were presented, he was described as, "An outstanding phonetician, linguistic analyst, and inspiring teacher of literally thousands ... a scholar whose influence is to be found wherever in this world 'linguistics' is a meaningful word."

In 1974 the College of Literature, Science and the Arts of the University awarded him a named professorship and he became the Charles Fries Professor of Linguistics. In recommending him for it, Dean Rhodes said, "Professor Pike's accomplishments and contributions to the field of linguistics coupled with his lifelong originality and energetic activity verge on the legendary."

Ken was especially happy to be named to the chair because Professor Fries had encouraged him, advised him, helped him from 1937 (the first year Ken was at the university), until he died in 1967. Also, when Ken traveled in Africa, the Philippines, Indonesia, and elsewhere, he found it to be advantageous to have his name connected with that of Professor Fries with whom he had worked on the English materials many years earlier.

When Ken was being considered for the professorship, a number of linguists wrote letters recommending that it be awarded to him. Excerpts from some of those letters are included here.

Thomas A. Sebeok from Indiana University wrote, "... Pike is one of the rare academic figures known to me whose eminence in research, versatility in public affairs, and skill in teaching is of equally extraordinary value to the institutions which are fortunate enough to enjoy his many sided services.... I know of hardly an American linguist whose writings, and lecture appearances, have carried his reputation to as many—even to the remotest—corners of our planet. How many linguists are known to the native peoples of Africa, South America, or New Guinea, or in the outbacks of Australia? From personal knowledge, I can report that Pike and his works are extremely well known both in Western and Eastern Europe, including the Soviet Union.... Besides his research, and associated editorial commitments, Pike is one of the most original and active forces in contemporary missionary activities ... he is obviously the *spiritus movens* behind the Summer Institute of Linguistics, and a world wide network of extremely productive Christian endeavor (the feedback of which into academic linguistics also has ramifications which are of capital importance).... Anyone who has heard Pike teach—large groups, as well as small seminars—knows that he is the supreme 'showman' in classrooms of linguistics. He is one of our few colleagues to whom pedagogical achievements mean as much as publications...."

M.A.K. Halliday wrote from Brown University, "Kenneth Pike is a scholar of the highest international standing in linguistics. His major contribution has of course been the development of tagmemic theory, which he initiated and in which he has continued to take the lead. Tagmemics is one of the most important of contemporary linguistic methodologies and has been more widely applied in the description of living languages than any other single approach.... Professor Pike's early work in phonetics and phonology, which first won him international recognition is still widely used and has in no way diminished with the passage of time. Mention might also be made of his outstanding practical ability as a linguist—I would say without hesitation that his combination of theoretical power, descriptive insight and practical facility is unique in the subject."

Eric P. Hamp of the University of Chicago wrote, "Pike's accomplishments and contributions to our field coupled with his lifelong originality and energetic activity verge on the legendary. It is well known that Pike has made fundamental and first rank contributions to several fields of the discipline of linguistics. His work in the field of phonetics makes his name a household word quite literally throughout the world. His book *Phonetics* revolutionized the thinking of the field nearly three decades ago; through advances made in the meantime other books take their places alongside his, but this stimulating classic will never be removed from basic bibliographies in the foreseeable future.... The contributions of Kenneth Pike to the whole gamut of descriptive grammar and syntax have been equally signal and distinguished. He is, after all, the originator of the approach to grammatical analysis known as tagmemics, which is surely one of the three or four major new thrusts in our approaches to grammar during the 20th century.... The interested reader with sufficient patience could easily pursue in Pike's many writings on numerous and often hitherto undescribed languages the rich array of grammatical insights that his perceptive and inquiring mind constantly discloses ... like most linguists of my age I have read large amounts of Pike's writings and can credit much of what I think I know to very direct learning from Kenneth Pike. Pike is not just a professor at Michigan ... he has been in many ways a teacher of us all. It is therefore easy to see that Kenneth Pike is a very eminent man, but his eminence grows out of a background that is truly unusual among academic scholars and that bears further witness to his personal greatness and accomplishment.... Kenneth Pike started out as a missionary who had mastered the language of one of the Mixtec groups in southern Mexico. This is not in itself unusual among linguists; our knowledge of numerous aboriginal languages has begun with the work of missionaries. But most such scholars live out even a distinguished career in considerable isolation and even loneliness. Pike immediately saw his own needs in linguistic knowledge (in the technical sense) and he rapidly came to see the very heart of basic and fundamental problems in their most general context. He has thus become not only a major theoretician but the principal trainer of the largest and most active group of descriptive linguists that the world has ever seen. His students and grand-students among missionaries are active on every continent of the world, and with notable and crucial effect in Mexico, South America, Southeast Asia, and New Guinea.... In bibliographic terms this means that in addition to Kenneth Pike's own prodigious personal output one must credit to his direct influence and teaching a bibliography on hundreds of aboriginal languages over the past two decades that now requires a fat booklet over a couple hundred pages merely to list in brief form. It is fair to say that something like one-half of all the raw data from exotic languages that has been placed at the disposal of theoretical linguists in the past quarter century can be attributed to the teaching, influence, and efforts of Kenneth Pike.... The boyish enthusiasm of Pike in all of his studies and his modesty in attacking every fresh problem would scarcely suggest to the unprepared onlooker that he was in the presence of one of the few really great linguists of the 20th century.''

Mary R. Haas of the University of California at Berkeley wrote, ''Kenneth Pike is an outstanding linguist known the world over for his many accomplishments. I do not think there is any man living who has had first-hand contact with as many totally diverse types of languages as he has, from high literary languages like Spanish and English to languages of the Mexican and South American jungles, the great deserts of Australia, the highlands of New Guinea and the vast plateaus of South Asia. This in itself is a truly stupendous achievement.... But he is not only a man of great practical exper-ience of languages; he is also a man of deep theoretical acumen. Early in his career he worked closely with the late Charles Fries and others in the strict Bloomfieldian tradition. But he was not content with this, particularly because of lack of attention to syntax, and so he developed his own approach, which is now known as tag-memics.... He is also famed as a teacher and as a lecturer and has trained large numbers of people. Many are working as missionaries but many others are teaching at various universities throughout this country and abroad.''

W.F. Twaddell of Brown University wrote, ''His early work on articulatory phonetics has remained substantially unchallenged and unimproved by other researchers. In the field of articulatory phonet-ics he is a virtuoso in practice as well as a formulator. Beyond that field, he has done work and developed techniques for grammatical and syntactic analysis; he has been a scientist in doing the hard work of mastering in depth the language under scrutiny.... His more general theories of linguistic structure and procedures of linguistic analysis are one set of doctrine among several that currently occupy the stage of controversy.... In general, his theoretical studies grow immediately out of his preoccupation with the real problems presented by the analysis of a very wide variety of real languages.... Related to Pike's own research has been his massive influence as an organizer of linguistic training programs and practical enterprises. The Summer Institute has probably turned out more competent producers of useful linguistic descriptions than any graduate school...."

Karl V. Teeter of Harvard University wrote, "For nearly thirty years Pike has been contributing practical and theoretical works of the first rank, from his 1943 book *Phonetics*, to the massive *Language in Relation to a Unified Theory of the Structure of Human Behavior* of 1967.... Everything he has written is significant, and more than one of his articles and books have become classics in the field, for example the book *Phonemics* and the paper "Grammatical Prerequisites to Phonemic Analysis".... He has been no less active as a teacher and lecturer and has freely given of his time to individual and small group discussion. A lecture of his illustrating monolingual elicitation and given in varying forms over a number of years has become internationally known and admired among linguistic scholars as a *tour de force*.... Through all his scholarly accomplishments Pike has consistently maintained a rare humanness, and a friendly and open personality in a field where abrasive types are legion. I first had the good fortune to meet him personally some fifteen years ago when I was a graduate student. I had accosted him at a learned society meeting with a disagreement over a paper he had just read, a disagreement expressed, I am afraid, in rather sharp terms.... Ken Pike's response, after a brief and temperate public answer, was to invite me to meet him a half hour later, at which time he devoted two hours to listening to me and patiently explaining his position. I do not recall whether he finally convinced me on this occasion—I have not always agreed with him—but I came away knowing that I had met a man who was a genuine and accomplished scholar and yet a warm and gentle human being, not a universally encountered combination."

Archibald A. Hill of the University of Texas at Austin wrote, "Professor Pike has been a most original investigator in linguistics, always one who blazed new trails, trails which were lonely when he started down them, but which soon ceased to be so when others followed him.... I will not dwell on Professor Pike's bibliography, except to say it is so copious as to be almost incredible. And in addition to this, it should be pointed out that he has been the principal mover in a whole school of linguists, who have done more to record the out-of-the-way tongues of the world than any group, governmental as well as private."

Albert H. Marckwardt of Princeton University wrote, "Professor Pike's reputation is truly international.... He has been an original force in the field of linguistics, in a certain sense the founder of a school. His driving energy has resulted in the extension of the work of the Summer Institute of Linguistics to almost unbelievable scope and proportion and has resulted in a firm disciplinary base behind the applied work which is its immediate concern. Aside from this one must take into account the personality and character of the man. The combination of kindliness, modesty, and utter devotion to a discipline and a cause is so rare as to be almost unique in the academic world as one encounters it today...."

The letter signed by his colleagues at Michigan said of him, "Kenneth L. Pike is the most distinguished scholar on our linguistics faculty. His contributions to the field of linguistics have been widely recognized both nationally and internationally. A glance at his curriculum vitae and bibliography makes it abundantly evident that this reputation as a leader and creative thinker in the field is well founded. He has pioneered in a variety of research areas in linguistics, and his teaching influence has been such as to have had an effect on literally thousands of students, many of whom have gone on to become outstanding linguists...."

In their recommendations, many of the linguists had mentioned Ken's connection with the Summer Institute of Linguistics. Also, when H.A. Gleason of the University of Toronto was asked what made Ken different from other linguists, he answered, in part, that, because of SIL, Ken had access to data from all over the world, and he got his ideas from data.

Ken, too, was aware of the debt he owed the SIL members. As he was giving his presidential report to the SIL biennial conference after he had received an honorary doctorate from the University of Chicago (1973) and had been named the Charles Fries Professor of

Linguistics (1974), he told his colleagues that he felt ridiculous taking credit for their work. He accepted the honors partly, he said, because he felt that it helped SIL too.

Ken was also very aware of the help he had received from the SIL members who had typed for him: the four girls who had typed the Mixtec New Testament, May Morrison who had typed the Phonemics book, and a sequence of somebodies who had typed umpteen articles and his correspondence.

Ella Marie Button told me about the time she and several others were in Mexico City helping at the biennial SIL conference. While delegates and visitors were in the auditorium listening to some vice president present a project, or perhaps the delegates from the Papua New Guinea branch debate an idea presented by the delegates of the Mexico branch, these girls were off in a room by themselves whacking away on typewriters. Their job was to type a motion from someone's hard-to-read scrawl, or perhaps put someone's report onto stencils.

One morning Ken appeared with a job for them, perhaps it was his presidential report. He handed it in to the one in charge; she took it and assured him that it would be ready by the next day. Then Ken sprang up on a table. He waved his arms, jumped, and shouted—he had become a cheer leader, leading an imaginary crowd in yelling approval of the stenos. Buttons says that it gave them all a big boost.

I don't know that Ken ever led in a cheer for Ruth Brend, but she has certainly deserved several. In 1957 when she became his secretary and research assistant, she not only took care of his correspondence, but she also helped by grading papers, and sometimes by making up exams. She typed manuscripts in the first, second, and third drafts—probably she learned to read Ken's almost illegible handwriting better than he himself could.

Ruth herself was interested in linguistics, but even while she was working on her Ph.D. she still managed to stay caught up with his office work.

When she became a Professor of Linguistics at Michigan State University in 1964, and was no longer working in Ken's office, the amount of work that she turned out that was helpful to SIL continued to be phenomenal. By 1977 she had edited three books: a selection of Ken's writings to commemorate his sixtieth birthday *(Kenneth L. Pike: Selected Writings,* 1972); a collection of works in tone and intonation by SIL members *(Studies in Tone and Intonation,* 1975); a collection of articles using tagmemic theory by numerous authors *(Advances in Tagmemics,* 1974).

Ruth was co-editor with Ken of three more books—but she did most of the work. They were: *Tagmemics: Aspects of the Field,* Vol. I; and *Tagmemics: Theoretical Discussion,* Vol. II, 1976; *The Summer Institute of Linguistics: Its Works and Contributions,* 1977.

One of Ruth's earlier duties had been to try to keep Ken reminded of appointments, but, she says, because of his preoccupation she sometimes had difficulty determining whether or not he had really heard her. At those times, just to be sure, she'd call Evie and give her the information too, hoping that Evie would remind him as the crucial time approached.

There was one appointment that neither Ruth nor Evie ever had to remind him of. In fact, if they tried to schedule something that might conflict with it, he would remind them. For years, three times a week, whenever he was in Ann Arbor, he went down to the pool to swim with the Flounders Club. The men who made up the Flounders were from the Michigan faculty, some graduate students, a few business men, and others. They gathered to play a variety of water polo. They had their own special rules which made Ken describe the game as more like football-in-the-water than like official water polo. The actual number of men who showed up on any one day varied greatly and there were no fixed teams, instead sides were chosen from whoever happened to arrive. Because of the constant rotation, yesterday's foes became today's colleagues.

One of the things Ken enjoyed especially about meeting with the Flounders was that it gave him contact with the men of the community as a whole. In the book *The Flounders: Fifty Years* (1976) by Clark Hopkins, there is a short biography of the members, giving the careers they have or have had. An idea of the breadth of experience represented by that small group of men is shown by the list of some of their fields: anthropology, biology, Eastern languages, forestry, fire department, fish and wildlife, football coach, geography, geologist, executive of the Standard Oil Corporation, judo expert, nuclear engineering, epidemiologist, physician, private law practice, registrar, surgeon.

After the game, the men would go to a restaurant to have lunch together and any topic could be brought up and discussed from multiple viewpoints by both the "specialist" and the "ridiculist." Ken loved it. As he wrote to a colleague in the anthropology department, "I have enjoyed more than you would suspect our too few contacts.... Life is richer for knowing people with basic convictions so different from one's own—and yet at points so close together (wearing camouflage)."

The thumbnail sketch of Ken that appeared in *The Flounders: Fifty Years* (1976, p. 32-33) is as follows: "A master of mind over matter. Trained to be a missionary and a linguist, he came to the English Language Institute from religious training in Oklahoma under a deep cloud of doubt among faculty here and so he became leader of them all—in worldwide travel—the transcription of strange languages—the ability to pick up and field a language from scratch—he turned out to be a genius, and has been sought in South America, Africa, and Asia—especially in the South Pacific—he has been an outstanding genius.

"Very thin, and seemingly frail he entered water polo with dynamic enthusiasm and no ability whatsoever. He could swim but not very well; he could throw but inaccurately; I forget if he could catch. He was all arms and elbows and thrashed unmercifully—worse than Ivan the Terrible he was, and like a leech in following an opponent to keep him out of the play. Tremendously enthusiastic about the game—he took to competition with zest and keeps his zeal undiminished. Slowly, slowly, slowly he obtained an inkling of what the game was about—improved his swimming, throwing, catching, and understanding until he has become a very respectable player but one always with dangerous elbows. An incurable optimist, he hoped to convert us all to the true religion—expounded in books which he wrote and presented to Club members. He brought up his son Steve in the right path to be a player of real ability."

Ken certainly likes telling people about things he reads in the Bible. He is delighted when someone turns the conversation in that direction. For example, a professor of philosophy from another university was visiting in Ann Arbor, and some philosophers and linguists were having lunch together, talking about language and communication. The guest was half-way around the table from Ken, but he boomed out, "Pike, I heard a strange rumor about you. I heard that you were a missionary. How about it?"

A little exchange while they defined terms, then Ken asked, "Would you say that God knows you by name?"

The philosopher thought a bit, "No," he answered, "I wouldn't."

"Well, I would," said Ken. "The character of God includes the fact that He knows us by name."

But sometimes it was the other way around. Sometimes one of his fellow professors would jog Ken's memory about a fact in the Bible. There was the time Ken had been at a gathering of linguists and some of them had been giving him a hard time about his theories. They disagreed with him about this, and they disagreed with him about that.

On the way home (he was riding with Professor Fries), he was in a rather discouraged mood, and he said with a sigh, "Sometimes I feel like I'm going out against those guys with nothing but five smooth stones."

Fries responded with a question, "Isn't that enough?"

He couldn't have given Ken a better answer (I Sam. 17:40-49).

Many linguists disagreed with Ken's theories, advocating theories of their own. Ken listened to them, perhaps asking himself some of the questions he advises students to ask, "Is the theory useful; is it fruitful? Will it be a good instrument of investigation?"

One of his former students said of him, "He dares to be different; he is eccentric and dares to be labeled that way.... Sometimes it takes courage to be different."

Another former student commented that Ken encouraged them to look at different points of view, and then added, "Pike expects a lot from his students."

Ken did expect a lot from them, and he enjoyed contact with them too. For years, every semester, Ken and Evie invited students to their home. They would have them out for a series of evenings, ten students at a time, until all of them had come. There would be a conversation starter, perhaps some of Ken and Evie's artifacts from Peru, or the students, many of them from abroad, would tell about their homelands. Evie would serve refreshments, and Ken would sometimes let them choose, as a party favor, one of C.S. Lewis's books.

Frequently Ken and Evie invited a foreign scholar home for dinner, and if he happened to be a vegetarian, that really tested Evie's ingenuity as she tried to prepare food that he would enjoy.

If the foreign guest had never seen a football game, Ken might take him to one, and he made sure the guest understood what was going on after he got there. Ken explained how points were made, the requirements for first downs, the cause and effect of penalties, the function of a quarterback, why a team punts, etc. The explanations were both thorough and interesting—but the guest was probably exhausted when the game was over.

The football season was apt to be a busy time for Ken and Evie. For a decade or more they invited anybody from the Inter-Varsity Christian Fellowship (in Ann Arbor), and anybody who attended the Bible class Ken taught on Sundays, to drop in after each football game. The largest number to accept the invitation was forty, and the smallest fifteen. Evie served refreshments, and everybody had fun rehashing the game.

Throughout the years Ken put quite a bit of thought and effort into teaching the Bible class. It was attended, for the most part, by university students. In 1962 he used his *With Heart and Mind* (1962) as a text book, and during the week the students talked about the assigned chapter with other students and then reported back any interesting problems or discussion that arose out of it. In 1973 Ken's topic was, "Biblical Biography," and when studying each character (Esau, Judah, Miriam, Balak, etc.) they tried to answer the question, "What personal, civic, and religious issues did he face? What character crisis did these provoke? How do these parallel dilemmas of our own?" Sometimes the discussions were profound, and the students seemed to find the class helpful.

Hearing about the Bible classes, some SIL members (who seldom call each other "missionaries") chuckled and called Ken and Evie "Michigan-aries."

23 LANGUAGE AND BEHAVIOR

(1948—1977)

In 1948 Ken became Associate Professor at Michigan, Professor Fries urged him to continue his research and to continue writing. Ken was wondering where he should put his attention. (Evie has long said that if she could once get Ken to put his attention on something, the problem was immediately half solved. Her trouble has been that she sometimes couldn't get him to focus on the thing she thought needed action.)

By 1948 Ken had been working on phonology for thirteen years and he wanted a change. So he decided to take a look at grammar. He started hunting for a unit in grammar that would be analogous to the phoneme in phonology. He had a hunch that he could make a generalized definition of any linguistic unit in terms of contrast between the unit under consideration and other units, the amount of variation which that unit had, and the place where the unit occurred—that is, the distribution (or the function) of that unit.

As he pursued the idea further, he found that he also wanted to define each specific language as a linguistic unit, but if he were to do that, then he would have to state into what that language was distributed. That was when he began to consider that language (verbal behavior) was embedded in culture—something larger than verbal behavior.

Then, in June of 1949, he was studying a business letter, intending to describe it as a linguistic unit. He was analyzing it as a unit with contrast, variation and distribution. (Various salutation forms could be substituted for one another in the space where the salutation usually occurs; different dates could be put into the space where the date was usually put, etc.) Everything seemed to be fine. Then suddenly, he realized that, in Bloomfieldian terms, the letter was not language at all because the message was on paper (not spoken) and writing was not considered to be speech. At that moment he also realized that he had crossed from language (verbal behavior) into nonverbal behavior. He said that it was like crossing the sound barrier, but he hadn't felt the bump that he had supposed would be there.

From then on he asserted that culture (behavior) and language could both be described within the same theory.

That was the way that Ken's tagmemic theory developed to include anthropology—it was a complete accident, unintended. He had not attempted to build such a theory, nor had he ever dreamed of it as a goal. Rather he had started out trying to find a practical way of handling language materials, something that would be useful to Bible translators; he had been trying to find generalizations that would help him to teach students how to analyze language.

When he realized that the theory could include nonverbal behavior, he intended to cover all phases of it. But time ran out. He had to settle for less anthropology and concentrate on linguistics. Hymes in his review (Hymes, 1969) was one who noticed and regretted that Ken had not carried on with anthropology.

That same business letter helped him to crystalize another idea. He noticed that there were breaks in the typed lines. That is, there were tiny breaks between the "letters"; there were bigger breaks between "words"; there were even bigger breaks between "sentences"; and bigger breaks still between things people call "paragraphs."

With an intuitive leap, he assumed that he was looking at a hierarchy, but it was a hierarchy that had nothing to do with meaning because he could still recognize it even when he was looking at a letter typed in a foreign language. So, this could not be a hierarchy that went from phonetics (or phonemes) to meaningful chunks (morphemes) as he, and others, had previously thought a linguistic hierarchy to be. Now he saw that language had a phonological hierarchy that was not entirely dependent upon the meaning of the words. The smallest unit of that phonological hierarchy was a phoneme which combined into syllables; and syllables combined into stress groups (phonological words); and stress groups combined into a still larger unit. He had already been considering a syllable to be a phonological unit, but it had not fit well into his model. Now, to his delight, it locked into place.

Once he was certain that he had a phonological hierarchy, he started looking for a hierarchy in grammar and he found one. Later he described a lexical hierarchy (then still later, because he wished to treat concepts more generally, he revised again to "referential" hierarchy). Later still, he looked at language from the static point of view—language as made up of sequences of discrete particles, and from the dynamic point of view—language seen as made up of waves of motion, etc. He also looked at it from a functional point of view—language seen as a patterned system. And from other points of view, and from other points of view, and from other... (Ken tells the history of tagmemic theory in the article, "Toward the Development of Tagmemic Postulates," 1976 and in "Crucial Questions in the Development of Tagmemics—the Sixties and the Seventies," 1971.)

But it didn't all happen at once. And it wasn't easy. In fact, sometimes he became very weary. Then he'd tell himself, and sometimes his colleagues, that being weary was a great privilege, because when he was weary at the end of the day, then he knew that he had given all that he had to the Lord—he had done all that was required of him. If at the end of the day he was thoroughly rested, it made him a little uneasy—perhaps he should have done more, he thought.

But he did need a good chance to work, and a grant for the academic year of 1952-53 from the Rockefeller Foundation helped give him that opportunity.

In 1954, Part I, the first seven chapters, of *Language in Relation to a Unified Theory of the Structure of Human Behavior* was published (by the Summer Institute of Linguistics of Glendale [now of Huntington Beach], Calif.) The next three chapters, Part II, was published in 1955, and the last seven chapters, Part III, was published in 1960. Then a revised edition, all in one volume with 762 pages, came out in 1967 (published by Mouton, The Hague, Netherlands). Ph.D. candidates found the discussion of the literature and the bibliography contained in the book to be helpful; a number have mentioned that it was a good place to begin most any linguistic study.

But Ken did not have to wait for the book to be published to be able to see that the results of his research were being put to practical use. He became really excited when he saw that the analysis of clauses and sentences (the old bothersome problem of syntax) was being solved by the new theory. Not only were some Ph.D. candidates using it in their theses, but it was almost immediately taught in at least two of the SIL schools.

Much of the spread and understanding of the theory was due to the excellent support Ken had from the SIL grammar staffs. In the early fifties, for example, at the University of Oklahoma, Velma Pickett, then head of the first-year grammar department, tutored her staff and led them and the students through clause analysis so smoothly that the students hardly knew that that part of Pike's theory had not been done by a class before. A mimeographed copy of her text, with the theory summarized and with language problems illustrating it, was published in 1956.

Ben Elson was also, with great success, teaching his staff and the students in the SIL school at the University of Washington. His textbook was published in 1958, and a revised edition in 1959.

Then in 1960, Ben Elson and Velma Pickett collaborated and wrote *Beginning Morphology-Syntax*. In 1962, with a revised edition in 1964, they wrote *An Introduction to Morphology and Syntax*. It has been widely used. For years it was the standard text not only in most of the SIL schools, but in some non-SIL schools as well. It was supplemented by the *Morphology-Syntax Laboratory Manual*, 1960, which had been compiled by William R. Merrifield, Constance M. Naish, and Calvin R. Rensch. In the laboratory manual forty-six languages were used in making up the problems which gave the students practice in applying the theory.

Ken was especially pleased when Walter A. Cook, S.J. of Georgetown University wrote *Introduction to Tagmemic Analysis* and used it in his courses there.

In 1971 and 1972, Darlene L. Bee in the SIL school in Auckland, New Zealand, was teaching what she called "Neo-Tagmemics" because, she said, it differed so much from tagmemics as defined by Ken. Both students and staff had been enthusiastic about the course, and she had her lectures typed up from a tape recording so that she could use them in a new textbook for beginning students. It was fortunate that she had made such careful notes and had prepared so well, because, when she died a little later, her colleagues, Alan Healey and Doreen Marks, were able to prepare the book for publication. *Neo-Tagmemics: An Integrated Approach to Linguistic Analysis* was published in 1973.

Bob Longacre, for many years the department head for the advanced grammar course, wrote a textbook for advanced students and field workers. His book, *Grammar Discovery Procedures*, was published in 1964. He was the one who pushed ahead on discourse theory and its practical application, and he and Ken both profited from their many discussions of tagmemic theory in general. (There is a beautiful summary of the development of discourse analysis in Longacre's article, "Discourse," [Longacre, 1976].)

Tagmemic theory was the topic of one entire section of the Eleventh International Congress of Linguists held in Bologna, Italy, in 1972. The papers were well received and a lively discussion followed each.

But Ken knew that not everything interesting and helpful about tagmemic theory, or any linguistic theory, had been discovered yet. He encouraged his students and colleagues on, telling them, "God will not rob our grandchildren of the fun and strength gained by their finding out linguistic information which is both useful and exciting. Otherwise His world would have been dull centuries ago. So, we cannot hope to finish all the practical or important discoveries, clean up the research task, and let our successors do the dull ditch digging. There will always be a horizon."

Sometimes he stimulated expectancy of discovery in a slightly different way, "You do not give the whole bowl of candy to the first child to reach the party, and God has both linguistic excitement and practical breakthroughs waiting for our grandchildren."

Probably none of the authors of the textbooks on tagmemics followed all of Ken's tagmemic theories, rather they modified parts here and there as it seemed useful to them.

That was also true of Ken's colleagues who were studying little-known languages all over the world. Many would gather for a month or two at workshops where they could receive help from someone who had more experience than they did, and who usually had a Ph.D. in linguistics. By 1978 there were over ninety-five SIL members who had Ph.D.'s in linguistics, and many of them helped their colleagues in language analysis and, subsequently, in writing an article setting forth that analysis.

Ken was always very aware that there was more to learn both about linguistic and nonlinguistic things, and he never lost an opportunity to get information from someone he considered competent in a specific area.

Professor Eric P. Hamp of the University of Chicago is a specialist in Indo-European languages and Ken's background included very little in that area. Hamp tells about the time he and Ken happened to be sitting together as they were flying from one city to another. Ken turned to him and asked, "While we're just sitting here undisturbed, could you outline for me what you think to be some of the major historical developments that led from Indo-European through the Greek of classical antiquity to what we find in the New Testament?" Hamp undertook the task while Ken listened, questioned, and asked for more.

Sometimes it seems that Ken is almost as eager as that to learn from a friend about the real estate business, or from another friend about the exploration of oil, or from a rock hound about why some rocks are more special than others.

Occasionally his search for wisdom gets derailed, like the time Joe Profita gave a three-day seminar on business management to some SIL directors. After it was all over, Ken woke up to the fact that he had missed something. He had a half hour between appointments, so he asked Joe if he would summarize for him the information he had given at the seminar. So Joe started. Ken listened for ten minutes, then something came up that to him seemed analogous to something in linguistics. That started him talking and for the next twenty minutes, it was Joe who listened—he was sort of relieved, glad not to have to try to summarize three days of lectures in a half hour.

But Ken doesn't forget the information that he picks up hither and yon. Bits of it come out in his linguistic lectures, or are used as examples in a devotional talk. Perhaps that is part of the reason why it seems to Evie and me that Ken never gives the same lecture twice. It keeps his grammar staff, and others, sitting in on his lectures—they can never predict what they are going to miss.

One summer at the SIL on the University of Oklahoma campus, Ken had about half a dozen people on his first-year grammar staff, and there were more than a hundred students taking the introductory grammar class. Ken didn't lecture every day, but on the days he did lecture, the students all met in one big auditorium-like classroom. On other days they were divided into sections and the assistants taught.

On the first day of classes, a couple of students arrived late, and by the time they had made their way to the building where the classes were held, Ken was already lecturing. The two students watched the numbers over the doors and found their way to the one listed on their sheet of instructions. Quietly they slipped into the back of the classroom. With students, plus staff, plus visitors, it had more people than they could ever imagine being in a grammar class. Then too, as they listened to the energetic man up in front, they didn't recognize a thing that seemed to them to be grammar. Quietly they slipped out and went back to Administration to tell them that the instruction sheet must be wrong; that room they had gone to didn't have a grammar class in it, at least not at this hour.

Administration asked them to describe the man who had been talking. Then they told them firmly that, indeed, that was the correct classroom. What was more, it was Dr. Kenneth L. Pike, President of the Summer Institute of Linguistics who had been teaching; they should return to the classroom at once—there was still time to get in on the last few minutes.

The news leaked to Ken's grammar staff. They laughed and shouted with glee—so did the phonetics staff. All up and down the corridor there were chuckles that day. Everybody knew that sometimes it is hard to keep Ken in sight—let alone to understand the entire lecture.

Probably Ken had been trying to stimulate the students to probe the horizons, or to at least realize that the horizons are there. He knew that parts of his lectures were over the heads of the beginners—but he kept right on including those parts in his lectures. He might justify that with one of his proverb-like sayings, "We cannot afford to ignore impractical theory.... Part of a student's job is to try to follow the most impractical material—there will be a little mental residue that may prove helpful later." And so he urged staff and students, not only to pay attention to all of his own lectures, but to others people's theories as well.

He knew that even important bits of the theory might not be applied for some time, but that objection could be pushed aside with another of his sayings, "As it takes time for rain on the mountain to reach the dry plain, so also from basic theory to application."

Ken wanted very much to be a help to those first-year students, and his choice to serve them influenced his decision as to where he would put his energy next. It seemed to Ken and Evie that the students needed to know more about meaning, discourse, paragraph structure, etc., and also the way one linguistic unit could affect another.

Ken and Evie knew that it was impossible to give the students a competely mechanical way of working toward an answer, but they wanted them to have a heuristic, a guess and check, procedure that would lead them to a good, helpful analysis of a language even when neither staff nor student had ever heard of that language before, and even when the language might have a type of structure that not even the staff member had imagined possible.

After talking it over, Ken and Evie came to the conclusion that they could present the material better with a new textbook. So, in 1971, they started work on a textbook for beginning grammar that would include parts of the theory that was not in the other books.

By 1975 Ken had made a good draft of the material as he thought it should be presented, but Evie, an expert pedagogue, was uneasy about part of it. For almost twenty years she had been teaching grammar to beginning linguistic students, and she had a well-developed feel for what the students would assimilate, and for the most successful sequence with which Ken's theories could be presented.

The 1975 draft did not follow that sequence, and some of the material, in her opinion, would not be useful for beginning students. She started pointing out to Ken some of the parts that she thought should be put first, versus parts that should be held until later on.

So Ken did something about it. He got out the scissors and cut his 1975 draft into paragraphs. Then he and Evie sorted the paragraphs into topics and made sections by clipping the topics together. Then they lined up the sections in the order of presentation that Evie thought was best for beginning students.

The next job, Ken said, was Evie's and he insisted that she do it.

Evie was to rewrite the material, making a continuity out of the uprooted paragraphs. She was to restate his ideas the way she did when she was teaching the theory—it would still be his theory, showing how he looked at language.

So Evie began, but she was slow—at least in comparison to the speed with which Ken did things. In order to spend more time at her desk, she limited her social life to a minimum. People weren't invited for dinner, and she was declining most invitations to go out. But it was apparent in the late fall of 1975 that Evie was not going to get the job done unless, somehow, more time was made available to her.

So, again, Ken did something about it. He washed both the breakfast and dinner dishes for the next four months, that is, during the time that Evie was rewriting the book. The very thought of Ken's washing dishes all that time appalled Evie; she knew how he hated routine, noncreative work. But Ken argued his point—she needed the time, and that was one way he could help to provide it.

As they worked together as a team, the book began to fall into shape.

Once Evie had rewritten a paragraph, however, the matter did not end there. Paragraph by paragraph, almost sentence by sentence, they discussed the way she had restated a portion. Sometimes she had misunderstood the theory and had to rewrite. A time or two, she convinced Ken that he should accept her way of looking at it. They kept discussing and rewriting until both were satisfied.

All that was not easy for Ken; he was accustomed to reworking a consultee's material—not to having his own material picked apart. But he valued Evie's help and he stuck with it.

One cause of disagreement between them was that Ken wanted to include more theory than Evie thought was possible for a beginning student to assimilate. In the end they came out with a good compromise—they put stars beside the paragraphs that the advanced students should have available, but that were not required by the beginning student at that point in the course.

Actually Evie restated about two-thirds of the finished copy. She says that she had not been competent to restate the other third; part of that third had to do with language units that were more inclusive than the sentence (discourse); the other part of the third had to do, not with the grammar or words, but rather with the people and events (real or imaginary) to which those words refer.

That last part which Evie says she was incapable of writing is just the part where, Ken says, she made an important theoretical contribution to him. She had pointed out that an adequate description of an event must include the people's explanation of why they did such a thing—knowing their purpose for doing it gives insight into their world view.

Ken and Evie had tested the material in class for several semesters before the time, in 1977, when *Grammatical Analysis* by Kenneth L. Pike and Evelyn G. Pike was finally in print. Both were satisfied that the effort and the long hours they had put on the project had been worth it; the book was proving to be helpful to the students.

24 PRESIDENT OF SIL

(1942—1979)

The Summer Institute of Linguistics was incorporated in 1942, and from then until 1979 Ken was President. Every two years delegates representing the SIL membership meet to elect the board of directors and conduct other business. They set policies which are to be followed throughout the corporation, hear reports from the various fields, and from the international administrators. When they take up different questions, the point of view of more than thirty countries may be considered, since each of them is either the home country of some of the delegates, or the place where they have been working.

The delegates from one part of the world may favor a very different solution from those from another part, and the discussion can be both lively and emotional.

As President, and therefore chairman of the SIL conference sessions, Ken tried to keep business moving on the floor, but at the same time he held things up enough to make sure that everyone knew which side of a question a "yes" vote represents. He was especially conscious of the new delegates, explaining the procedures to them, telling them, "The rules are designed to help you get what you want."

After a count was made and a motion was carried, Ken's fist slapped the podium, "Passed!" At the beginning of a conference, that startled the newcomers and there was a slight chuckle, but soon it was ignored as just another Pike characteristic.

Ken valued discussion, convinced that a group could come to a better decision if various aspects of a problem has been presented, and that a group worked together better if those in the minority had had a chance to express their opinions. At times he said, "We've had three people speak in favor of this motion; now I'd like to hear from someone who is against it."

Frequently the discussion of a motion went on for hours. A particularly hard problem may have had considerable committee work, then floor discussion, and more committee work. When the motion was finally passed, it was usually with a good majority, because it had been discussed, or modified until most of the delegates had been convinced of its value.

After a very difficult problem had been resolved, and Ken had whacked a firm, "Passed!" he sometimes stood and shouted, "Praise the Lord!" Others stood with him and he led them in singing some favorite such as, "It will be worth it all, when we see Jesus...."

Once, as part of his presidential report to conference, Ken burst out with, "God alone could have taken us to 560 language groups.... He alone could have called out such a strong, competent crew. He alone could have raised up the millions in support.... He alone opened doors ... and He alone keeps shut the doors we think He ought to open. He reigns! He rules! He's Boss. And I bow and say, 'Thank you, Lord.' "

Especially when giving his report as President of SIL (but at other times as well), Ken urged his colleagues to put all they have into the job of Bible translation. Sometimes he told them to hurry, "Pretend that today is tomorrow. Tomorrow 'tomorrow' may be too late."

Sometimes he reminded them that translating the New Testament for minority groups is a team job, "Not one of us can handle it by ourselves.... We need to be sensitive to when our brother needs help and try for just a moment to carry that load—even if just for a moment." He said that every weak man must carry his own little load, and that the strong must carry part of the load for the weak, but that the strong man's back would break if he had to carry all the little loads of all the weak.

Sometimes he urged the administrators to have some of their workers take time out to get Ph.D. degrees. "Degree credentials are needed for teaching in our schools, and for some government and academic contacts.... Yet far more important is the fact that during the training the students learn how to survive a difficult problem, how to walk around it if unsolvable, how to check the literature so they don't lose years 'reinventing the wheel', and ... something of the technique of helping others." He adds, "Good technology gives rapid success, but breadth of exposure to theoretical conflict gives independence and flexibility in times of stress."

When someone objected to the time that must be spent in acquiring a degree, he said, "An oak tree does not give bananas, but its boards stand up to a lot of stepping on, so persons trained slowly and at length may help us survive the trampling of hostile forces."

Even back in 1957 he was reminding the administrators that some of the women were very well able to fill high academic positions; and he was urging the women to be willing to take high academic positions. But he added the caution (for both men and women) that graduate work should follow personal interest, if at all possible. He said, "Graduate work along the lines of sheer duty is usually unproductive on the Ph.D. level."

Sometimes he supported Dick Pittman's insight, that the SIL linguists needed to co-author articles with national scholars wherever feasible. Ken asked, "Do you suppose that loving your neighbor as yourself would overlap with helping a national to get material ready to publish under his own name?"

Sometimes he reminded members that producing and publishing technical linguistic papers and monographs was an essential and substantial part of their task, reminding them of the importance of the translation-linguistic-literacy triangle established by Uncle Cam, the founder of Wycliffe Bible Translators and the Summer Institute of Linguistics. Ken urges his colleagues not to neglect any of the three.

Sometimes he reminded the members of how important the administrators are to SIL. He says that the difference between SIL and other organizations in terms of turning out linguistics and Bible translations, is not in the personnel involved, but in the administration which encourages the presence of linguists, and arranges people's programs so that some of the members can specialize in the academic side of the work. Ken considered simple linguistic chit-chat to be important and urged the administrators to encourage an atmosphere where members could swap ideas with one another. And those ideas didn't have to be based on Ken's own theory—tagmemics. During the 1966 conference he sponsored a motion that the SIL schools should not be restricted to any one linguistic theory, but that all theories should be allowed.

Sometimes he reminded his colleagues that they should think of themselves as servants of local scholars and government officials. In fact, they should count their masters "worthy of all honor" (I Tim. 6:1). One of his ways of emphasizing that point of view was to say, "Choose to be a servant of man and you can be under no threat of losing status—a doormat cannot be lowered lower."

Ken frequently reminds himself that he is a servant, especially when he is working with his colleagues. If he is a servant, then it is the colleague who is boss, and even if the colleague angers him, he mustn't snarl because a servant is not allowed to snarl at his boss. That is not easy for Ken to remember; for years he has struggled to be gentle and it grieves him when he fails.

When Ken was acting as chairman of the conference sessions he had to be constantly alert as he guided the motions through the parliamentary process and made sure that people with differing opinions about the topic had a chance to express their views. The chairman's spot was a tension-filled, tiring place to be. Ken knew that eventually someone else would have to be chairman. His comment, "Why wait until I retire? These people are capable; let them begin now!" So, Cal Rensch, Frank Robbins, and Sarah Gudschinsky began to chair the meetings. Ken liked it that way; he was able to relax, and even slip out once in a while to do something else while the meetings were going on.

As the organization grew bigger, the responsibilities of the administrators increased and Ken felt that if he were to give top priority to workshops and to helping the young scholars of SIL to develop, then he would not be able to give as much time to administration as he felt it needed. His load was made lighter in 1972 when the Board appointed Calvin Rensch to be Linguistic Coordinator for the corporation. Ken shed a few more responsibilities still, when the Board appointed Frank Robbins to be Vice President of Academic Affairs. (Robbins had already been Coordinator for the eight SIL schools for a year previous to that time.) Ken was delighted and grateful for how well the men picked up and carried the load. It meant that he could spend more time in research and writing.

For years he had been grateful to George Cowan who, since 1958, has been President of Wycliffe Bible Translators. When George was contacting people and preparing schedules for the Board meetings of WBT, or for the WBT conferences, the arrangements he was making for WBT were also applicable to the SIL Board meetings and to SIL conferences. Because he did more than his share of the work, Ken, as chairman of the SIL Board, was saved days of time.

When the Summer Institute of Linguistics and the Wycliffe Bible Translators were about to be incorporated in 1942, William G. Nyman had been asked to be the Secretary-Treasurer. Before he would accept, he insisted that he with Uncle Cam, Eugene Nida, and Ken kneel in prayer and promise the Lord that none of them would quit the organization until at least five years had passed. Those four would be the founding core of the Board, and Mr. Nyman considered that all of them had strong opinions, and that without that promise things would soon fly apart. He figured that if they managed to stay together for five years, the team might then have a chance to last considerably longer than that.

There is no doubt that Nyman had been wise. Ken remembers that but for that promise he himself would have quit. The board meetings (with about twenty members) were tension-filled as someone (in the early days it was usually Uncle Cam) tried to persuade those of differing opinions to yield to his. Usually Uncle Cam succeeded.

Each board meeting was a crisis. Those with non-Townsend opinions did not give up easily and the debates were long and earnest. For the first twenty years, Ken, except for once or twice, backed Uncle Cam. Perhaps he helped most by making explicit some of Uncle Cam's ideology. Ken figures that an organization can get underway as people follow someone with charisma and personal strength. Then, however, if the organization is going to be maintained after the leader is gone, or after the organization has a large number of members (so many that the new member does not have personal contact with the leader), the ideological factors must be made explicit. If they are explicit, then someone else can pass them on to the newcomers.

Ken has great admiration for Uncle Cam and confidence in him. He admires his insights and the way he can judge the national situation in a Latin American country. But, as time has passed, he has also seen that Uncle Cam can misjudge. Perhaps, because he has learned so much from Uncle Cam, that is why he becomes so tense when he finds that his judgment and conscience make him take the non-Townsend side of an argument.

The Board-meeting days are not easy on the other men either. Tensions rise as this policy is discussed, that program is reviewed, and that action of a vice president is questioned. (The Hefleys have described some of the more outstanding issues in their book *Uncle Cam,* Word Books, Waco, Texas 1974.) As one man after another gives his opinion (or as the same man keeps giving one more reason why his opinion is right), the meetings get quite tedious, or exhausting, or distressing. Occasionally Ken's ability to be explicit about a policy is used on the non-Townsend side and that is especially distressing to both Ken and Uncle Cam.

At especially strenuous times, Ken's tension may be manifested by a mouthful of canker sores, or by blisters on his feet. To try to keep the blisters to a minimum, Ken pulls off his shoes—the blisters don't form as quickly when his feet are cool. And he tries, not very successfully, to be relaxed.

All that can give a strange appearance to the Board meetings: the chairman (Ken), conducting the meetings with his shoes off, and, at least once, while he lay flat on his back. The first time they attend the sessions, that startles even Americans who are accustomed to a relaxed atmosphere.

For Ken the hard sessions are endurable because he is convinced that the organization is held together by the very fact that everyone is given a chance to express his opinion, and that others, therefore, have the chance to hear those opinions refuted or modified.

After the May 1978 meeting, he wrote one of his colleagues on the Board why he thought there was so much tension. His conclusion was that, "We have for years specifically set ourselves up as *servants* of the membership. Had the opposite been true, with the Board being *directors* in fact, then with very quiet voices we could say 'no' or 'come' and there would be no decision problem remotely such as we have—but neither would there be the likelihood of remotely as many people in the organization as we have. I believe God guided us—but He sure guided us into tension."

Ken compares SIL to a human body with muscles. Each muscle can pull but never push. When a person holds his hand steady, it isn't because a lot of muscles are all pulling in the same direction, but because some are pulling upward, some sideways, some downward, etc., and all of them are obeying the head. In that same way SIL has a job to do, and the Holy Spirit as the head guides each member. Some members are pulling one direction and some another. Because they balance each other, SIL stays on course, doing linguistics and literacy, and translating the New Testament into the languages of people who have not had it before.

Ken is also helped to carry on because he knows that none of the members want to bruise or destroy one another. As one pulls this way, and one pulls that, they are working together to get the job done that each believes the Lord has given SIL to do.

25 TEACHER

The job of translating the New Testament for minority peoples seemed to be getting bigger and bigger as the SILers kept learning of more and more groups in more and more countries who were preliterate. But the members of SIL worked together well and with drive and energy. By 1977 they were working in more than 650 languages.

One important facet of the job was giving linguistic training to the young folks who were looking forward to learning one of the little-known languages. To make it easier for them to get training, other schools were started in the USA and one each in Australia, England, West Germany, and for several years in Canada and New Zealand. Also, in order to cooperate with local educational institutions, SIL provided staff for linguistic training in Brazil, Guatemala, India, Mexico, Nepal, Nigeria, Papua New Guinea, Peru, the Philippines, and Viet Nam, and for Native Americans in Santa Fe, New Mexico. (For a history of the SIL schools, see Robbins, 1977.)

The main emphasis had been on linguistics, but translation theory and translation techniques were also developed. (For a summary of those most involved in the development of the theory, see Moore, 1977.) Because students who expected to work with people who spoke a minority language usually found themselves living in a culture different from their own, and because they needed a knowledge of the culture in order to translate, more and more time was spent on teaching anthropology. (For a summary of SIL research in anthropology, see Dye and Merrifield, 1977.) From the very beginning, literacy had been considered an important part of the program.

The SILers wanted to help their new friends to read and write, to have an opportunity for personal growth, and to integrate with the national culture (see Gudschinsky, 1977). All of that took a lot of good and capable staff, and it was a relief to Ken when he saw his colleagues develop and then assume responsibility.

Once his head was aching, literally, because of the pressure of all the things he saw that needed to be done. Then he saw George Cowan move in and pick up the responsibility. Ken's head stopped aching right then.

Of course as his colleagues developed linguistically, they did not necessarily follow his theories—although it pleased him when they did. Ken liked metaphors and as he thought of his colleagues, he applied this metaphor. "When a person lights a fuse to a bomb, or dynamite, he runs and ducks. Only a fool hangs around. I have been desperately trying to light fuses to Ph.D. growers. Shouldn't I jump, duck, and be found somewhere else? How sad to stick around and be splattered about...."

Sometimes his comment was sweeter. "As an Institute ... we must somehow cover as much of the field as possible. For a long time we have had people studying for their doctorates in a variety of places, with a variety of viewpoints. We must continue to welcome this variety, as we do the varieties of spring flowers—with different odor, for a different soil ... and attractive to different creatures.... We need a matrix of corporate understanding, rather than total understanding in a single individual. We must encourage our internal communication network so that those with special knowledge from one theory can talk with those who have a different theory.... The normal barriers to such talking are severe, sometimes accompanied by emotional overtones."

Meanwhile, in Australia a group of men were concerned for the aboriginese there, and for the people of Papua New Guinea. They contacted SIL and asked to have a school started in Australia so that the young folk there could have the advantage of linguistic training. The SIL members were delighted at the news that others would join them in the job of Bible translation, so the staff at the Oklahoma SIL voted that $1,500. of the funds of their school (Oklahoma SIL) be given to Ken and Evie to help pay their transportation to Australia. (Actually in giving that $1,500. they were giving almost half of the balance that the school had at the end of the summer.)

Most of the money had come from "The Book Fund." In the early years the students were not charged enough to pay all expenses, and the Board had no money to give. But both Gene Nida and Ken were turning out textbook material; Gene was preparing materials for grammar (Nida, 1946), and Ken was beginning his *Phonemics* (Pike, 1947). In 1943 the Oklahoma school ran off a half-million sheets of paper on a $35. second-hand mimeograph machine —the crank was turned by one-hour-a-day volunteer labor. Then the students were charged for the mimeographed materials. The cash received was then returned toward the running expenses of the school. In that way the pattern was set, and even after the books were published, the royalties continued to go to the organization. It seemed logical to use some of that money to pay Ken and Evie's way to Australia.

Ken went in November of 1949. He wanted to be there ahead of time so that he could study up on (listen to) some of the aboriginal languages of Australia. He also went to Papua New Guinea and spent a few days on languages there. He was especially excited when, in those few days, he was able to determine that at least one of the languages was tonal. Then, having listened to some of the languages of the area, he felt ready to teach the Australian students how to analyze them.

Evie, with year-old Stephen, went over in December. Barbara stayed with her Griset grandparents, and Judith was with friends in Philadelphia. That was hard on Evie—her thoughts were across the ocean much of the time—but, with only Stephen actually with them, she was able to carry the heavy, heavy load of tutoring the new staff and heading up the phonetics department.

The language course was well worth the effort. That first year more than thirty-five students took the course; they were from eight denominations, and were candidates or applicants of sixteen different mission boards. Some of the most enthusiastic students were those who had already been trying to learn one of the little-known languages. Everybody agreed that there should be a session each year, and the men who had assumed the responsibility for that first session asked that SIL send them help again.

To make it possible for Ken to be there in the Spring of 1950, I had taught his phonology class the first few weeks of the semester at the University of Michigan, and Professor Fries had taught his seminar. Ken and Evie hurried back from Australia to Michigan just as soon as they could, so that Ken could take over and teach the greater part of the semester. Dick Pittman headed up the Australia SIL in 1951, and I started the semester at the University of Michigan for Ken again in 1952. In 1953, Howard McKaughan headed up the Australia SIL, and by 1954 the staff there had developed enough so that they could carry on their program without help from the outside.

Some leaders in evangelical circles in England were also thinking of asking SIL to give linguistic training there. They too had become convinced that it would be helpful to those who wanted to learn little-known languages. So it was arranged that Ken and Evie, and George Cowan should go over in the summer of 1953. The leaders were enthusiastic, but somehow students were slow in applying. A week or two before the starting date, only three or four had applied. The leaders stood by their decision to start the school anyway.

After getting to England, Ken and George scurried around and managed to persuade a few more. Partial scholarships helped. In the end, the number of students was just under fifteen. Two of those were John and Pam Bendor-Samuel (at that time Pam was still Pam Moxham) and the course would have been worthwhile if just for those two. In a few years John became the director of the school and Pam is one of his very good staff members.

Ken enjoyed contact with the linguists in England, and he was especially delighted when Professor Firth (an eminent linguist at University College, London) wrote him enthusiastically about the research British members of SIL were doing, and were about to do, in American Indian languages.

Well, the British SIL had gotten off to a slow start, but the number of students began to increase and by 1970 it was averaging nearly 200 students each session. (For a description of the beginnings of the Summer Institute of Linguistics and the Wycliffe Bible Translators in England, see, Thompson, 1974.)

Ken was not the first director of the other SIL schools; some of his colleagues were, and he delighted to see them in action. In fact, in 1971 he even persuaded Frank Robbins to become director of SIL in Oklahoma. Ken found that as his administrative duties lessened he was able to spend more time on research; he also preferred teaching to administrative duties.

When he taught, he liked to have the students see the whole picture, to know the relation of the information they were receiving to other information. The way he started the beginning grammar class in 1973 is quite typical of the way he tried to show how their classwork fitted into a larger view of linguistics.

That first day he said, "What is a theory? A theory is like a window. Suppose you have a house; if you look out a window of that house, you see certain materials. If you turn around and look out a different window, you see different materials, and if there is no window, you see nothing. Here in this classroom we have a window about three inches wide and two feet long. That's a pretty poor theory—it allows us to see a little bit but not very much.

"But note. From this point of view, a theory can look at only part of the data at any one time. A theory is constrained by its nature; it doesn't let you see everything. This implies that you may need several theories if you want to look in several directions.

"Now, if you are in a house with no windows, you are blind (as far as the outside world is concerned), and even if you have only a small window, or a window with wavy glass which distorts the view, that is better than having no window at all. In that same way, a poor theory is better than no theory.

"A theory can also be called a model. Suppose, for example, that we are building a model of a bridge, and we want to test that bridge. It is easier to build a model than it is to build a bridge, because a model *leaves out* material. If the model were as complicated as the data, the model would be pointless—you might as well have the whole data. So the point to a model—or a theory—is to leave something *out,* to select the things you want to look at.

"Notice now, you *hope* that the data that your theory leaves out are not the data which will ruin the purposes for which you want that theory. So, a theory leaves out material and a good theory leaves out wisely. That is, it leaves out materials which are irrelevant to your particular purpose.

"Now there is a philosopher by the name of Frank, and I enjoy some of his material.... Now one of the things he says is that a theory has a pragmatic component, a practical component, in that a theory is a tool.

"Now, *that* you need to understand. A theory is a *tool* to let you *see* something, and therefore the tool you should choose is dependent upon what it is you want to see.

"Suppose you want to buy an airplane. Well, what airplane do you want? Do you want an airplane like a helio-courier which will land on a three-hundred-foot airstrip in the jungle, in mud, under full power, and with five people in it? (I've flown in them.) And they have to take off on that same three-hundred-foot airstrip, in the mud, fully loaded.

"But there are times when the helio-courier is not so good. If you want to cross the Atlantic...

"So, Frank says (Frank, 1957) that a theory is like an airplane, and it is chosen for much the same reason—it is chosen to get you where you want to go.

"Now note. The theory I am using in this course is chosen because it takes you where I want to take you. Where do I want to take you? I want to take you into a language which you have never studied, for which you have no teacher, for which there are no books, no alphabet, no dictionary, no helps of any kind. And I want you to understand something about that language fast and efficiently.

"After that, other theories may be better for your purpose. You may want to describe the language in some way which is considered esoterically beautiful—in which case this theory may seem esoterically unbeautiful to you."

Sometimes Ken would be so busy giving the overall view that he'd forget to teach something that the students needed to know in order to do their homework. It was Evie who was up on those mundane things. A little before it was time to dismiss the class, Ken would glance in her direction to see if he had covered the material that was vital from her point of view.

They made a good team; she tutored the staff, made the assignments, and saw that the tests were graded. Ken's lectures were supposed to stretch the students' horizons and give them background theory. But he didn't want the students, nor the staff, to hear only his theory, he took considerable pains to have them come in contact with other linguists.

One of the ways he had of doing it was to have a seminar of staff and advanced students. Then at the seminar he'd pretend that he was some outstanding linguist. He would present material from that linguist's point of view and the staff and students would try to refute what he had said. Ken would respond with the arguments he thought the linguist would have used. By the time the hour was over everybody had a better idea of at least some of the points in that linguist's theory.

Every year he'd invite a linguist or two to spend a couple of days at Oklahoma SIL, and he made sure that the ordinary staff members had contact with them. He'd have a secretary set up a series of fifteen or twenty-minute appointments. The staff member was instructed to have some linguistic or anthropological item ready to discuss with the visitor. (Most of the staff members had already done field work in Mexico, Peru, or in some other country.) The result was interesting to the visitor and very good for the young staff member.

At meal times a group of four or five staff members took the guest out to dinner, and in that way a few more had good contact with a real live linguist.

The linguists enjoyed it too. For example, Robert A. Hall, Jr., Professor of Linguistics at Cornell University and author of many linguistic books, wrote back, "It was extremely good to be with you folks at Norman.... I was favorably impressed beyond all my expectations; I liked the people, the atmosphere, the spirit with which both staff and students were working...."

Ken himself has enjoyed the atmosphere at the SIL schools. In part, he has been molded by the students and young field linguists who constantly surround him, looking for answers. He says that his choice to serve the students, the team doing translation work, helped keep him on course. His desire to be useful kept him from getting pulled off into purely scholastic arguments, and from going after some theory just to be in style. He feels that his contribution to society has been greater because he has been kept in contact with all kinds of languages and the analytical problems found in them.

But not even Ken expects students to study all the time. He thinks they do better if they get away from linguistics at least for a little while—he advocates volleyball. Someone hangs up a sheet where prospective players can sign up for the summer; then the players are arranged into teams. Ken is assigned to a team, and when they play he is always there. When there are challenge games (staff versus students, over-forty versus under-forty, fathers versus nonfathers), Ken's loud chatter about the event brings out spectators, so that more than just the players get relaxed.

Then there are Friday night parties—a special time for relaxing. Every summer one of the parties is put on by staff, and Ken is apt to have a conspicuous part, usually doing something crazy. He may sing a solo in falsetto while wearing a straw wig, or demonstrate how he could bounce from one side of the room to the other, feet in the air, and without touching his hands to the floor. The students love it and I've had some tell me thirty years later what Ken did when they were beginning students. From Ken's point of view, it is all part of the same job. If the students need to relax in order to go back to work again, full steam ahead, on their studies, then Ken goes at the party as enthusiastically and as deliberately as he gives a linguistic lecture. He is all teacher.

Dr. Eugene Loos who has been working with the Capanahua-speaking people of Peru tells about the time Ken was conducting a workshop there. He was working with one of the wise old Capanahua-speaking people. The man said a word. Ken wrote it down. He said another, and another, and some more. Ken wrote them down. Then he studied them a moment and read them all back. The old man was delighted! With a big smile he told Ken, "You say them very well. You learn fast. Some day you're going to be a teacher!"

26 FEELING IGNORANT

(1964—1969)

Ken grew up a monolingual, speaking English only. In 1938, one of the reasons he hesitated about working for a Ph.D. degree was because his top priority was translating the New Testament for the Mixtec people of San Miguel, and he felt that he couldn't take the time to study German. A knowledge of German was usually a requirement for a Ph.D. degree, but Professor Fries said that Ken would be allowed to fulfill the language requirement with Spanish, since Spanish was needed in Latin America where he was working. So it was arranged that way.

But Ken felt ignorant. His fellow students at Ann Arbor, and the young Ph.D.s with whom he was associating, all knew German, and some of them spoke it fluently.

As time passed and Ken became recognized as a linguist, he still felt ignorant. He explained his uneasiness by saying that every competent linguist was expected to know German. He said that for a hundred and fifty years 'linguistics' had meant 'historical linguistics.' A large percentage of that had been initiated by German linguists and the results had been published in German. It bothered him that, because he did not know the language, he did not have direct access to much of the literature on the comparative-historical method. He had to use translations. He felt bad about that for years.

The climax of wistfulness—wishing to know German—came when SIL started a linguistic school in Germany. Ken was expecting to go there in the summer of 1964. It seemed to him that it would be difficult to explain to the people there how the Summer Institute of Linguistics could run a linguistic school, especially one that emphasized the need of speaking a people's mother tongue, while he, the President of SIL, couldn't speak their language.

He decided that something must be done, so, in Michigan, in the spring of 1964, in addition to his regular duties as professor of linguistics, he began sitting in on a reading course for German. It was a course for graduate students who needed to be able to read German, but who were not required to speak it. He started working on verbs and pronouns, but the irregularities were extremely annoying.

In order to help him remember them, he began applying to them his matrix theory that had been so successful in analyzing some of the irregularities of Foré in Papua New Guinea, and of Navaho and Potawatomi in the United States (Pike 1963, Pike and Becker 1964, Pike and Erickson 1964).

Ken set the verb paradigms in rows and columns in such a way that the bits of the words with the same pronunciation fell together in blocks within the square that had been formed by the rows and columns. He rearranged the order of the words several times, and each time different blocks or patterns were formed. Seeing the various patterns helped him to correlate the pronunciation of the different bits with the different fragments of the meanings. Such correlation helped, but remembering still wasn't easy.

Ken was scheduled to spend a short time at the SIL school in Germany, and in Freiburg, and also in Münster at an international Congress of Phonetic Sciences. He chose to travel by boat because many of his fellow passengers would be German and he would have a week to immerse himself in the language before reaching Germany.

He had borrowed some language-learning phonograph records and had listened to the first few lessons, but when he arrived on the boat, on July 9, 1964, and heard someone speaking, it was just one indistinct rumble. Several days passed before he could begin to pick out words inside the German sentences. At his table in the dining room, everyone spoke German, and Ken found himself with symptoms of culture shock. He wrote Evie, "It's hard for me to accept the lack of communication while trying to learn. I feel ignored and abused and rebellious."

He found it difficult to remember the agreement between articles, adjectives, and singular and plural nouns. He complained that he could hardly utter two consecutive words without pausing between them. A linguist? Him? How could the Lord choose a person like him to do linguistic work? The answer to that was not clear to him. "But," he wrote Evie, "nor does it have to be clear. His to wield the ax; mine to surrender the edge to the grindstone." Then he began to feel a little more encouraged. Someone who knew no English conversed happily with him for a whole hour—of course it was about very simple things. And he went to a German-speaking movie and found that he could understand snatches of it.

When he arrived in Freiburg, West Germany, on July 16, 1964, one of his friends, Professor Herbert Pilch of the University of Freiburg, was a tremendous help to him. He explained points about the grammar and conversed with him in German. But they had one problem. Both Ken and Pilch had linguistic ideas that they wanted to discuss together. They hated to be restricted by Ken's lack of knowledge of German, so most of the time they used English to talk about the things they were really interested in.

Henning Wode, one of Professor Pilch's assistants, spent considerable time with Ken, conversing with him, answering his innumerable questions, and giving him drills to try to make automatic some of the agreement between words. Wode had been writing his dissertation on the intonation of English, and Ken, in exchange for his time, read the dissertation and discussed it with him.

Both Wode and Pilch were interested in Ken's matrix theory and how he had applied it to the German verb 'to be' and fused pronouns. It gave them insights into the structure that they had never seen described. Pilch suggested that Ken write it up and publish it in Germany.

Ken was beginning to chit-chat with more people, and he was really encouraged when he went out shopping and was able to buy a map and some paper without the use of English. But not all days were that successful. He went to a railroad station and tried to get information about a certain train. After he had come out with several badly constructed German sentences, the clerk interrupted sharply with, "Do you speak English?"

"Yes."

"Then why don't you use it?"

Language learning. What a pain. The utter hopelessness of dominating automatically the arbitrary agreement between words, and of remembering the correct form of the irregular verbs. Memorization of vocabulary. Again Ken felt culture shock, a revolt against all foreign customs, sounds, and language. He felt nauseated. Trying to tell Evie a little of his struggle, he wrote, August first, the following poem. (It was later published in *Stir-Change-Create*, 1967, p. 109.)

CRUSHED

Through culture strain
Where words like spears
Pierce rebel ear
Where screams with pain
Both dumb and blind

(How *can* man love—

Or cope with woe—
Where systems wildly smash
Each other's proud unconscious plan?)

Our Father—to whom
All speech is one
And tongues of man
But image thin of Thine—
Help me now.

Ken got his courage back when he reached the SIL school. He had been in Germany a little more than three weeks by that time and he was doing all right with simple chit-chat. The students and staff were appreciative of his efforts, and that encouraged him. Also, he was doing pretty well with linguistic terminology in German. A member of the German staff worked with him in making up a summary lecture on linguistics. He memorized it and that helped him when talking about linguistic things much the way memorizing Mixtec stories had helped him to talk Mixtec years before.

Some of his lectures he gave in English and a staff member interpreted them. Three he gave in German. He says his syntax was terrible, but the message understandable. He was grateful to the Lord that somehow he had managed to do it.

He also gave one of his chapel talks in German. For the most part he just read verses from the German Bible and put his own connecting sentences in between.

After a week at the school, he went on to Münster to attend the Fifth International Congress of Phonetic Sciences. He had been to international congresses before, but this one was special. It wasn't the paper that he gave that made it special, nor the papers that anyone else gave, but because this time he was able to greet people in German and even explain a linguistic point if the person listening was willing to give him time to put his words together.

He was back in Michigan, ready to start the fall semester by the end of August, but his encounter with German was not over yet. At the December meeting of the Linguistic Society of America, he gave a paper on the German verb 'to be,' the personal pronouns, and the definite article, as viewed through matrix theory. In an expanded form, "Non-linear Order and Anti-redundancy in German Morphological Matrices," it was published in 1965 in the journal *Zeitschrift für Mundartforschung*. Learning a little German had been a real, but worthwhile, struggle for Ken.

Now he was feeling ignorant about something else.

In the 1960s, mathematics was very much in focus. It was influencing some linguists in their mode of argumentation and in their way of presenting evidence.

Ken didn't know math and he wondered if he could do a better job for Bible translators if he did. Just in case, he started reading math books. It was an example of what Robert A. Hall of Cornell University said in his book *Stormy Petrel in Linguistics*. He said that Ken tried "to seek out and adopt whatever there might be of merit in any point of view, no matter how different from his own" (1975 p. 125).

When Ken was invited to spend the academic year 1968-69 as a Fellow at the Center for Advanced Study in Behavioral Sciences, adjacent to the campus of Stanford University, it was math that he wanted to study. He was looking for ways that mathematics could contribute to linguistic analysis. A couple of years previously, working with Ivan Lowe (a Ph.D. in physics from Cambridge University), he had been able to apply group theory to a problem about pronominal reference, and they had written an article on it, "Pronominal Reference in English Conversation and Discourse—A Group Theoretical Treatment" *Folia Linguistica* 3.68-106 (1969).

But in spite of the reading he had already done, and in spite of his success in applying group theory to one problem, he found the work with math at the Center to be extremely difficult for him. Sometimes he found himself staring at a problem and he was sure that a good freshman would have seen the answer ten times faster than he had done.

Even though he was slow at solving some of the problems in the math books, he was enjoying the contact with the other professors there. One of them especially, a theoretical physicist, found it exciting that there was a possibility that Ken could formalize mathematically some of the characteristics of conversational structure, and he urged Ken to keep working on it.

As his stay at the Center was coming to a close, Ken assessed the situation. He decided that he had not gotten as far along in math as he had hoped. He did not have the independence or scope that he would have liked, but he now felt better able to guide younger scholars who were already mathematically competent, helping them to integrate linguistics with math.

Ken had spent those months working on math at the Center and considerable time reading before then. He didn't want that time to be wasted as far as his own production was concerned. As usual, he thought of a verse in the Bible that could apply to the situation. He remembered that the Lord had said that He would help the Israelites and not let their fruit fall to the ground—without being harvested, that is (Amos 9:9, Malachi 3:11). Ken felt that after spending all the time on math, that he should have some kind of harvest from it. So he prayed that his efforts might not be without fruit, that somehow he could have at least a small harvest.

He made up his mind to again concentrate on using his own linguistic tools—those found in tagmemics—but before turning from math, he would make an all-out effort to crystalize something of what he had done. He succeeded. He finished up for publication the article, "Sociolinguistic Evaluation of Alternative Mathematical Models: English Pronouns" *Language* 49: 121-60 (1973). As it said in the opening summary, it was an article that "studies in the interplay of linguistics, social situations, and mathematical formalisms, as they affect certain speaker-addressee relationships involving three people."

His stimulus for that article came from the time he was helping Jean Soutar, a missionary with the Sudan Interior Mission, with the Bariba language. She had been having trouble translating John 14:6 (RSV), "Jesus said ... no one comes unto the Father, but by me." When a missionary was quoting that verse to the people, it confused them. Many thought they were being told that Jesus said that they should follow the missionary. Ken helped Jean unscramble the situation. Then he began considering still other problems in indirect discourse. From there he moved into group theory.

Something like that has happened many times. As Ken helps a Bible translator, he himself profits from it.

27 CHAPEL SERVICES

In the SIL schools, chapel services were scheduled for a half hour on each school day. Even though attendance was voluntary, most students made it a habit of going, since their very reason for taking linguistics was to acquire some of the tools they would need for spreading the truth about Christ.

For years at the SIL in Oklahoma, Ken had led two of those services each week. Then when he dropped part of his administrative responsibilities, he also stopped leading part of the services. Like many who lead chapel services at SIL, Ken is not ordained. When he teaches others about Christ and how to apply Scripture to their lives, he is merely trying to fulfill the responsibility he feels he has as a Christian layman.

One of the things the students remember most vividly about Ken is the way he led the singing. Some of the students talk about it with distaste. They didn't like it. Ken sped up the singing of some of the words and had them sing others very slowly. They said the timing was so terrible it ruined the hymns, and that it was almost impossible for the organist to stay with him.

Other students liked the way he led. The originality of it so burned the hymns into their memory that they remembered them years later—the words with their comforting or prodding message, the togetherness of the whole crowd united as they sang about the Lord, and Ken up front directing. For example, Myron Bromley wrote back from West Irian at least fifteen years after he had been a student at SIL, "Sometimes when I think I just can't make it, I'm reminded of your wiry, intense, arm-flailing frame leading a chapelful of us singing 'Faith, Mighty Faith'—and faith lights a lamp in the gloom.''

Ken enjoyed it when the rhythm of spoken speech was reflected in the way the hymns were sung. He liked it too when meaning was emphasized by a change in the dynamics.

Ken's intonation was very expressive throughout the chapel talks and was accompanied by changes of voice quality and facial expression. It helped even simple statements like these to stick in the memory:

"Disaster is God's opportunity to teach us comfort. Let's not miss it.''

"What is God like? We ought to be interested because He's boss.''

"Don't faint by the way. The row you have chosen to hoe is a long one, but the fruit of it is good.''

"God won't give up when it is shown that we are weak, since He choose us *because* we are weak.''

"It's not our privilege to be so disturbed by another person's failure that we look on that failure rather than on the sovereignty of God.''

"Can you imagine God saying, 'I will identify myself by saying, I am the God of Jacob, Job, Jim, George, *you?'* Well, as a matter of fact, He does. You represent God, right where you are. People say, 'God's the God of that bloke.' ''

"We must not, on the one hand, ignore that we are in a battle, or we won't have the armor ready. On the other hand, we mustn't quit because it's a battle.''

"If you give thanks to God, He will give joy to you.''

"God said to Solomon, 'Choose.' It takes courage to choose, knowing that if we choose wrong, things will look pretty bad—except for the mercy of God.''

For years many of Ken's chapel talks were taped and transcribed. From these Ken selected some for publication. Twenty-five came out in *With Heart and Mind: A Personal Synthesis of Scholarship and Devotion* (1962). Six more were published in *Stir-Change-Create* (1967). In addition to these two books, more than forty articles have been published in various journals. Portions from a number of his talks are given here.

Ken talked about balance in relation to the way he and his colleagues tried not only to concentrate on doing a good linguistic job, but also to concentrate on living in accordance with Matthew 28:19 "Go ... and teach...," and other Scriptural injunctions. He rejected any suggestion that a person try to walk a line half way between two viewpoints, that he look for a happy medium. A half-way-between-something job was a mediocre job and excellent in nothing. He insisted that a person deliberately cultivate a vibration, shifting his focus back and forth between two or more points of view, similar to the way a person stays on course as he walks, alternating between his left foot and his right. In chapel, he told the SIL students, "I've thought a great deal recently about the problem of walking. How does one walk? It has to do with balance.

"When a person walks, he doesn't stay in balance by just keeping all his weight on one foot. A one-legged man doesn't have better balance than a two-legged man. And yet the two-legged man maintains balance by first putting all his weight on one foot and then moving all his weight to the other foot.

"Balance is a kind of vibration between different kinds of outlook."

There was another figure of speech that Ken thought of in relation to his own work, and that he tried to pass on to others. He said, "Drive the well deep and irrigate widely." By that he was advocating concentration on a small area, combined with less concentration and a quick sweep over a wide area. He applied this, not only to linguistic study, but also to contact with people. He advocated that a teacher, a leader, concentrate his efforts on a few specific people, but that he also put at least some effort on many people. He backed up his point of view with incidents in the life of Christ. He pointed out that Christ chose twelve men. Concentrating on them, He drove the well deep so that there might be a few who understood His teachings as much as they could at that time. It was on those men that He was to support the building of his church.

On the other hand, Ken pointed out that in Mark 1:38 Jesus did the exact opposite. In verse 37 Simon and his companions had gone to Jesus and told him that everyone was looking for him. But Jesus did not restrict His activities to that one area, He said, "Let us go into the next towns, that I may preach there also: for therefore came

I forth." Christ went throughout all Galilee. He did not strike a happy medium. He was in balance between driving the well deep as He taught the twelve, and irrigating widely as He went to many different places in order to reach all who would respond after a brief hearing.

Ken pointed out, too, that Paul advised Timothy to drive the well deep. That is, in II Timothy 2:2 (RSV) he told Timothy, "and what you have heard from me before many witnesses entrust to faithful men who will be able to teach others also." On the other hand, Paul advocated that Timothy irrigate widely when he told him in II Timothy 4:2 (RSV), "preach the word, be urgent in season and out of season, convince, rebuke, and exhort, be unfailing in patience and in teaching."

Ken knew that his colleagues could not expect a life of ease, and he reminded them that they should look to God for comfort (II Corinthians 1:3-7). He said, "We're told about the God of all comfort, but there's no comfort if there is no distress. If there is no weakness, no problem, no difficulty, no pain, there is no comfort. Pain and comfort come together as a composite.

"Why should the Lord design it so that we will have pain? Perhaps because pain jolts the self-sufficiency of even the hardiest. It is pain that lets a person see that he is incompetent. We have pain when we are unable to do what we ought to do. It hurts. But there is comfort when one admits that he is incompetent and looks to God for help to do what God has built him to do. God chose us because of our weakness. How amazing! But He can't help us if, in our own eyes, we are strong. It is only when we know we are weak that He can send His power through us."

Ken knew that most of his colleagues were goal-oriented. Most were working hard to have something to show in heaven, and sometimes they were hurting because they knew that they hadn't done as much as they had wanted to do. So he reminded them of the passage in Luke 10:17-20 where the seventy people Jesus had sent out returned joyful because the demons had obeyed them. But Jesus told them not to rejoice about that, instead, Jesus said, 'rejoice that your names are written in heaven' (Luke 10:20b RSV). That is, they should rejoice because they belonged to God. Belonging to God is important. For each one of us, belonging to God is more important than all the work, all the preaching, all the teaching that any of us can do.

A favorite thesis of Ken's was our relationship with other people. We are to remember that relationship even while working our hardest. "There is a social responsibility implied in the Scriptures for us today. It will not do to assume that the Gospel is merely for salvation without reference to living. Our lives should be different because we know the Lord. Our lives should be kindly, and our lives should be honest and in good report.

"The prophet Jeremiah has a message for us in terms of our social situation, 'Woe to him who builds his house by unrighteousness, and his upper rooms by injustice; who makes his neighbor serve him for nothing, and does not give him his wages' (Jeremiah 22:13 RSV). What is the underlying principle in this verse, and how does it apply to us here in this room? As I see it, the underlying principle is, woe to the man who builds up his ego at someone else's expense.

"That can apply to anyone of us. It also applies whenever anyone deliberately tries to make someone else look bad so that he himself can look good. Climbing at someone else's expense is sin. It is possible to write linguistic articles at someone else's expense, not in honest criticism (which I for one insist is part of science), but to deliberately tear him down in order to build oneself up. That is wrong.

"Now, what is the relation of this sin to drive? to competition? We have to have drive to succeed. We have to have drive to serve the Lord. Competition, where one is not pulling the other man down, is shown in the Scriptures to be o.k. In I Corinthians 9.24 (RSV) we read, 'Do you not know that in a race all the runners compete, but only one receives the prize? So run that you may obtain it.' It is the will of God that we compete to do His will with our best. But we can get the prize only if we run without tripping the opponent. We must run fairly, honestly, encouraging our opponent to do his best too."

Ken knew that the students and his colleagues were working hard and were sometimes discouraged. One of his ways of encouraging them was by telling them about struggle or tension as one facet of tribulation. "Paul was teaching the disciples, 'exhorting them to continue in the faith, and saying that through many tribulations, we must enter into the kingdom of God' (Acts 14:22b RSV). How does this about tribulation apply to us? For most of us it must mean something different from torture—none of us are hanging by our thumbs. If we are facing tribulation, but haven't labeled it as that, God who is to comfort us in every tribulation (II Corinthians 1:3-4) may not be comforting us the way He would like to.

"What could be tribulation to you this week? I'll tell you. Struggle, tension, frustration. The frustration that comes when you are given a job that is not in your line. Or, perhaps when you are struggling to keep from getting bitter about someone, someone who has been inconsiderate. Perhaps you have a struggle between conflicting duties—trying to do three things at once. Perhaps you are struggling to continue on with a job when you feel incapable of that job. All this causes tensions—tribulation—and we need to look for comfort from God."

Ken reminded the students that they could have success only with God's help, but that they couldn't sit on their hands and expect God to do the job without them. "We are told in Psalm 127:1, 'Except the Lord build the house, they labor in vain that build it [Unless God labors with us, we might as well quit]: 'except the Lord keep the city, the watchman waketh but in vain.' It is possible to have built a city, but if it depends on us to make it last, it will fall. There is a sense in which only in God is there any permanancy.

"The book of Isaiah reminds me that God is in history as an active, personal, conscious, vigorous, directing force. (Not a dynamo, not energy, not abstract power, but person.) What I want to do today is to remind you that as far as we are concerned, unless God is involved, we cannot succeed in a long-term contribution.

"I also want to emphasize the opposite of that—the other approach to the same truth. It's this. If the Lord is building the house, we don't have to worry about its being built if we keep swinging the hammer. If we stop swinging the hammer, well, God has not promised to build the house. He built the universe so that we have to do these things together.

"God's side will win; we can't lose if we're on that side and swing the hammer. And yet what a mess we appear to be in—pressures, tensions, upsets, failure, work not done, behind schedules…. •

"Why this struggle if God is that big? Why this struggle if we can win? Well, think about playing volleyball. It's no fun to win all the time by huge scores. None of the good volleyball players want to win all the time and never have a good sharp close game. Human beings are unhappy unless there is a battle, and God has given us what we want—a battle. So accept it. Without it you'd be crying of boredom. God has built the world to give us fun. So accept the battle and rejoice in the struggle. It's character that we want more than success, so ask the Lord to give you love, joy, peace, gentleness, goodness, meekness—those things come only from Him."

Ken wanted the students to realize that God had a special interest in each of them. "God knows our names. He knew Samuel by name and He called him, 'Samuel! Samuel!' (I Samuel 3:4-10). An astonishing thing.

"God not only remembers names and knows names, but He gives names. In Genesis 17:5-6 (RSV) He told Abram, 'No longer shall your name be Abram [that is, exalted father], but your name shall be Abraham [that is, father of a multitude]; for I have made you the father of a multitude of nations. I will make you exceedingly fruitful; and I will make nations of you, and kings shall come forth from you.'

"To me Romans 4:17 is one of the most exciting verses in the whole Bible. It says, God '... calleth those things which be not as though they were.' God, by giving a name to somebody, sets in motion a whole chain of events which determines that the man will become what God has called him. He not only knows our names and calls us by name, but he can give us a name.

"Our God is not some kind of vague mist. He is not energy, as such, alone. God is personal. Perhaps the most potent evidence of this, from the Scriptural point of view, is that He knows us by name.

"We mustn't forget that, when we get tired and weary of the struggle, the chaos, the controversy, the misunderstandings, the lack of clarity about what we should do. In the midst of these things, I don't know anything more cheering than to say, 'Don't worry, God knows you by name.' Tonight if He chose, He could call out, 'John, wake up! I've got something to say to you.' or 'Susan! Listen a minute.'

"Knowing our names may seem such a small thing, but it is no small thing at all. It shows the degree of commitment and interest which is involved."

Ken told the students that God has a plan for each of us. There is a pattern to our lives and it is not completed here on earth. We won't understand the meaning of our lives until we see the whole—and part of the whole is completed only in eternity. He said that is similar to the way that the entire meaning of a sentence doesn't come in the first words of the sentence, but must include the words at the end too.

Ken reminded them of I Corinthians 13:12b (RSV). "Now I know in part; then I shall understand fully, even as I have been fully understood." We understand only part because we are still on the earthy level. When we get up above and we see all the parts together, we'll see what God has planned for us and how everything fits into the pattern. Somehow, God sees us as part of a whole.

Referring to Psalm 31:15a, "My times are in thy hand..." and Psalm 31:17a (RSV), "Let me not be put to shame..." Ken said, "We're under the control of God. Our future is under the control of God. Our development is under His control. Our times are in His hands. And if our times are in His hands, our enemies—if there are any—are under His control.... Even our embarrassments are under His control."

Ken considered that the set of the mind was important. He told the students, "The Scriptures tell us in Colossians 3:2 to set our minds on things that are above. There is a sense in which a person can deliberately set his mind to think about things above, and to deliberately shut out from it things which are ugly and hateful.

"There is another very wonderful thing about the mind. A person can, to some degree, think of two things at once. In speech, we have our words, and we have our intonation. Our intonation gives a different message from our words. We have simultaneous messages. Similarly, in our psychology, we have simultaneous messages going on inside ourselves. For example, we are told in Ephesians 5:19 that we should make melody in our hearts to the Lord. And one of the things which I consider most to be prized is those times when I wake up in the morning and find that without effort a hymn is running through my mind. Sometimes, as I'm talking with someone, if I relax a minute, this hymn comes back into the foreground. It's like having a tape recorder on at dinner, playing lovely music while you're having conversation.

"Ideally, our psychology should have, at the background of our mind, a tape recorder with a hymn going all day long, so that whenever we relax, we relax back into making melody in our hearts to the Lord, instead of relaxing back into horror, and fuss, and anger, and hatred.

"As I see it, the structure of the human spirit is intricate, detailed, and beautiful. But is a monstrous mechanism when out of control, when the gears clash, when sand gets in them.

"When under control, our body, mind, and spirit are intricately, beautifully, elaborately worked out according to the plan of God, so that every part supports every other part. It can lead to character and joy and service and cleanness in the eyes of God, whose we are and whom we serve. This is mature man.

"This is the way I want to be, serving God, so that my feet carry me where they should go; serving God, so that my mind concentrates only on the things which it has a right to concentrate on, and my spirit concentrates on the walk of service with God. This is to be 'a new man' created after the image of Christ Jesus" (Colossians 3:10).

When Ken's chapel talks were taped, usually his prayer at the end was taped also. Those prayers were a kind of instant application of the message. They also give an idea of the things Ken was concerned about, his goals, and the source of his drive. Some of them are included here. The prayers were short, and are usually given in their entirety, except that his ending, "In Jesus' name," or "For Jesus' sake" has been omitted.

(1) "Father, comfort those today who don't feel important."

(2) "Our Heavenly Father, we ask You to give us the character that You want us to have (like that of Christ's), and then use it to help feed the world in its great need."

(3) "Father, we don't know why our souls are disquieted within us. We pray that Thou wilt build joy into us so that it will last."

(4) "Lord, we thank Thee that we are weak, because, Lord, we want Thy power. We choose, and ask Thee to help us to choose, to be weak when it can lead to strength in others."

(5) "Lord, we yield again today, as we yielded yesterday, and as we want to yield tomorrow, to Thy will, that we might not please ourselves and be sharp and bitter, or selfish and envious."

(6) "Father, we thank Thee for Thy goodness to us. We pray for these our younger colleagues, who are just beginning to come into areas which will bother them a lot. We pray that Thou wilt give them strength and courage to believe. Thy mercies fail not; they are new every morning. Great is Thy faithfulness."

(7) "Father, we thank Thee for anxieties, upsets, difficulties, troubles, in order that Thou canst use these things to keep us humble before Thee, and that Thou canst make Thy power known to us."

(8) "Lord, help us to obey. Help us so we won't feel that it is safe to disobey just a little bit."

(9) "Our Heavenly Father, thank you for calling our father Abraham of whom we are heirs—but not very satisfactory ones. "

(10) "Our Heavenly Father, Thou art in the heavens and Thou dost do whatsoever Thou wilt. Work in us a heart (like Daniel's) of courage, of wisdom, of understanding, of scholarship, of study, of application, of work, of fearlessness, and give us the courage of persistence to last all our lives, for this long long task of getting out the Word of God to every tongue and nation where they don't have it.... Help us to be willing to do what Thou wouldst have us to do, that in all these languages, they might have the message."

(11) "Our Heavenly Father, Thou hast called us to be men and we're afraid. We ask Thee to help us and guide us. And, dear Lord, help us to win some showpieces for heaven that'll be to the glory of our Lord Jesus Christ."

(12) "Father, we thank Thee that Thou dost have a plan for our lives. We pray that Thou wilt develop it in us."

(13) "Our Heavenly Father, help us to realize the seriousness of getting on with our business while we are here, that we might seek *now* to make our characters like that of Christ, that we might seek *now* to follow Christ, so that throughout eternity our characters will have the benefit of the imprinting of the nature and image of God in Jesus Christ."

(14) "Our Heavenly Father, when we say what we want from Thee, it is Christ's righteousness in us. We want character more

than we want success. We want integrity of spirit more than we want our name known. We want joy of heart more than we want money. We want love, joy, peace, gentleness, goodness, meekness, mercy—all of these characteristics which are so far from us, which are so hard to come by, because they don't come on the open market, but they come only from Thee. Teach us to rest in Thy power, in Thine ultimate victory, and in these precious things which above all Thou wouldst have for us."

(15) "Our Father, we have been talking about things which are too deep and wonderful for us—things about which we know not. And yet, Lord, we see that Jesus Christ loves us and wants us to be happy, and that He came, not to chastise us, not to boss us, but He came to help us to live abundantly. We are very grateful for this. Help us to live abundantly in the Spirit."

(16) "Our Heavenly Father, Thou has condemned us for those times when we sing praises with our lips, but are hard on our brethren. Thou hast condemned us for those times when we've talked about love and have refused to give up that which is our own when somebody needed it. And Thou dost condemn us when we claim to be religious and have theology but fail to see it made concrete in our lives. And so forgive us, dear Lord, for the day's journey today, with our feet soiled in the dust. Cleanse us again for tomorrow that we might walk set in Thy will."

(17) "Our Heavenly Father, we look to You to guide us and bless us. Help us to value one another. Help us to serve one another with joy and not to be touchy when someone isn't quite courteous within our definition of courtesy, or when, in fact, they damage us deliberately—as we have damaged others deliberately. Forgive us both, Father, through the blood of Jesus Christ and help us to grow into a coherent community, serving one another, helping one another, admiring one another, strengthening one another. If a brother be taken in a fault, help us to be gentle and restore him so that our community is retained."

(18) "Lord, we are grateful that You are giving us a chance to work for You. We are sorry when we blow it."

(19) "Our Lord, teach us to walk, that we might not be children falling down all the time, stumbling all the time, weak. Teach us so that we might grow up and be mature and wise."

(20) "Father, help us to serve, not claiming privileges or status, but help us to serve as Jesus served."

(21) "Heavenly Father, take care of us. Help us to be what You want us to be."

(22) "We pray, O Lord, that Thou wilt help us to trust in Thee and not in ourselves, and not in our logic, nor in anything else, but in our Lord."

(23) "Our Heavenly Father, we pray that we might not be afraid of what Thou dost have in store for us or for the world. Help us that with courage we might look to Thee to guide us forth in the face of winds and clouds, knowing that Thou dost rule in the kingdom of men, and that Thou wilt guide us surely."

(24) "Our Heavenly Father, we commit to Thee our lives, and our strength, that we might carry on when we feel futile."

(25) "Lord, help us not to bury our talents in the sand, nor to complain, nor to quit."

(26) "Father, protect us from pride, from bitterness, in Jesus' name Who taught us to be kind one to another, tenderhearted, forgiving one another, by showing us that we should walk in His steps."

(27) "Help us, Lord, to carry our share of the load."

(28) "Father, help us to not be scared of the giants. Help us not to refuse to believe."

(29) "Thank You, Lord, for taking care of us."

(30) "Father, we thank You for your grace and your goodness. Help us to rejoice and laugh in the midst of our failures...."

(31) "Lord, we are ignorant. We are stupid. We sin. We're incompetent, and yet we are under your orders to act anyhow.... Help us...."

(32) "Father, You have chosen us. You ordained us. You've sent us out—incompetent, but with your power. Thank You."

(33) "We thank You, Father, for making us in your image. We thank You for giving us language so that we can talk and think and ponder things from different points of view. We thank You for making us all alike so that we can be a team working together. We thank You for making us all different so that none of us is unnecessary, but each is needed for his particular bit. Help us in our fallen state to learn to enjoy one another—which comes hard."

28 WORKSHOPS—A WAY OF HELPING COLLEAGUES

Very soon after going to Mexico in 1935, Ken began to feel responsible for helping his colleagues. Mainly he focused on giving aid linguistically by developing linguistic theory that would answer their problems, by working with the languages they were studying, or by teaching others how to do consultant work. He also helped with public relations in any country where he happened to be, and occasionally he gave advice about personal matters. Actually he seldom helped exclusively in just one way over any extended time; instead, the various activities frequently overlapped. Eventually it became apparent that he could help the greatest number of people at one time when they gathered at a workshop. In a workshop setting, while he was helping one person, several others could be listening in, while still others were studying ahead on different projects.

Ken's present program of helping hundreds did not have an instant start. Actually, as he tried to be useful, the workshop—a more formal, more efficient way of helping—sort of evolved.

Ken seems to have been born a teacher, that is, born with a built-in desire to help somebody benefit by something he himself had learned. Even in those early years in Mexico he would spend hours and days trying to pass on anything that he thought might help one of his colleagues to do the job of Bible translation.

An example of that was a letter he wrote to Max Lathrop in December of 1937. Max had written telling him that he was having difficulty with the verbs of Tarascan, the language he was studying. Ken wrote back pointing out the difference between 'tense', 'aspect', and 'mode'. He went on to talk about gender and classes of verbs. Then, because Max asked about suffixes, Ken described a way to recognize the different suffixes with their meanings—'morpheme identification' we'd call it now. That letter was twenty-three pages long, typed and single spaced. He sent a copy to me so that I could learn from it too.

In those days he was reading *Language* by Bloomfield (1933), and every time he found something that he thought might help me as I studied the Mazatec language, he'd dash off a letter, summarizing some parts of it and expanding others. In such ways as that, I benefited by the reading that he was doing.

Remembering those old letters, Ken says that he benefited too. He says that's when he learned to write. Back in his college days, he hated trying to write on an assigned topic or to write a prescribed number of pages. He wrote the letters to me and other SIL members to tell us something that he felt we needed to know. Once he had told us, he stopped. Somehow that made it easier.

Basically Ken was responsible only for the translation of the Mixtec of San Miguel, but he felt burdened for all his colleagues. Whenever he met one of them anywhere, it was only a matter of minutes before he was asking questions about the language they were studying. A few minutes later, he was offering suggestions.

Although for years he had been helping his colleagues one or two at a time, his first workshop-type situation was in the fall of 1950. At that time translators from several different Mixtec languages met for three weeks in Mitla, Oaxaca. They all brought a speaker of the language they were studying, and Ken worked with each language, helped the translators with the analysis, and advised them how to carry on from there.

Howard Klassen remembers some nonlinguistic help that he received at that time. It had bothered him that he'd fall asleep while he was trying to study. Ken told him that he fell asleep because it was a strain to live in a culture different from his own. Because of that strain, he needed more sleep than usual. Ken's suggestion was that he set a timer and snooze for ten minutes, then he could get back at his studying again. Howard felt that the advice had been a great help to him.

Ken's desire and drive to help his colleagues never lessened. All his energy would go into the task, whether he was helping one, two, or dozens. Little by little the number of field linguists who had been guided by him increased. Voegelin in the *International Journal of American Linguistics,* 23:219 (1957) said (in his review of *Dictionary of Anthropology* by Charles Winick) "... a whole army [of field linguists]... led by Kenneth Pike, have announced their intention to give us information on morphology-syntax, as well as on phonology, in a freshly innovated set of technical terms...."

The 'freshly innovated set of technical terms' that Voegelin was talking about were coming from Ken's tagmemic theory as set forth in his *Language in Relation to a Unified Theory of the Structure of Human Behavior.* Voegelin was well aware of the number of linguists using that theory since he was editor of the *International Journal of American Linguistics* where numerous articles by SIL members had been published. In fact, the third issue of that journal in 1957 was special in that all the articles in it were based on Ken's tagmemic theory. Voegelin had also helped train several of the SIL members who received Ph.D. degrees.

Ken's (and SIL's) aim was threefold: to serve God, to serve our neighbors, and to serve science. The publication of the material presenting the languages the SILers had studied as they prepared for Bible translation was in line with 'serving science', and part of the reason Ken and Evie (with Judith, Barbie, and Steve) went to Peru in October 1955 was not only to help the translators with their problems in language analysis, but also to help them to write up the solutions.

Every morning Ken worked on two different languages, two hours each. He discussed the language analysis with the field linguist involved and, when there were problems, they often listened again to the native speaker of that language.

One of the languages, Campa, had a hard-to-solve problem in stress—Ken and Will Kindberg struggled with that for about three months before finding the solution. Ticuna, the language Lambert and Doris Anderson were working with, had contrastive tone (five levels). That was a surprise because it had been assumed that there were no tone languages in South America. Ken was happy at the way the Andersons had hung on until they had the problem licked. For some of the translators, it was in grammar that they were making exciting discoveries.

In the afternoon, three times a week, Ken lectured on some aspect of linguistics, and three times a week somebody else presented a language problem either showing its solution, or hoping for advice that would lead to one. By having the seminars, the linguists were able to learn from each other. In fact, some of them were training as junior consultants and were having a part in helping others.

When not in conference with Ken, Evie, or some other colleague, the linguists were either working ahead on the language analysis by themselves, or they were writing up a description of it. They really worked hard, but when they saw how much progress they were making, that encouraged them so much that they worked harder than ever. As somebody said, "When Pike arrived, he was tired; now everybody is tired."

Evie was coauthoring a paper on Cocama with Norma Faust, and one on Ocaina with Arlene Agnew. They were all delighted when the papers were published a year or so later. Ken, of course, expected that the people he was helping would end up with something in print, but it was a new triumph for Evie.

Evie had a triple job at the time. She was a housewife; she'd helped with the analysis of two languages; and she taught Spanish to the SIL school children. She wanted language learning to be fun for them, so one of the things she did was to help them to memorize riddles in Spanish. That gave them a conversation piece they could use with almost any adult. The children loved it, and some of them memorized between thirty and forty riddles, and (at least when they were telling riddles) the Spanish rippled off the end of their tongues.

In November it was rain, rain, rain, there in the jungle beside a lake that was several miles long and about a quarter of a mile wide. When it wasn't raining, it was blistering hot, hot enough to make studying an effort and a swim in the lake very welcome.

Evie wrote about a family of frogs that lived in the rafters of their house. They peeped loudly and she said they sounded like a lot of large squeaky doors. Then one day she started to put on her swim suit and a frog jumped out. She was grateful for Stephen who came to the rescue and carried the creature away.

With swimming, and all kinds of animals for pets, the SIL center was a fun place for the children. One little boy pulled a snake out of his desk and played with it while Evie was teaching. That didn't bother her as much as the three-foot alligator that Steve was trying to make friends with. He tied it, inside the house, with a long leash to the foot of the stairs—Evie decided that she didn't have to use those stairs as soon as she had thought she was going to. Then there was a parrot that the Goodalls had. He'd peck at Barb, but he'd sit on Steve's shoulder and stay there even while Steve ran and jumped with him. And there were fun things to see, like the bulge in the middle of the twelve-and-a-half foot boa constrictor that had just swallowed an alligator.

Parents couldn't study well unless their children were happy and making good progress in school, so for a workshop to be successful, school teachers were needed. And there had to be a place for the families and their language helpers to stay, so builders were needed.

Actually the SIL center was like a small city, developed to provide for the translators as they worked among the ethnic groups who were scattered hundreds of miles up and down the rivers. Of course after growing up in the jungle, a person did not immediately change his appearance and habits. Part of the fun of the center was to see the individuality of the different language groups. There were the Campas, for example. The language helper from there wore a straw crown with one very long feather sticking straight up from the back of it. When he dressed carefully, he painted geometric designs across his nose and on both cheeks. He used orange, red, and black paint, so when the sun was shining, it was startling and beautiful. The paint was soluble, however, so when it rained the beautiful design smeared.

The SIL center had a doctor, nurses, a clinic, and a store. There were pilots to fly the translators out to, and in from, the various spots on the rivers that were close to the places where the people lived. Mechanics kept the planes flying. Radio personnel kept the pilots in contact with the center while they flew. It was the radio, too, that let the translators in the faraway places hear news from the outside world, and because of the radio, people at the center were able to know that the translator was all right—or that he needed help. To have a successful workshop it took all these people plus secretaries, bookkeepers, librarians, and others. Then, of course, there was the director of the branch. At that time the director was

Harold Goodall. He planned, organized, and kept people working together as a team. Yes, the workshop was a success.

Between October 26, 1955, when the workshop started, and March 31, 1956, when it officially closed, Ken listened to more than twenty languages and helped analyze the phonology or grammar of those languages. He also guided the translators as they wrote up their findings, or had coauthored articles with them. About twenty articles, which were later published in linguistic journals, came up through that workshop.

While Evie, with the rest of the family, stayed on in Peru, Ken went to Brazil. He was welcomed by the chief of the Research Section of the Indian Protection Service, and by the head of the Anthropology Section of the National Museum. They had received reprints of the SIL scientific publications describing linguistic systems in other parts of the world, and when they saw the summary of the Peru workshop that had just taken place, they wanted to have the same type of linguistic help. Especially they considered it important that data be gathered so that there could be a revision of the classification of the languages of Brazil.

It was encouraging to Ken, who had just come from the workshop, to see how the effort that the SILers had put forth in writing up their linguistic findings was immediately useful in helping their colleagues to get started some place else. SIL was given an invitation to begin work in Brazil. That included, not only living in some of the areas where the indigenous groups were and doing linguistic analyses of their languages, but also, it was understood that they would be allowed to translate the Bible into those languages.

While in Brazil Ken gave a series of lectures in binational centers. (The centers were in part under the control of the U.S. State Department.) These lectures emphasized the role of rhythm and intonation in the teaching of English to Latin Americans. At the Museum of Rio de Janeiro, and at the University of Brazil, he lectured on verbal versus nonverbal behavior, and on current trends in linguistics, etc. Everywhere his lectures were well received.

Ken also called on government officials at various levels, both Brazilian and American, and in all his interviews, he interpreted the signs as saying that SIL should go ahead and begin work in Brazil. He was grateful to the Lord for guiding and helping him. Yet, although the contacts had gone well, Ken did not consider public relations and administration to be his forte. Even while doing a good job, he sometimes could feel pressure building up inside himself.

He went to Ecuador soon after leaving Brazil and as part of his responsibilities there, he discussed with the SIL powers-that-be in Ecuador the location in which they should build the SIL center. (It was from there that the translators would fly to and from the various indigenous groups of people who were living in the jungle.) He discussed with them, too, the decisions they were making about the flying program itself.

The whole Branch also needed counsel in interrelating with other organizations that were also contacting the indigenous people—how SIL could help and encourage them, rather than be a part of a bite-and-devour-one-another program (Galatians 5:15). Much of the tension came from the fact that Townsend and the Branch leaders were not in agreement about what the answers should be, and Ken did not find standing between the various parties to be easy. He wrote Evie that the tensions had caused several canker sores to break out in his mouth and that he didn't think he would be able to put up with such a strain for any very long period of time. (A few days after leaving Ecuador, Ken wrote a report to Townsend, and just thinking about the problems there started his head aching again.)

Ken didn't find it easy to lecture with canker sores in his mouth, but fortunately "linguistics" which included lecturing, doing research, writing, and consulting, didn't cause the same type of pressure that "administration" did. In fact, even as he became tired carrying a heavy load of linguistics, the tensions which had been caused by administration lessened.

So, when Ken left Ecuador and went on to Venezuela, the canker sores started to fade. Probably a letter from Wm. G. Nyman, Sr. helped too. Nyman had been secretary-treasurer of SIL ever since it was incorporated in 1942. He wrote Ken thanking him for "the tremendous lift you have been to all of our group" and telling him that his report of the time in Brazil "makes us ever grateful for your inspired leadership in the work which the Lord has called you to do."

In Venezuela, Dr. Martha Hildebrandt, Professor Norman Painter, Professor George W. Hill, and Professor Rosenblat had been expecting Ken, and posters announcing his coming lectures had been displayed throughout the university. The day after he arrived, he began lecturing for the Department of Sociology and Cultural Anthropology, for the School of Humanities, and for the School of Economics. Some of his topics were the syllable, air mechanisms and segmentation, American intonation, language and behavior, voice quality, etc. The schedule included a lecture every day, with interviews or casual chit-chat at other times. On the last day there, he did his language-learning-by-gesture demonstration, this time with a Guajiro Indian. It was written up in the English language newspaper of Caracas. The reporter wrote that she asked the taxi driver to wait for her, so he went in to watch the demonstration too. The report told how the students and professors were all "looking on avidly and taking notes," and how even the taxi driver had "followed every gesture with consummate interest."

From Caracas, Venezuela, Ken went to Bogotá, Columbia for two days. It had been announced by radio and advertised in bulletins that he would speak there, but his plane was late, so he missed the engagement. It was rescheduled, and even though his lecture now came at an awkward time, Ken was very satisfied with the attendance and the people he met there. Professor Jean Caudmont had made arrangements for the main lecture and another at the binational center.

Then it was back to Ecuador to lecture at the University of Guayaquil and to pick up Evie and the rest of the family. From there they went to the USA and then to SIL at Norman, Oklahoma, for the summer.

In the spring of 1958, Ken and Evie went again to Mexico to help with more than ten languages there. During that time, Ken took a few days off to go to the University of Texas at Austin to take part in a Religion and Life week. One of the pleasant things about it, from Ken's point of view, was that the week combined a religious emphasis with an academic program. Ken gave linguistic lectures to the linguistic staff and students, but he also gave lectures as part of the religious series. Then, in at least one lecture, he combined the two by showing the implications of linguistic material to Christian living. (Several years later, when commenting on Ken's book *With Heart and Mind,* Professor Warner G. Rice, Chairman of the

Department of English Language and Literature of the University of Michigan, wrote, "It seems to me that you have been remarkably successful in bringing your scholarship and your special knowledge to bear on problems of faith and conduct." Professor Rice had put his finger on the very thing that Ken loved to do.)

In September 1960, Ken was back in Ecuador helping again with the languages there. Part of the fun of studying with people who spoke Auca was to learn the 'phonetics' of how to shoot a dart from a blowgun. He wrote, "You don't just blow hard. I know. I tried and failed to move the dart down the barrel. The Aucas puff their cheeks wide, take a deep breath, and cough with one convulsive brief squeeze of lungs, stomach, and cheeks—and away darts the dart. Even so, when I tried to shoot, I had to rest the heavy end of the blow gun on something in order to take a nonwobbly aim—and I hit a papaya at some thirty feet distance. I had aimed at the whole bunch, but then Kimu, an Auca, aimed at the one I had shot, and hit it."

Ken was somewhat disappointed in the SIL center in the Ecuadorian jungle because he couldn't go swimming in the lake. That was because there were electric eels there with a six hundred volt discharge, also sting rays, boa constrictors, cannibal fish (piranha), and alligators (caiman).

In November, 1960 Ken joined Evie in Peru. During that stay he had eight people understudying him, helping him carry the load of advising others, and gaining experience that they could use as consultants in the future. The SIL program was growing so rapidly that there was need for many consultants.

From the first week of February 1962, until the latter part of May, Ken was in Papua New Guinea—except for about three weeks that he spent in Australia. SIL hadn't started work in Papua New Guinea until 1956, but already translators were working in about thirty-five languages there.

The translators who attended the 1962 workshop had been working in twenty-two languages. Of course Ken couldn't give everybody all the help they needed in that limited time, and leaders in the Papua New Guinea branch needed experience in helping others, so it was arranged that about ten of the translators would be junior consultants. They would fill a double role; they would work part time on the languages they had been studying, and spend part of the time guiding others. Howard McKaughan, in connection with a University of Washington project, also helped by serving as a consultant.

A junior consultant was expected to work four hours daily on his own language, two hours in group seminar, and two hours either working with his consultee or sitting-in to watch Ken while he worked with someone. A junior consultant wasn't responsible to solve the problems of his consultees, but he was to see that the consultee was moving in the right direction and making progress toward a solution.

The first three days of the workshop Ken checked through the materials of each member of the workshop: his files, publications, tentative manuscripts, etc. The purpose was to get an idea of what each knew and what he had already done, and to help him decide on a goal for the workshop. Usually there were two workers for each language, and each had one project, or maybe two.

Every week everybody had a half-hour appointment with Ken to show him what they had been doing. That let him know that they were making good progress, or, if they had bogged down on some problem, then he could help them figure out a new plan of attack.

Two or three times a week Ken gave lectures on some aspect of linguistic theory that some of those in the workshop would apply immediately to the analysis of the language they were studying. It always delighted him when he could see that the theory had helped someone. An example of that was his talk on the phonemic implications of the phonetics of high-level phonology. He not only talked about it, but he demonstrated on one of the languages how to do it. When some of the translators began to apply it, they found their pronunciation improving as they mimicked the pitch contours, the stresses, and the rhythm of whole sentences. It also helped in the analysis of stress and tone.

Other lectures that immediately paid off were on syntax and the use of a matrix as a tool for showing the relationships between grammatical constructions. Because it showed a pattern, a matrix helped the researcher to know what to expect in the language and gave him an idea of where to look for more grammatical constructions.

Ken was so excited about how much the matrix theory had helped, and how well a number of folks were doing on syntax, that for several nights he couldn't sleep. He kept thinking of still other ways he could use the theory. Once, he got out of bed, and by flashlight jotted down an idea. Then, when he got back in bed again, he still couldn't sleep. He said that he couldn't find the switch to turn off the computers.

Pattern was also useful in tone analysis. For example, it was used when checking to see if each tone preceded all other tones. Many of the languages in Papua New Guinea were tonal, and Ken was giving priority to helping in the analysis of two of them. Such an analysis could take a long time, and it was a big relief to him when, after some weeks, Joice Franklin had the tone data of Kewa lined up in a way that made it apparent that the backbone of the problem was broken. Then Alan Healey was able to give a clear-cut presentation of the solution to the Telefomin tone analysis.

But Ken was even more delighted when Dottie James analyzed the tone of Siane without his help. She had attended the lectures and seminars, and had sat in a time or two when he was helping Joice and Alan. She had understood the method and then had applied it to Siane. That gave Ken courage to think that others would be able to do the same, or that she would be able to help them.

Not only was Dottie James able to help others, but in countries all over the world many SIL members who have had success in language analysis, language learning, Bible translation, or literacy were (and are) helping their colleagues. Some of it was done informally, and some was done in workshops much like the one that was being held at that time in Papua New Guinea.

The purpose of some of Ken's workshop seminars was to give him the opportunity to explore any special problems that the consultees were having. The consultee would present the data, pointing out the source of the problem as best he could. Then Ken would start asking questions. If the consultee didn't know the answer, Ken would sometimes work directly with the language helper who was usually present. Often Ken was able to suggest a new direction that the consultee could take to conquer the problem. Usually by the time the seminar was over, the consultee had new ideas on how to proceed, and had already made a big step toward the answer. Since many of the languages in Papua New Guinea were related, some of the other consultees who were attending the seminar also got ideas that they could apply to the languages they were studying. When the answer did not materialize, or when Ken did not have time to spend with all the consultees who were having problems, then he could feel pressures and tension building up inside himself. The result was canker sores in his mouth and blisters on his feet— even though the pressure was coming from linguistics and not from administration. He wanted very much that everybody finish the workshop confident about the alphabet he was using to write the language that had been assigned to him, and confident that he had the grammar under control. Sometimes Ken and the junior consultants knew the answers, but they had to be sure that the consultees had been taught the solution thoroughly enough so that they were comfortable using it—sometimes that was difficult. Therefore Ken's canker sores and blisters.

Some of the seminars were on writing up the solutions, writing a paper for publication, revising a paper, and editing a paper.

Whenever Ken was at one of the SIL workshops, he gave a number of devotional talks. While he was in Papua New Guinea, he talked one day about John 3:17 and Isaiah 42:3, "A bruised reed shall he not break, and the smoking flax shall he not quench...." Ken explained the verse by comparing the smoking flax to a bit of straw, or a little wheat stubble, that he had seen used by some of the poor people in the mountains of southern Mexico. They took a little bunch and lit it by holding it against the hot coals of their open fire. It became their torch as they looked around their hut for something in the rafters or in a dark corner. That little torch smoked and made Ken's eyes smart. You might say, "It's smoking. Put it out!" but if it was put out, the people would be in the dark. They had nothing else. That smoking straw was a poor person's flashlight; it didn't give a very good light, but it was all he had. God tells us in John 3:17 that Jesus didn't come to condemn, in Isaiah 42:3 that He isn't going to destroy a person just because his work is like a torch that gives a flickering, smoky light.

Ken pointed out that the verse had a message for the consultants. The role which God gave them was to help the consultees; their role was not to destroy, to criticize, to tear down. Even though a consultee might seem to be incompetent and not living up to their expectations, the consultant's role was to build him up and help the smoking flax to give a better light.

The verse Isaiah 42:3 had a message for the consultees too. If they thought they were not doing a good job, they could take courage, because God had said that He would not destroy them when they didn't give the best possible light; He would strengthen them and let them serve Him.

One of Ken's prayers shows that he, at times, regarded himself as a piece of smoking flax: "Dear Father, we're grateful to Thee that Thou hast told us that Thou hast not come to condemn us, even though our light be smoky. We thank Thee that Thou wilt not stamp on it and put it out. We're sorry for the smoke that gets in people's eyes when we're grouchy. We ask You to give us grace and make our characters what they should be."

In the summer of 1962, Ken, with his family was back teaching at the SIL in Norman, Oklahoma. The fall semester he spent at the University of Michigan. Then, in the spring of 1963, he was off to help at another workshop. This time the workshop was to be at the SIL center in the Philippines.

On his way there, Ken stopped in Hong Kong to visit with a friend who worked with Inter-Varsity Christian Fellowship. After a meeting in which Ken spoke to the Inter-Varsity folks who were there, the friend took Ken on a quick tour of the island.

Ken wanted very much to look into mainland China. It was about thirty years since he had been told that he could not go to China, but he had continued praying for the people there, and since he couldn't go, he wanted the chance to look at it at least. It reminded him of Moses who had wanted very much to lead the Israelites into the promised land, but the Lord had told him no. Instead, He told him (Deuteronomy 3:37), "Get thee up into the top of Pisgah, and lift up thine eyes westward, and northward, and southward and eastward, and behold it with thine eyes: for thou shalt not go over this Jordan."

So Ken's friend drove with him up a mountain, around a peak, and Ken saw China, twenty-five miles away. Then Ken went on to do the job the Lord had lined up for him in the Philippines.

At that workshop about sixty people, working on thirty languages, were attending. As in Papua New Guinea, Ken was helped by a crew of junior consultants. The workshop went very well. Ken learned lots; the junior consultants learned lots; the consultees were encouraged and guided over the hard parts of the languages they were studying. Numerous articles were written and published from which others could benefit.

Evie had stayed in Michigan again, and Ken was missing his family. Perhaps that is part of the reason for his reaction when the school children at the SIL center had a field day. There were numerous children there because their parents, who were usually living in a village somewhere, had come in to attend the workshop. Somehow Ken found out that only one child lacked a parent.

Willis and Virginia Kramer, the parents of Nancy Kramer, were not there because Willis was in charge of radio communication and had had to stay on in Manila. Nancy was six and in the first grade. The evening before the field day, Ken took her a tiny airplane as a present (the kind that had a rubber band and could actually fly). He told her that his children were in the USA, so he didn't have anybody to cheer for when the students were competing. Her parents were in Manila, but, if he could be her "Daddy-for-a-day," he would be her cheering section. Agreed.

As the sports events got under way, Ken was there with flowers over his ears and waving a big banana leaf. Whenever Nancy was in a race, he was at the finish line, yelling her in. For the high jumps, too, Ken cheered her on, loudly, enthusiastically.

In 1963, Ken's program at the University of Michigan was changed. Instead of teaching there every fall semester and spending the spring at workshops, he started to spend both semesters at the University. Then, every third year, he spent the whole year somewhere in service for SIL.

In the spring of 1966 Ken was in Africa helping the SIL members in a workshop there. His report to the U.S. Department of Health, Education, and Welfare (which had helped fund his research) included articles written by consultees and a 155-page summary by Ken (*Tagmemic and Matrix Linguistics Applied to Selected African Languages,* 1966).

John Callow, a linguistic consultant who has spent considerable time in Africa, wrote about the report saying that it was, "going to be very useful indeed to us who work in West Africa...."

Jim Dean as Branch Director played an important part in getting SIL underway in Papua New Guinea, then India and Nepal, later on in Indonesia. He wrote, 'Ken poured himself out unstintingly in lectures, counselling and public relations work in each country. The production of articles at each workshop was a special help...'

About the workshop in Indonesia in 1975, Professor Ignatius Suharno, Director of the Institute for Anthropology, Cenderawasih University wrote about the SIL members, "Theirs is a dedication of highest quality. Despite the harshness of the terrain and climate, the problem of communication and transportation characteristic of jungles in this part of the world, little experience of most of the participants in dealing with the autochthones whose very tongues they were just beginning to learn, all the participants worked very hard in the short time available and came out with respectable papers. The linguistic activities would not have been possible had not the non-linguistic teams bent their backs to prepare the place and organize the maintenance of the well-being of participants and their belongings. The third group we will never be able to take for granted consists of the skillful and friendly MAF [Missionary Aviation Fellowship] pilots, who may well be human representations of God's angels.... As a loving and responsible head of family, Dr. Pike managed to make the young participants work very hard and enjoy what they were doing. The modern world surely needs scholars who are really good humans like Dr. Pike...."

In the fall of 1977, Bob Goerz, Public Relations Coordinator, and his wife Joyce wrote from Mexico, "Mexico was his [Ken's] first stop on a trip that will take him and his wife Evelyn to all the countries where we work in Latin America during the next seven months. They were with us for three weeks, and he and Bob hardly stopped. Pike lectured in the main universities and institutes, and we were astounded at the way the Lord enabled them to make friends with the students and faculty members, in a way that promises to be fruitful for months and years to come...."

Then Ken and Evie went to several other Latin American countries. Jim Wroughton, one of the directors of the Peru Branch wrote of the time they were in Peru, "... It was a real joy to work with Ken and Evie.... Especially significant to me was the Thursday evening lecture and dialogue to which we invited a limited number of top Peruvian scholars in the Social Sciences and Humanities.... Ken's lecture on 'Philosophy of Sciences in Relation to Linguistics' was followed by a lively and cordial discussion...."

Other branch directors, as well as grassroots members, wrote saying how much they appreciated Ken and Evie's help. In fact, the value of the various workshops is well recognized, and, over the years, other SIL members have been working as consultants and directors of them. Some of those who have headed up numerous workshops are Joseph Grimes (Professor of Linguistics at Cornell University), Robert Longacre (Professor of Linguistics at the University of Texas at Arlington), Kenneth Gregerson, and Austin Hale, David Thomas, and Doris Bartholomew. Actually in 1978 SIL had twenty-five international linguistic consultants, and most of them have directed large or small workshops. All of the consultants (most of them with Ph.D. degrees) have been a help and an encouragement to their colleagues. In addition to the international consultants, there are also branch consultants who help their colleagues within one country. And in addition to the linguistic consultants, there are translation consultants and literacy consultants who conduct workshops.

While in Africa in 1978, Ken set up "talk partners." The idea was to help members get started in consulting even while they felt so inexperienced that they hesitated about being called "consultants." Sometimes the "inexperienced" ones discovered that just being interested was supportive, and that they could even come up with a good idea once in a while.

But in spite of consultants, and more consultants, there is always somebody else who needs help. So it was that Ken, retiring from his position as Professor of Linguistics at the University of Michigan, decided that he wanted to spend the rest of his strength, "as long as Evie and I can toddle up a mountain," going from one country to another helping the translators.

They didn't waste any time getting started. Most of September to December, 1978, they spent in Ivory Coast. They took a couple of weeks to go to Germany for the Board meetings of WBT and SIL.

Ken was sixty-six and he felt that he did not stand stress as well as he used to, and it is still stress from organizational leadership responsibilities that is the more burdensome to him. So, he decided to move out of it. At the Board meeting he expressed his gratitude to God and to his colleagues on the Board for the privilege of working with them, but he told the committee who makes nominations for the office of president of SIL that he would not accept the nomination for president in 1979, nor would he agree to be on the Board after 1979. He felt that without administrative responsibilities he could concentrate all available energy on linguistics and on helping the translators.

In December, Ken took another couple of weeks off. This time it was to go to Paris to give a lecture, "Here We Stand—Creative Observers of Language," as part of the reception ceremonies at which he received an honorary degree from the University René Descartes, at the Sorbonne, Paris.

Then back to Ivory Coast to join Evie there. Together they went on to Cameroun, Kenya, Thailand, and Malaysia, helping their colleagues each step of the way.

The next year they stayed in Texas most of the time. But by the fall of 1980 they were off again. They spent a month in India teaching linguistics in the Central Institute of Indian Languages, Mysore. From there they went on to the People's Republic of China where both Ken and Evie lectured in the Institute of Foreign Languages of Beijing.

Ken was thrilled. He had started for China in 1932, convinced that the Lord had a job for him to do there. He had made every effort to go, but it was not until 1980 that he arrived. He could be there only a month, but he had a dream that even that short time would be fruitful. He hoped that one of the young professors he was teaching would some day teach the type of linguistics that would be helpful to translators, as Bloomfield and Sapir, back in the 30's, had taught the type of linguistics needed by Bible translators. He hoped that the professor would some day come in contact with a "Townsend" of China. He hoped that this "Townsend" would inspire young folk to get the linguistic training they needed to do Bible translation in China. He remembered how Townsend had sent him, Ken, off to study with Sapir, and how, because of Townsend's vision and drive, many peoples all over the world have Scriptures in their own languages. Ken hoped and prayed that somehow a "Townsend" would be raised up for China.

THE END

REFERENCES CITED

**(Except for items where Pike is sole or first author;
for those items see Pike's bibliography.)**

Agnew, Arlene, and Pike, Evelyn G. 1957. "Phonemes of Ocaina (Huitoto)." *International Journal of American Linguistics* 23:24-27.

Bee, Darlene L. 1973. *Neo-Tagmemics: An Integrated Approach to Linguistic Analysis and Description.* eds. Alan Healey and Doreen Marks. Ukarumpa, Papua New Guinea: Summer Institute of Linguistics.

Bloomfield, Leonard. 1933. *Language.* New York: Henry Holt and Co.

Bolinger, Dwight L. 1951. "Intonation: Levels versus Configuration." *Word* 7:199-210

Brend, Ruth M. 1970. "Tagmemic Theory: An Annotated Bibliography." *Journal of English Linguistics* 4:7-41.

Brend, Ruth M. ed. 1972. *Kenneth L. Pike: Selected Writings.* The Hague: Mouton.

————. 1974. *Advances in Tagmemics.* Amsterdam: North Holland Publishing Co.

————. 1975. *Studies in Tone and Intonation.* Bibliotheca Phonetica 11. Basel: S. Karger.

Brend, Ruth M., and Pike, Kenneth L. eds. 1976. *Tagmemics: Aspects of the Field,* Vol. 1; *Tagmemics: Theoretical Discussion,* Vol. 2. The Hague: Mouton.

————. 1977. *The Summer Institute of Linguistics: Its Works and Contributions.* The Hague: Mouton.

Cook, S.J., Walter A. 1969. *Introduction to Tagmemic Analysis.* New York: Holt, Rinehart and Winston, Inc.

Dowling, Elisabeth. 1975. "Smashing the Language Barrier: An Expert Shows How." *The Charlotte Observer* Aug. 1, p. 18A.

Dye, T. Wayne, and Merrifield, William R. 1977. "Anthropology." In *The Summer Institute of Linguistics: Its Works and Contributions,* eds. Ruth M. Brend and Kenneth L. Pike, pp. 165-82. The Hague: Mouton.

Elson, Benjamin. 1958. *Beginning Morphology-Syntax.* Glendale [now Huntington Beach], Calif.: Summer Institute of Linguistics.

Elson, Benjamin, and Pickett, Velma. 1960 *Beginning Morphology-Syntax.* Santa Ana [now Huntington Beach], Calif.: Summer Institute of Linguistics.

————. 1962. *An Introduction to Morphology and Syntax.* Santa Ana [now Huntington Beach], Calif.: Summer Institute of Linguistics.

Executive Committee of the Linguistic Society of America. 1948. "Proceedings of the Ann Arbor Meeting 1947." *Supplement to Language* 24:3.3-5

Faust, Norma, and Pike, Evelyn G. 1959. "The Cocama Sound System [with Portuguese version, O Sistema Fonemico de Kokama]." Publicacões de Museu Nacional: *Série Lingüística Especial* 1:10-55.

Fischer-Jørgensen, Eli. 1949. "Kenneth L. Pike's Analysis of American English Intonation." *Lingua* 2:1.3-13.

Frank, Phillip. 1957. *Philosophy of Science: The Link Between Science and Philosophy.* Englewood Cliffs, N.J.: Prentice-Hall, Inc.

Gudschinsky, Sarah C. 1977. "Literacy." In *The Summer Institute of Linguistics: Its Works and Contributions,* eds. Ruth M. Brend and Kenneth L. Pike, pp. 39-56. The Hague: Mouton.

Hall, Robert A. Jr. 1975. *Stormy Petrel in Linguistics.* Ithaca, N.Y.: Spoken Language Services, Inc.

Hefley, James and Marti. 1974. *Uncle Cam.* Waco, Texas: Word Books.

Hockett, Charles F. 1942. "A System of Descriptive Phonology." *Language* 18:3-21.

Hopkins, Clark. 1976. *The Flounders: Fifty Years.* Ann Arbor.

Hymes, Dell. 1969. Review of "Kenneth L. Pike. *Language in Relation to a Unified Theory of the Structure of Human Behavior.*" *American Anthropologist* 71:361-63.

Jesperson, Otto. 1922. *Language, Its Nature, Development, and Origin.* London: G. Allen.

Jones, Daniel. 1940. *An Outline of English Phonetics.* 6th ed. New York: E. P. Dutton and Co.

Kenyon, John Samuel. 1943 [1935]. *American Pronunciation.* 9th edition. Ann Arbor: George Wahr.

Longacre, Robert E. 1964. *Grammar Discovery Procedures: A Field Manual.* The Hague: Mouton.

————. 1976. "Discourse," in *Tagmemics: Aspects of the Field,* Vol. 1. eds. Ruth M. Brend and Kenneth L. Pike. The Hague: Mouton. pp. 1-44.

Martin, Howard R., and Pike, Kenneth L. 1974. "Analysis of the Vocal Performance of a Poem: A Classification of Intonational Features." *Language and Style* 7:209-18.

Merrifield, William R.; Naish, Constance M.; Rensch, Calvin R.; and Story, Gillian. 1967. *Laboratory Manual for Morphology and Syntax.* 4th ed. rev. Santa Ana [now Huntington Beach], Calif.: Summer Institute of Linguistics.

McQuown, Norman A. 1974. Review of *"Kenneth L. Pike: Selected Writings."* *American Anthropologist* 76:931-32.

Moore, Bruce R. 1977. "Translation Theory." In *The Summer Institute of Linguistics: Its Works and Contributions,* eds. Ruth M. Brend and Kenneth L. Pike. The Hague: Mouton. pp. 147-64.

Nida, Eugene A. 1946. *Morphology: The Descriptive Analysis of Words.* Ann Arbor: University of Michigan Press.

————. 1960. *A Synopsis of English Syntax.* Linguistic Series 4. Norman, Okla.: Summer Institute of Linguistics and University of Oklahoma.

Pickett, Velma. 1956. *An Introduction to the Study of Grammatical Structure.* Glendale [now Huntington Beach], Calif.: Summer Institute of Linguistics.

Pike, Evelyn G. 1949. "Controlled Infant Intonation." *Language Learning* 2:1.21-24.

Pike, Evelyn G. and others. 1954. *Laboratory Manual for Pike's Phonemics.* Glendale [now Huntington Beach], Calif.: Summer Institute of Linguistics.

Robbins, Frank E. 1977. "Training in Linguistics." in *The Summer Institute of Linguistics: Its Works and Contributions,* eds. Ruth M. Brend and Kenneth L. Pike, pp. 57-68. The Hague: Mouton.

Sapir, Edward. 1921. *Language: An Introduction to the Study of Speech.* New York: Harcourt, Brace and Co.

Taylor, Howard, Dr. and Mrs. 1911. *Hudson Taylor in Early Years: The Growth of a Soul.* Philadelphia: China Inland Mission.

Thompson, Phyllis. 1974. *Matched With His Hour.* London: Word Books.

Townsend, William Cameron, and Pittman, Richard S. 1975. *Remember All the Way.* Huntington Beach, Calif.: Wycliffe Bible Translators.

Trager, George L. 1943. Review of "Kenneth L. Pike, *Phonetics: a Critical Analysis of Phonetic Theory and a Technic for the Practical Description of Sounds."* *Studies in Linguistics* 2:1.16-20.

Trager, George L., and Smith, Jr., H.L. 1951. *An Outline of English Structure,* Norman, Okla.: Battenburg Press.

Voegelin, C.F. 1957. Review of "Charles Winick, *Dictionary of Anthropology."* *International Journal of American Linguistics* 23.219-23.

Wallis, Ethel E., and Bennett, Mary A. 1959. *Two Thousand Tongues to Go.* New York: Harper and Brothers.

Waterhouse, Viola G. 1974. *The History and Development of Tagmemics.* The Hague: Mouton.

Pike's Bibliography*

Secular

Books and Monographs

1942   *Pronunciation.* Vol. 1 of *An Intensive Course in English for Latin American Students.* Ann Arbor: English Language Institute of the University of Michigan.

1943   *Phonetics: a Critical Analysis of Phonetic Theory and a Technic for the Practical Description of Sounds.* University of Michigan Publications in Language and Literature 21. Ann Arbor: University of Michigan Press.

1945   *The Intonation of American English.* University of Michigan Publications in Linguistics 1. Ann Arbor: University of Michigan Press.

1947   *Phonemics: A Technique for Reducing Languages to Writing.* University of Michigan Publications in Linguistics 3. Ann Arbor: University of Michigan Press.

1948   *Tone Languages: A Technique for determining the Number and Type of Pitch Contrasts in a Language, with Studies in Tonemic Substitution and Fusion.* University of Michigan Publications in Linguistics 4. Ann Arbor: University of Michigan Press.

1951   *Axioms and Procedures for Reconstruction in Comparative Linguistics: An Experimental Syllabus.* Santa Ana [now

---

* In this bibliography, for the years 1937-1971, I have relied heavily on that compiled by Ruth M. Brend and published in *Kenneth L. Pike: Selected Writings* (pp. 326-31). ed. Ruth M. Brend. The Hague: Mouton, 1972. Also, very helpful have been *Bibliography of the Summer Institute of Linguistics 1935-1972* compiled by Alan C. Wares. Mexico, D.F.: Summer Institute of Linguistics, 1974, and S.I.L. Bibliographer's Bulletin no. 1 (January, 1973) - No. 10 (July, 1978) compiled by Alan C. Wares.

Huntington Beach], Calif.: Summer Institute of Linguistics. Revised, 1957.

1954   *Language in Relation to a Unified Theory of the Structure of Human Behavior,* Part I; 1955, Part II; 1960, Part III. Glendale [now Huntington Beach], Calif.: Summer Institute of Linguistics. (2nd ed. rev. The Hague: Mouton. 1967)

1966   *Tagmemic and Matrix Linguistics Applied to Selected African Languages.* (Final Report, Contract OE 5-14-065) Washington, D.C., U.S. Office of Education). Reprinted: 1970 in Summer Institute of Linguistics Publications in Linguistics and Related Fields 23—Appendix omitted.

1970a   and Young, Richard E.; and Becker, Alton L. *Rhetoric: Discovery and Change.* New York: Harcourt, Brace and World.

1970b   and Hale, Austin. eds. *Tone Systems of Tibeto-Burman Languages of Nepal.* Part I: Studies on Tone and Phonological Segments; Part II: Lexical Lists and Comparative Studies; Part III: Texts I; Part IV: Texts II. Occasional Papers of the Wolfenden Society on Tibeto-Burman Linguistics, Vol. III. Urbana: University of Illinois.

1976a   and Suharno, Ignatius, eds. *From Baudi to Indonesian.* Jayapura, Irian Jaya, Indonesia: Cenderawasih University and the Summer Institute of Linguistics.

1976b   and Brend, Ruth M. eds. *Tagmemics: Aspects of the Field,* Vol. 1; *Tagmemics: Theoretical Discussion,* Vol. 2. The Hague: Mouton.

1977a   and Brend, Ruth M. eds. *The Summer Institute of Linguistics: Its Works and Contributions.* The Hague: Mouton.

1977b   and Pike, Evelyn G. *Grammatical Analysis.* Summer Institute of Linguistics Publications in Linguistics 53. Dallas, Texas: Summer Institute of Linguists and University of Texas at Arlington.

1977c   and Pike, Evelyn G. *Instructor's Guide for Use with Grammatical Analysis.* Huntington Beach, Calif.: Summer Institute of Linguistics.

(in press)   *Concepts with Special Reference to Language as Seen from a Tagmemic Viewpoint.* Lincoln: University of Nebraska Press.

(in press)   "Tagmemics, Discourse, and Verbal Art." *Michigan Studies in Humanities,* ed. Richard Bailey. Ann Arbor, Michigan.

Articles and Pamphlets

1937a   "Likenesses, Differences and Variations of Phonemes in Mexican Indian Languages and How to Find Them." *Investigaciones Lingüísticas* 4:1-2.134-39.

1937b   "Una Leyenda Mixteca." *Investigaciones Lingüísticas* 4:3-4.262-70.

1938a   "Practical Suggestions Toward a Common Orthography for Indian Languages of Mexico." *Investigaciones Lingüísticas* 5:1-2.86-97.

1938b   *Phonemic Work Sheet.* Santa Ana [now Huntington Beach], Calif.: Summer Institute of Linguistics. Reprinted: 1977. *Grammatical Analysis* pp. 469-474, Dallas Summer Institute of Linguistics and University of Texas at Arlington.

1943   "Taxemes and Immediate Constituents." *Language* 19:65-82.

1944   "Analysis of a Mixteco Text." *International Journal of American Linguistics* 10:113-38. Reprinted: 1972. *Kenneth L. Pike: Selected Writings.* ed. Ruth M. Brend. pp. 11-31. The Hague: Mouton.

1945a   "Mock Spanish of a Mixteco Indian." *International Journal of American Linguistics* 11:219-24.

1945b   and Traver, Aileen; and French, Virginia. "Step-by-step Procedure for Marking Limited Intonation with its Related Features of Pause, Stress, and Rhythm." *Teaching and Learning English as a Foreign Language* by Charles C. Fries. Ann Arbor: English Language Institute, University of Michigan. pp. 62-74.

1945c   "Tone Puns in Mixteco." *International Journal of American Linguistics* 11:129-39.

1946a   "The Flea: Melody Types and Perturbations in a Mixtec Song." *Tlalocan* 2:128-33.

1946b   "Another Mixteco Tone Pun." *International Journal of American Linguistics* 12:22-24. Reprinted: 1975. *Studies in Tone and Intonation.* ed. Ruth M. Brend. Basel: S. Karger. pp. 57-61.

1946c   "Phonemic Pitch in Maya." *International Journal of American Linguistics* 12:82-88.

1946d   and Merecias, Angel; and other Mixtecs. *Cuendu Nanga* [Funny Stories]. Mexico, D.F.: Instituto Lingüístico de Verano.

1947a   "A Text Involving Inadequate Spanish of Mixteco Indians." *International Journal of American Linguistics* 13:251-57.

1947b   "On the Phonemic Status of English Diphthongs." *Language* 23:151-59. Reprinted: 1972. *Phonological Theory: Evolution and Current Practice.* ed. Valerie Becker Makkai. N.Y.: Holt, Rinehart and Winston, Inc. pp. 145-51.

1947c "Grammatical Prerequisites to Phonemic Analysis." *Word* 3:155-72. Reprinted: 1972. *Kenneth L. Pike: Selected Writings.* ed. Ruth M. Brend. The Hague: Mouton. pp. 32-50. Reprinted: 1972. *Phonological Theory: Evolution and Current Practice.* ed. Valerie Becker Makkai. N.Y.: Holt, Rinehart and Winston, Inc. pp. 153-65. Reprinted 1973. *Phonology: Selected Writings.* ed. Erik C. Fudge. Middlesex, England: Penguin Books. pp. 115-35.

1947d and Pike, Eunice V. "Immediate Constituents of Mazatec Syllables." *International Journal of American Linguistics* 13:78-91. Reprinted: 1975. *Studies in Tone and Intonation.* ed. Ruth M. Brend. Basel: S. Karger. pp. 62-83.

1948a "Problems in the Teaching of Practical Phonemics." *Language Learning* 1:3-8.

1948b and Sinclair, Donald. "The Tonemes of Mezquital Otomí." *International Journal of American Linguistics* 14:91-98.

1948-1949 "Cuento Mixteco de un Conejo, un Coyote, y la Luna." *Revista Mexicana de Estudios Anthropológicos* 10:133-34.

1949a and Fries, Charles C. "Coexistent Phonemic Systems." *Language* 25:25-50. Reprinted: 1972. *Kenneth L. Pike: Selected Writings.* ed. Ruth M. Brend. The Hague: Mouton. pp. 51-73.

1949b "A Problem in Morphology-Syntax Division." *Acta Linguistica* 5:125-38. Reprinted: 1972. *Kenneth L. Pike: Selected Writings.* ed. Ruth M. Brend. The Hague: Mouton. pp. 74-84.

1951a *Bibliography of the Summer Institute of Linguistics.* Glendale [now Huntington Beach], Calif.: Summer Institute of Linguistics.

1951b "The Problems of Unwritten Languages in Education." Report in the UNESCO meeting of Experts in the Use of the Vernacular Languages. Paris: UNESCO.

1952a "More on Grammatical Prerequisites." *Word* 8:106-21. Reprinted: 1972. *Phonological Theory: Evolution and Current Practice.* ed. Valerie Becker Makkai. N.Y.: Holt, Rinehart and Winston, Inc. pp. 211-23.

1952b "Operational Phonemics in Reference to Linguistic Relativity." *Journal of the Acoustical Society of America* 24:618-25. Reprinted: 1972. *Kenneth L. Pike: Selected Writings.* ed. Ruth M. Brend. The Hague: Mouton. pp. 85-99.

1953a "Intonational Analysis of a Rumanian Sentence." *Cahiers Sextil Puscariu* 2. University of Washington, Seattle, Dept. of Romance Languages and Literature pp. 59-60.

1953b "A Note on Allomorph Classes and Tonal Technique." *International Journal of American Linguistics* 19:101-05.

1955a   "Meaning and Hypostasis." *Monograph* 8. Georgetown University, Institute of Languages and Linguistics 134-41.

1955b   and Pike, Eunice V. *Live Issues in Descriptive Linguistics.* Santa Ana [now Huntington Beach], Calif.: Summer Institute of Linguistics. 2nd ed. 1960.

1956a   "As Correntes da Linguistica Norteamericana." *Revista Brasileira de Filologia* 2:207-16.

1956b   and Kindberg, Willard. "A Problem in Multiple Stresses." *Word* 12:415-28. Reprinted: 1975. *Studies in Tone and Intonation.* ed. Ruth M. Brend. Basel: S. Karger. pp. 212-26.

1956c   "Toward a Theory of the Structure of Human Behavior." *Estudios Anthropológicos Publicados en Homenaje al Doctor Manuel Gamio.* Mexico, D.F. pp. 659-71.

1957a   "Grammemic Theory in Reference to Restricted Problems of Morpheme Classes." *International Journal of American Linguistics* 23:119-28.

1957b   "Grammatical Theory." *General Linguistics* 2:35-41.

1957c   and Beasley, David. "Notes on Huambisa Phonemics." *Lingua Posnaniensis* 6:1-8.

1957d   "Abdominal Pulse Types in Some Peruvian Languages." *Language* 33:30-35. Reprinted: 1975. *Studies in Tone and Intonation.* ed. Ruth M. Brend. Basel: S. Karger. pp. 204-11.

1957e   "Language and Life: A Training Device for Translation and Practice." *Bibliotheca Sacra* 114:347-62. Reprinted: 1972. *Kenneth L. Pike: Selected Writings.* ed. Ruth M. Brend. The Hague: Mouton. pp. 117-28.

1958a   and Matteson, Esther. "Non-Phonemic Transition Vocoids in Piro (Arawak)." *Miscellanea Phonetica* 3:22-30.

1958b   "Interpenetration of Phonology, Morphology, and Syntax." *Proceedings of the Eighth International Congress of Linguists.* Oslo: University Press. pp. 363-74.

1958c   "On Tagmemes, *née* Gramemes." *International Journal of American Linguistics* 24:273-78.

1958d   and Saint, Rachel. "Notas sobre Fonémica Huaraní (Auca)." *Estudios Acerca de las Lenguas Huaraní (Auca), Shimigae y Zápara: Publicaciones Científicas de Ministerio de Educación del Ecuador* 4-17.

1959a   and Barrett, Ralph P.; and Bascom, Burt. "Instrumental Collaboration on a Tepehuan (Uto-Aztecan) Pitch Problem." *Phonetica* 3:1-22.

1959b "Language as Particle, Wave, and Field." *The Texas Quarterly* 2:2.37-54. Reprinted: 1972. *Kenneth L. Pike: Selected Writings.* ed. Ruth M. Brend. The Hague: Mouton. pp. 129-43.

1960a "Linguistic Research as Pedagogical Support." *Papers of the National Conference on the Teaching of African Languages and Area Studies.* ed. John G. Broder. Georgetown University. pp. 32-39.

1960b "Toward a Theory of Change and Bilingualism." *Studies in Linguistics* 15:1-7.

1960c "Nucleation." *The Modern Language Journal* 44: 291-95. Reprinted: 1961. ILT *News* [Journal of the Institute of Language Teaching, Waseda University, Tokyo] 6:1-5. Reprinted: 1963. *Philippine Journal for Language Teaching* 1:1-7, 20. Reprinted: 1965. *Teaching English as a Second Language.* ed. Harold B. Allen. N.Y.: McGraw-Hill. pp. 67-74. Reprinted: 1972. *Kenneth L. Pike: Selected Writings.* ed. Ruth M. Brend. The Hague: Mouton. pp. 144-50.

1960d "Building Sympathy." *Practical Anthropology* 7:250-52.

1961a "Stimulating and Resisting Change." *Practical Anthropology* 8:267-74.

1961b "Compound Affixes in Ocaina." *Language* 37:570-81.

1961c and Warkentin, Milton. "Huave: A Study in Syntactic Tone with Low Lexical Functional Load." *A William Cameron Townsend en el Vigesimoquinto Aniversario del Instituto Lingüístico de Verano.* Mexico, D.F.: Instituto Lingüístico de Verano. pp. 627-42.

1962a and Saint, Rachel. "Auca Phonemes." *Studies in Ecuadorian Indian Languages* I. Norman, Okla.: Summer Institute of Linguistics and the University of Oklahoma. pp. 2-30.

1962b "Practical Phonetics of Rhythm Waves." *Phonetica* 8:9-30. Reprinted: 1975. *Studies in Tone and Intonation.* ed. Ruth M. Brend. Basel: S. Karger. pp. 11-32.

1962c "Dimensions of Grammatical Constructions." *Language* 38:221-44. Reprinted: 1972. *Kenneth L. Pike: Selected Writings.* ed. Ruth M. Brend. The Hague: Mouton. pp. 160-85.

1963a and Scott, Graham. "Pitch Accent and Non-Accented Phrases in Fore (New Guinea)." *Zeitschrift für Phonetik, Sprachwissenschaft und Kommunikationsforschung* 16:179-89.

1963b "Choices in Course Design." *The Teaching of Linguistics in Anthropology.* Memoir 94, American Anthropological Association 315-32.

1963c   "Theoretical Implications of Matrix Permutation in Fore (New Guinea)." *Anthropological Linguistics* 5:8.1-23.

1963d   "A Syntactic Paradigm." *Language* 39:216-30. Reprinted: 1974. *Advances in Tagmemics.* ed. Ruth M. Brend. Amsterdam: North-Holland Publishing Co. pp. 235-49.

1963e   "The Hierarchical and Social Matrix of Suprasegmentals." *Prac Filologicznych* 18:95-104.

1964a   "A Linguistic Contribution to Composition: A Hypothesis." *Journal of the Conference on College Composition and Communication* 15:82-88.

1964b   and Larson, Mildred. "Hyperphonemes and Non-Systematic Features of Aguaruna Phonemics." *Studies in Languages and Linguistics in Honor of Charles C. Fries.* ed. A. H. Marckwardt. Ann Arbor: The English Language Institute of the University of Michigan. pp. 55-67.

1964c   and Erickson, Barbara. "Conflated Field Structures in Potawatomi and in Arabic." *International Journal of American Linguistics* 30:201-12. Reprinted: 1974. *Advances in Tagmemics.* ed. Ruth M. Brend. Amsterdam: North-Holland Publishing Co. pp. 135-46.

1964d   "Beyond the Sentence." *Journal of the Conference on College Composition and Communication* 15:129-35. Reprinted: 1972. *Kenneth L. Pike: Selected Writings.* ed. Ruth M. Brend. The Hague: Mouton. pp. 192-99.

1964e   "Discourse Analysis and Tagmeme Matrices." *Oceanic Linguistics* 3:5-25. Reprinted: 1974. *Advances in Tagmemics.* ed. Ruth M. Brend. Amsterdam: North-Holland Publishing Co. pp. 285-305.

1964f   and Becker, Alton L. "Progressive Neutralization in Dimensions of Navaho Stem Matrices." *International Journal of American Linguistics* 30:144-45.

1964g   "Stress Trains in Auca." *In Honour of Daniel Jones.* ed. D. Abercrombie; D. B. Fry; P. A. C. MacCarthy; N. C. Scott; and J. L. M. Trim. London: Longmans, Green. pp. 425-31. Reprinted: 1972. *Kenneth L. Pike: Selected Writings.* ed. Ruth M. Brend. The Hague: Mouton. pp. 186-91.

1964h   "Name Fusions as High-Level Particles in Matrix Theory." *Linguistics* 6:83-91.

1964i   "On Systems of Grammatical Structure." *Proceedings of the Ninth International Congress of Linguists.* ed. H. G. Lunt. The Hague: Mouton. pp. 145-54. Reprinted: 1972. *Kenneth L. Pike:*

Selected Writings. ed. Ruth M. Brend. The Hague: Mouton. pp. 200-08.

1965a "Language—Where Science and Poetry Meet." *College English* 26:283-92.

1965b "Non-Linear Order and Anti-Redundancy in German Morphological Matrices." *Zeitschrift für Mundartforschung* 32:193-221.

1966a "A Guide to Publications Related to Tagmemic Theory." *Current Trends to Linguistics* 3. ed. T. A. Sebeok. The Hague: Mouton. pp. 365-94.

1966b "On the Grammar of Intonation." *Proceedings of the Fifth International Congress of Phonetic Sciences.* ed. E. Zwirner and W. Bethge. Basel: S. Karger. pp. 105-19. Reprinted: 1975. *Studies in Tone and Intonation.* ed. Ruth M. Brend. Basel: S. Karger. pp. 33-44.

1967a "Suprasegmental in Reference to Phonemes of Item, of Process, and of Relation." *To Honor Roman Jakobson.* The Hague: Mouton. pp. 1545-54. Reprinted: 1975. *Studies in Tone and Intonation.* ed. Ruth M. Brend. Basel: S. Karger. pp. 45-56.

1967b "Tongue-Root Position in Practical Phonetics." *Phonetica* 17:129-40. Reprinted: 1972. *Kenneth L. Pike: Selected Writings.* ed. Ruth M. Brend. The Hague: Mouton. pp. 221-30.

1967c "Grammar as Wave." *Monograph* 20. Georgetown University, Institute of Languages and Linguistics 1-14. Reprinted: 1972. *Kenneth L. Pike: Selected Writings.* ed. Ruth M. Brend. The Hague: Mouton. pp. 231-41.

1968a "How to Make an Index." *Publications of the Modern Language Association of America* 83:991-93.

1968b and Jacobs, Gill. "Matrix Permutation as a Heuristic Device in the Analysis of the Bimoba Verb." *Lingua* 21:321-45. Reprinted: 1972. *Kenneth L. Pike: Selected Writings.* ed. Ruth M. Brend. The Hague: Mouton. pp. 242-62.

1968c "Indirect Versus Direct Discourse in Bariba." *Proceedings of the Conference on Language and Language Behavior.* ed. M. Zale. N.Y.: Appleton-Century-Crofts. pp. 165-73.

1969a "Language as Behavior and Etic and Emic Standpoints for the Description of Behavior." *Social Psychology: Readings and Perspective.* ed. E. F. Borgatta. Chicago: Rand, McNally. pp. 114-31. Reprinted from *Language in Relation to a Unified Theory of the Structure of Human Behavior.*

1969b and Lowe, Ivan. "Pronominal Reference in English Conversation and Discourse: A Group Theoretical Treatment." *Folia*

Linguistica 3:68-106. Reprinted: 1972. *Kenneth L. Pike: Selected Writings*. ed. Ruth M. Brend. The Hague: Mouton. pp. 263-97.

1970a "The Role of Nuclei of Feet in the Analysis of Tone in Tibeto-Burman Languages of Nepal." *Prosodic Feature Analysis*. eds. Leon, and Faure, and Rigault. *Studia Phonetica* 3:153-61. Reprinted: 1970. *Tone Systems of Tibeto-Burman Languages of Nepal*, Part I. eds. Austin Hale and Kenneth L. Pike. pp. 37-48.

1970b and Hari, Maria; and Taylor, Doreen. "Tamang Tone and Higher Levels." *Tone Systems of Tibeto-Burman Languages of Nepal*, Part I. eds. Austin Hale and Kenneth L. Pike. pp. 82-124.

1971a "More Revolution: Tagmemics." Ch. 7 of *Reading About Language*. eds. C. Laird and R. M. Gorrell. N.Y.: Harcourt, Brace, Jovanovich. pp. 234-47.

1971b "Implications of the Patterning of an Oral Reading of a Set of Poems." *Poetics* 1:38-45.

1971c "Crucial Questions in the Development of Tagmemics—the Sixties and the Seventies." *Monograph* 24, Georgetown University, Institute of Languages and Linguistics 79-98.

1972a and Schoettelndreyer, Burkhard. "Paired-Sentence Reversals in the Discovery of Underlying and Surface Structures in Sherpa Discourse." *Indian Linguistics* 33:1.72-83. Reprinted: 1973. *Clause, Sentence, and Discourse Patterns in Selected Languages of Nepal*, Part I. Summer Institute of Linguistics Publications in Linguistics and Related Fields 40. ed. Austin Hale. pp. 361-75.

1972b and Gordon, Kent. "Preliminary Technology to Show Emic Relations Between Certain Non-Transitivity Clause Structures in Dhanger (Kudux, Nepal)." *International Journal of Dravidian Linguistics* 1:1.56-79.

1972c and Pike, Evelyn G. "Seven Substitution Exercises for Studying the Structure of Discourse." *Linguistics* 94:43-52.

1973a "Comments on Gleason's 'Grammatical Prerequisites'." *Annals of the New York Academy of Sciences*. 211: 34-38.

1973b and Schoettelndreyer, Burkhard. "Notation for Simultaneous Representation of Grammatical and Sememic Components in Connected Discourse." *Clause, Sentence, and Discourse Patterns in Selected Languages of Nepal*, Part I. *Summer Institute of Linguistics Publications in Linguistics and Related Fields* 40. ed. Austin Hale. pp. 321-60.

1973c and Gordon, Kent H. "Paired Semantic Components, Paired Sentence Reversals and the Analysis of Dhanger (Kudux) Discourse." *International Journal of Dravidian Linguistics* 2:1.14-

46. Reprinted: 1973. *Patterns in Clause, Sentence, and Discourse in Selected Languages of India and Nepal.* Part I. Summer Institute of Linguistics Publications in Linguistics and Related Fields 41. ed. Ronald L. Trail. pp. 313-43.

1973d "Sociolinguistic Evaluation of Alternative Mathematical Models: English Pronouns." *Language* 49.121-60.

1973e "Science Fiction as a Test of Axioms Concerning Human Behavior." *Parma Eldalamberon* 1:3.3-4.

1974a "Agreement Types Dispersed into a Nine-Cell Spectrum." *On Language, Culture, and Religion: In Honor of Eugene A. Nida.* ed. Matthew Black and William A. Smalley. The Hague: Mouton. pp. 275-86.

1974b "Recent Developments in Tagmemics." *Proceedings of the Eleventh International Congress of Linguists, Bologna-Florence, 1972.* Vol. I. ed. Luigi Heilmann. Bologna: Mulino. pp. 163-72. Reprinted: 1977. *Linguistics at the Crossroads.* eds. Adam Makkai, Valerie Becker Makkai, Luigi Heilmann. Lake Bluff, Ill.: Jupiter Press, pp. 155-66.

1974c and Pike, Evelyn G. "Rules as Components of Tagmemes in the English Verb Phrase." *Advances in Tagmemics.* ed. Ruth M. Brend. Amsterdam: North-Holland Publishing Co. pp. 175-204.

1975a "Focus in English Clause Structure Seen Via Systematic Experimental Syntax." *Kivung* 8:3-14.

1975b "On Describing Languages." *The Scope of American Linguistics.* ed. Robert Austerlitz. Lisse, The Netherlands: The Peter de Ridder Press. pp. 9-39.

1975c "On Kinesic Triadic Relations in Turn-Taking." *Semiotica* 13:389-94.

1976a and Sterner, Robert; and Suharno, Ignatius. "Experimental Syntax Applied to the Relation Between Sentence and Sentence Cluster in Indonesian." *From Baudi to Indonesian.* eds. Ignatius Suharno and Kenneth L. Pike. Jayapura, Irian Jaya, Indonesia: Cenderawasih University and the Summer Institute of Linguistics. pp. 95-117.

1976b "Pike's Answers to 12 Questions for Conference on Language Universals." held at Gummersbach, October 4-8, 1976. In *Materials for the DFG International Conference on Language Universals* AKUP (Arbeiten des Kölner Universalien - Projekts) 25:170-76.

1976c and Pike, Evelyn G. "The Granular Nature of a Construction as Illustrated by 'Flying Planes'." *From Baudi to Indonesian.* eds.

Ignatius Suharno and Kenneth L. Pike. Jayapura, Irian Jaya, Indonesia: Cenderawasih University and the Summer Institute of Linguistics. pp. 29-37.

1976d   "The Meaning of Particles in Text: A Random Note." *From Baudi to Indonesian.* eds. Ignatius Suharno and Kenneth L. Pike. Jayapura, Irian Jaya, Indonesia: Cenderawasih University and the Summer Institute of Linguistics. pp. 41-44.

1976e   "Toward the Development of Tagmemic Postulates." in *Tagmemics: Theoretical Discussion.* Vol. II eds. Ruth M. Brend and Kenneth L. Pike. The Hague: Mouton. pp. 91-127.

1977a   and Huttar, George L. "How Many Packages?" *Hemisphere* 21:12.26-29.

1977b   and Pike, Evelyn G. "Referential Versus Grammatical Hierarchies." *The Third Lacus Forum* 1976. eds. Robert J. DiPietro and Edward L. Blansitt, Jr. Columbia, South Carolina: Hornbeam Press. pp. 343-54.

1977c   ed. *Pilot Projects on the Reading of English of Science and Technology.* University of Michigan Papers in Linguistics Special Publications in Applied Linguistics, 1. Ann Arbor: Department of Linguistics, University of Michigan.

1977d   "Introduction: On the Relation Between Modes of Argumentation in Linguistic Analysis Versus the Documentation of Change of Behavior in Reading." *Pilot Projects on the Reading of English of Science and Technology.* ed. Kenneth L. Pike. Ann Arbor: Department of Linguistics, University of Michigan. pp. 1-5.

1977e   and Bernstein, Jared. "The Emic Structure of Individuals in Relation to Dialogue." *Grammars and Descriptions,* eds. Teun A. Van Dijk and János S. Petöfi. Berlin: Gruyter. pp. 1-10.

1978a   "Particularization Versus Generalization, and Explanation Versus Prediction," *The Teaching of English in Japan,* eds. Ikuo Koike, Masuo Matsoyama, Yasuo Igarashi, and Koki Suzuki. Tokyo: Eichosah Publishing Co., Ltd. pp. 783-85.

1978b   "Thresholdism Versus Reductionism," *Language Universals.* ed. Hansjakob Seiler. Tübingen: Gunter Narr Verlag. pp. 53-58.

1978c   "Social Interaction as the Break-in Point for the Analysis of Verbal Behavior." *Proceedings of the Twelfth International Congress of Linguists, Vienna, August 28-September 2, 1977.* pp. 739-41.

1979a   "Linguistics—From There to Where? *The Fifth Lacus Forum 1978.* eds. Wolfgang Wölck and Paul L. Garvin. Columbia, S. Carolina: Hornbeam Press. pp. 3-18.

1979b   "Universals and Phonetic Hierarchy," in *Proceedings of the Ninth International Congress of Phonetic Sciences, Copenhagen, August 6-11, 1979.* eds. Eli Fischer-Jørgensen, Jørgen Rischel, and Nina Thorsen, pp. 48-52.

1979c   "Social Linguistics and Bilingual Education," *System* 7:99-109.

1979d   "On the Extension of Etic-Emic Anthropological Methodology to Referential Units-in-Context." *Lembaran Tengkajian Budaya* 3.1-36.

1980a   and DuBois, Carl D. and Upton, John. "Constraints on Complexity Seen via Fused Vectors of an n-Dimensional Semantic Space (Sarangani, Manobo, Philippines)." *Semiotica* 29:3-4. pp. 209-43.

1980b   "Here We Stand—Creative Observers of Language." *Approches du Langage: Colloque Interdisciplinaire.* eds. Reuchlin and François. Publications de la Sorbonne, Série "Études" 16:9-45.

1980c   "A Mixtec Lime Oven," SIL Museum of Anthropology, Publication 10.

1981   "Wherein Lies 'Talked-About' Reality?" *A Festschrift for Native Speaker.* ed. Florian Coulmas. The Hague: Mouton. pp. 85-91.

(in press) "Nonsense in the Service of Sense." *Language and Communication.*

Educational Television Programs

1977   *Pike on Language,* series. On 3/4 inch videocassettes (NTSC standard) and on 16mm kinescopes, Ann Arbor: University of Michigan Television Center. The University of Michigan.

Program No. 1: "Voices at Work [Phonetics]"
Program No. 2: "The Music of Speech [Pitch and Poetry]"
Program No. 3: "Waves of Change [The How and Why of Change in Language]"
Program No. 4: "The Way We Know—The Value of Theory in Linguistic Study"
Program No. 5: "Into the Unknown [Learning an Unknown Language by Gesture—a Monolingual Demonstration]"

Religious

Books

1946   and Stark, Donald; Pike, Evelyn; and Merecias, Angel. *Cuendú Ndaã [True Tales]* (in Mixteco). México, D.F.: Instituto Lingüístico de Verano.

1947a   and Merecias, Angel. *La Epístola del Apóstol San Pablo a los Filipenses.* (diglot, Mixteco-Spanish). México, D.F.: Sociedad Bíblica Americana.

1947b   and Stark, Donald; and Merecias, Angel. *El Santo Evangelio según San Marcos.* (diglot, Mixteco-Spanish). México, D.F.: Sociedad Bíblica Americana.

1950   and Stark, Donald. *Las Epístolas de San Juan Apóstol* (diglot, Mixteco-Spanish). México, D.F.

1951   and Stark, Donald; and Merecias, Angel. *El Nuevo Testamento do Nuestro Señor Jesucristo.* (diglot, Mixteco-Spanish). Cuernavaca, México: Tipografía Indígenia.

1957   and Stark, Donald. *El Santo Evangelio según San Juan* (diglot, Mixteco-Spanish). Cuernavaca, México: Tipografía Indígena.

1960   and Stark, Donald. *Los Hechos de los Apóstoles* (diglot, Mixteco-Spanish). Cuernavaca, México: Tipografía Indígena.

1962   *With Heart and Mind: A Personal Synthesis of Scholarship and Devotion.* Grand Rapids, Mich.: Wm. B. Eerdmans Publ. Co.

1967   *Stir-Change-Create: Poems and Essays.* Grand Rapids, Mich.: Wm. B. Eerdmans Publ. Co.

1971   *Mark My Words.* Grand Rapids, Mich.: Wm. B. Eerdmans Publ. Co.

1977   and Pike, Stephen B. *Songs of Fun and Faith.* (By Fish and Chip, words by Kenneth L. Pike, music by Stephen B. Pike.) Edward Sapir Monograph Series in Language, Culture, and Cognition 1. Supplement to *Forum Linguisticum* 1:3. Lake Bluff, Ill.: Jupiter Press.

Articles and Pamphlets

1947   *God's Guidance and Your Life's Work.* Chicago: Inter-Varsity Christian Fellowship. Reprinted: 1955 by Wycliffe Bible Translators, Santa Ana [now Huntington Beach], Calif.

1948   "Living on Manna." *The Sunday School Times* May 1, pp. 3-4.

1951   "We'll Tell Them, But in What Language?" *His* 12:2.8-11, 14.

1957a   "Gold, Frankincense, and Myrrh." *The King's Business* 42:12.16-17.

1957b   "Why I Believe in God." *His* 18:2.3-7, 32-33.

1957c   "Prescription for Intellectuals." *Eternity* 8:8.11, 44-45.

1957d   "A Stereoscope Window on the World." *Bibliotheca Sacra* 114:141-56.

1957e   "Slots and Classes in the Hierarchical Structure of Behavior." *Bibliotheca Sacra* 114:255-62.

1957f   "A Training Device for Translation Theory and Practice." *Bibliotheca Sacra* 114:347-62.

1958a   "Tristructural Units of Human Behavior." *Bibliotheca Sacra* 115:36-43.

1958b   *Language and Life.* The four preceding articles reprinted from *Bibliotheca Sacra.*

1958c   "Serving our Colleagues." *His* 18:5.5-7.

1958d   "The Sin of Independence." *His* 18:8.5-7.

1958e   "The Individual." *Eternity* 9:9.18-19.

1959a   "Marriage." mimeograph.

1959b   "Our Own Tongue Wherein We Were Born: The Work of the Summer Institute of Linguistics and the Wycliffe Bible Translators." *The Bible Translator* 10:2.3-15.

1959c   "Intellectual Idolatry." *His* 19:5.5-6.

1959d   "Walking." *The King's Business* 50:4.10-11.

1959e   "A Linguistic Parable." *His* 19:6.39-40.

1959f   "Why the Angels Are Curious." *The King's Business* 50:9.12-13.

1959g   "Cause-and-Effect in the Christian Life." *His* 20:1.33-34.

1960a   "Players." *His* 20:9.41-42.

1960b   "When Failure is Success." *The Alliance Witness* 95:21.5.

1960c   "Why There is a Moral Code." *The King's Business* 51:10.10-11.

1961a   "Strange Dimensions of Truth." *Christianity Today* 5:690-92. Reprinted: 1972. *Kenneth L. Pike: Selected Writings.* ed. Ruth M. Brend. The Hague: Mouton. pp. 301-06.

1961b   "Current Strategy in Missions." *His* 22:1.9.13-14.

1962   "Left-Handed." *His* 22:9.36-47.

1963   "Modern Christianity's Crucial Junctures [a note in a list of comments by scholars]." *Christianity Today* 8:1.32.

1964   "Man or Robot." *Eternity* 15:2.9-11, 46.

1965   "Christianity and Science." *The Church Herald* 22:4.4-6.

1966a   "Tempted to Quit." *The Church Herald* 23:6.14-15. Reprinted: 1968. *The Christian Athlete* Feb. p. 11.

1966b   "The Disillusioned Scholar." *The Church Herald* 23:30.15, 30.

1966c   "God in History." *The Church Herald* 23:2.4-5, 22.

1967a   "The Courage to Face Tension." *The Church Herald* 24:21.11.

1967b   "Abraham My Father." *The Alliance Witness* 102:25.9, 19.

1968a   "Intergenerational Cleavage." *Translation* (Jan.-Feb.), 4-5.

1968b   Review of *You! Jonah!* (by J. T. Carlisle). *Christianity Today* 13:2.22-23.

1968c   "Mental Tension." *The King's Business* 58:2.30-31.

1968d   "Mission and Social Concern [a letter to the editor]." *His* 28:[Mar.].26.

1968e   "Termites and Eternity." *His* 28:7.4-5.

1969   "Guest editorial: On Finding God's Role for You." *Missionary Messenger* (organ of the Eastern Mennonite Board of Missions and Charities) 45:8.23-24.

1970   "Good Out of a Student Strike [a letter to the editor]." *The Church Herald* 27:18.17.

1971   "The Linguist and Axioms Concerning Language of Scripture." *Interchange* 3:2.77-84. Reprinted in *Journal of the American Scientific Affiliation* 26:47-51 (1974).

1972a   "Language." *Christ and the Modern Mind.* ed. Robert W. Smith. Downers Grove, Ill.: Inter-Varsity Press. pp. 59-67.

1972b   "Language and Faith." *Language and Faith.* Santa Ana [now Huntington Beach], Calif.: Wycliffe Bible Translators. pp. 18-30.

1972c   "Morals and Metaphor." *Interchange* 12:228-31.

1972d   *Use What You Have* (Six cassette tapes, twelve religious talks, published as a set.) Costa Mesa, Calif.: One Way Library.

1973a   "[Jesus Choosing His Disciples]" in Seed Thoughts, *His* 34:2.7.

1973b   "Language and Self Image." *The Scientist and Ethical Decision.* ed. Charles Hatfield. Downers Grove, Ill.: Inter-Varsity Press. pp. 69-82.

1974a   "[The Sluggard]" in Seed Thoughts, *His* 34:4.13.

1974b   "[A Chain Reaction]" in Seed Thoughts, *His* 34:6.22.

1974c   "[Attacked—Nehemiah]" in Seed Thoughts, *His* 34:8.4.

1974d   "[Flagellation]" in Seed Thoughts, *His* 34:9.21.

1974e   "[God Remembers Us By Name]" in Seed Thoughts, *His* 35:1.23.

1974f   "[Power When We're Weak]" in Seed Thoughts, *His* 35:3.23.

1974g   "The Linguist and Axioms Concerning Language of Scripture." *Journal of the American Scientific Affiliation* 26:47-51. Reprinted from *Interchange* Vol. 3:2.77-84 (1971).

1975a   "Analogies to the Good News." (Review: 1974 *Peace Child* by Don Richardson.) *Christianity Today* (Oct. 24) 20:91-92. A different review, also of *Peace Child,* in *His* 36:5.26 (1975).

1975b	"[In the Interest of Others—Diotrephes]" in Seed Thoughts, *His* 35:5.21.
1975c	"[Jacob Valued the Birthright]" in Seed Thoughts, *His* 35:7.27.
1975d	"[A Spiritual Democracy—Korah]" in Seed Thoughts, *His* 35:8.5.
1975e	"[Two Timid Men—Joseph of Arimathea and Nicodemus]" in Seed Thoughts, *His* 35:9.12.
1975f	"[An Unforgiving Spirit—Ahithophel]" in Seed Thoughts, *His* 36:1.26.
1976a	Review of *Naked and Not Ashamed,* by Lowell L. Nobel. *Christianity Today* 21:4.42.
1976b	"A Mighty Coral Reef" in Seed Thoughts, *His* 36:8.7.
1976c	"How to Sin Righteously—[Balaam]" in Seed Thoughts, *His* 36:9.22.
1976d	"Well Worth Doing" in Seed Thoughts, *His* 37:2.8.
1977a	"[Serving One Another]" in Seed Thoughts, *His* 37:4.31.
1977b	"[The Excuse Is Gone]" in Seed Thoughts, *His* 37:6.15.
1977c	"[Practical Advice in Marriage]" in Seed Thoughts, *His* 37:7.9.
1979a	"Truth and Responsibility—[Pilate]" in Seed Thoughts, *His* 39:5.13.
1979b	"Love God with Mind—and Bless Babylon." *The Gordon Alumnus* 8:4.6-7.
1979c	"Christianity and Culture I. Conscience and Culture." *Journal of the American Scientific Affiliation* 31:8-12.
1979d	"Christianity and Culture II. Incarnation in a Culture." *Journal of the American Scientific Affiliation* 31:92-96.
1979e	"Christianity and Culture III. Biblical Absolutes and Certain Cultural Relativisms." *Journal of the American Scientific Affiliation* 31:139-45.
1979f	"Emotion in God, and its Image in Us." *The Banner* 114:45.4-5.
1979g	"Intellectual Initiative: the Image of God." *The Banner* 114:46.10.
1980	"An Image of His Debating Technique." *The Banner* 115:14.6-7.

Poetic

1958	"Flaming Candle." *His* 18:7.30.
1966	"Crushed." *Translation.* Spring, p. 12. Reprinted: 1967. *Stir-Change-Create.* Kenneth L. Pike. Grand Rapids, Mich.: Wm. B. Eerdmans. p. 109.
1968a	"In War—or Fuss." *Overflow* 2:1.16.
1968b	"The Day Before Christmas." *Overflow* 2:1.8.

1969   "Fear." (two poems), *His* 29:9.13.

1970   "Five Poems." *Essays in Honor of Claude M. Wise.* eds. A. J.
           Bronstein; C. L. Shaver; and G. Stevens. Hannibal, Mo.: The
           Standard Printing Co. pp. 67-72.

1971   "Implications of the Patterning of an Oral Reading of a Set of
           Poems." *Poetics* 1:38-45.

1974a "Don't Jitter." *The Forum* p. 14.

1974b "New Year's Resolutions." *The Forum* p. 13.

1974c and Martin, Howard R. "Analysis of the Vocal Performance of a
           Poem: A Classification of Intonational Features." *Language and
           Style* 7:209-18.

1976   "A Poem on Disconnecting Form and Meaning." *Linguistic and
           Literary Studies in Honor of Archibald A. Hill: Vol. I General
           and Theoretical Linguistics.* eds. Mohammad Ali Jazayery, Edgar
           C. Polomé, Werner Winter. Lisse, The Netherlands: The Peter de
           Ridder Press. pp. 233-34.

1979   [Ten Poems, reprinted]. *Linguistic Muse* eds. Donna Jo Napoli
           and Emily N. Rando. Carbondale: Linguistic Research Inc. pp.
           138-44.

(**Books:** *Stir-Change-Create, Mark My Words,* and *Songs of Fun and Faith*
are listed under Religion.)